THE DECORATED STYLE

Architecture and Ornament
1240–1360

NICOLA COLDSTREAM

UNIVERSITY OF TORONTO PRESS
TORONTO BUFFALO

To Nicolas

© 1994 Trustees of the British Museum

Published by British Museum Press
First published in North America by University of Toronto Press Incorporated Toronto Buffalo

ISBN 0–8020–0700–7

Canadian Cataloguing in Publication Data available from the publisher

Designed by Roger Davies

Typeset by Create Publishing Services, Bath, Avon
Printed in Great Britain by The Bath Press, Avon

Frontispiece Beverley Minster, the Percy tomb, *c.*1340. It was possibly that of Eleanor Percy, d. 1328, and is the last of the so-called Court series of canopied tombs (see pp. 43 and 138), with a vast ogee arch and heavily crocketed gable. The sculptures include figures of Christ, censing angels, grotesque heads and figures holding heraldic shields.

Right The Peterborough Psalter (see plate VI).

Contents

Acknowledgements

The interpretation of the Decorated style put forward in this book has evolved over a long period, during which friends and colleagues have been generous with both information and opinions. Even twenty years ago, the book could not have been written in this form, for much new and valuable work has been done by younger scholars in the last two decades. My debt and thanks to them all are expressed in the bibliography. The following, to whom I am very grateful, read and commented on sections of the text: Paul Binski, Michael Clanchy, Jean Givens, Sandy Heslop, Virginia Jansen and Caroline Shenton. My greatest thanks, however, go to John Cherry, Christopher Wilson and, above all, Veronica Sekules, who read the whole typescript and made very helpful suggestions and corrections. None of the above is responsible for errors that remain. Veronica Sekules has also, with great generosity, allowed me to refer to material in her unpublished doctoral thesis, *The Sculpture and Liturgical Furnishings of Heckington Church and related monuments: Masons and Benefactors in early fourteenth-century Lincolnshire* (University of London, 1990).

Other assistance has been given by David Carpenter, Richard Marks, Richard Morris, Pamela Tudor Craig (Lady Wedgwood) and Neil Stratford. Anne Booth Thompson and Stephanie Wilson helped with angels. Nicolas Coldstream read the proofs. Most of the illustrations were supplied by the efficient staff at the National Monuments Record and the Conway Library at the Courtauld Institute of Art. Catherine Macduff was a tactful copy editor and Sarah Derry, Susanna Friedman and Joanna Champness have seen the book into production.

London, May 1994   NICOLA COLDSTREAM

The Decorated Style

In the years around 1240 architects in England were presented with a new stylistic phenomenon: window tracery. Bar tracery, thin bars of stone fashioned into circles to fill the blank head of a window, had been devised probably at Reims Cathedral in France about a generation before; and once its implications were appreciated, tracery became one of the principal decorative motifs of late medieval architecture. It was not wholly cosmetic. It forced architects to think anew about the relationship of structure to ornament.

The immediate change to the look of English buildings caused by the arrival of tracery was superficial, but it was combined with a slower and more profound change that had been taking place for some time and was now to be fully developed: the tendency, always strong in English architecture, towards a highly ornamented, coloured and burnished interior. The decorative possibilities offered by the fusion of tracery and ornament gave rise to some of the most beautiful and spectacular buildings of medieval England, among them the cathedrals of Lincoln, Exeter, Wells and Bristol, chapels such as the Lady chapel of Ely Cathedral, and parish churches such as Winchelsea in Sussex and 1 Patrington in Yorkshire.

The style of these and other buildings that are the subject of this book has been known as Decorated ever since styles were first classified early in the nineteenth century. The term was originally coined to denote the period following the arrival of window tracery, which was even then seen to be its most diagnostic feature; but it was later extended to embrace other aspects of the buildings such as patterned vaults, undulating, soap-like mouldings and abundant surface decoration. The Decorated style encompassed the period from about halfway through the reign of King Henry III (*reg* 1216–72), to a similar point in the reign of his great-grandson, Edward III (*reg* 1327–77). It is peculiar to the British Isles, more particularly to England. In these years, although the kings of England claimed sovereignty over Scotland, Wales and Ireland, only Wales was conquered; and although in Wales there was some English building and English influence had been strong in the south since the

1 Patrington church, Humberside, view looking from the nave south-eastwards into the south transept and Lady chapel. Built in the first half of the fourteenth century, the church displays the complicated mouldings, bubbly, stylised foliage carving and curvilinear window tracery typical of the later Decorated style.

Norman Conquest of 1066, the Decorated style appeared only fitfully. In England, however, the style can be found right across the country, recognisable in the sculptured Angel choir at Lincoln, the naturalistic leaves in the chapter house at Southwell, the great heart-shaped tracery design of the west window in York Minster and the extraordinary scissor arches supporting the central crossing at Wells. Yet, despite the fame of these and other buildings, Decorated has suffered rather at the hands of writers on architecture, both in general surveys and in full-length studies, of which there have been only two in the last thirty-five years. Until relatively recently architectural history, like the history of art in general, was perceived as a cyclical process: the classification of styles in the nineteenth century was inspired by the fever for scientific classification and a biological approach by which every period was divided into early, middle and late phases, as if forming a lifespan; and as in life, the zenith of the cycle came in the early-middle period, after which the style was seen to decline. English medieval architecture thus reached perfection in the thirteenth century and declined from the fourteenth, the signal for decline being a decidedly anti-structural feature, the ogee, a reversed, S-shaped curve that is one of the defining characteristics of later Decorated. All cyclical views of artistic styles also contain an inherent, if unspoken, belief that the decline is not only visual but moral, so that later phases are deemed somehow impure; in contrast to the clear, easily read muscularity of Anglo-Norman and Early English architecture, Decorated was infected with an element of moral degeneracy.

Two further problems have added to the complications. Decorated architecture has little cohesion. Its buildings are not structurally uniform. Indeed, many of them are extensions to earlier structures that dictate their proportions; and rather than conveying a coherent visual

2 York Minster, the great west window, given by Archbishop Melton, 1338. The heart-shaped main motif of the design is composed of leaf-stem patterns of curvilinear tracery.

message they seem to constitute a collection of daring individual architectural feats. Whether studied chronologically, regionally or formally, Decorated buildings are extraordinarily disparate, especially in comparison to those that preceded them and to the Perpendicular style that followed, all of which seem to have an inner coherence that Decorated buildings lack. The absence of unity would not, however, have affected attitudes to Decorated in itself were it not for the Perpendicular style. This had appeared, seemingly without warning or precedent, at Gloucester Abbey (now the Cathedral) in the mid-fourteenth century, and it lasted into the sixteenth, manifest in such splendid buildings as the nave of Canterbury Cathedral and the chapel of King's College, Cambridge, as well as numerous parish churches, whose square, battlemented towers represent to many a symbol of rural England. Contemporary with the various styles of late Gothic architecture in continental Europe, Perpendicular is nevertheless so distinct that for a time it was considered to be the English national style. This had further unfavourable consequences for Decorated, the blowsy abundance of which had no chance against the austere 'English' purity of Perpendicular. Then, in the search for origins, the sources of Perpendicular were discovered deep in the Decorated period; and so Decorated was explained as a series of unsatisfactory experiments from which architecture was rescued by Perpendicular.

This is all past history, and none of it would matter were it not for the repercussions that still linger in the literature. The entire debate contains a central confusion, which arises from concentrating on the way Decorated is perceived. It is almost invariably treated solely as an architectural phenomenon, with attention devoted to such formal aspects as plans, elevations, vaults and mouldings, and little notice accorded to the sculpture, paint, glass and metalwork that adorned it. Decorated is not primarily concerned with structure. Its main characteristics, which create what we identify as a style, are not structural but decorative. The architects of the time were interested only indirectly in structural problems. Their main preoccupations were with ornament and shapes, whether in ground-plans, vault patterns or window tracery, and structural changes were made primarily to accommodate new ideas about forms. The blanket of decorative coverage fell without distinction on three-storey basilicas, box-like chapels, thinly-walled parish churches and solid monastic choirs. The structural basis was less important than the decorative idea. Beyond some compromises in designs for clerestory windows, few new technical solutions were explored; but what emerged from the years around 1300 was the fusion of structure with decoration. Decorated motifs, ogees, nichework, foliage and rosette diaper, were deployed with equal success on liturgical furniture, shrines, tombs and memorial crosses, which themselves made their own contribution to architectural developments. The same devices were echoed in stained glass, embroideries, paintings, ivory carvings and

89

metal objects, so that a building resonated with designs on the largest and smallest scales that constantly reflected each other's appearance IV and meaning. In its universal application and sometimes wilful disregard of established structural logic, the Decorated style could be thought of as anti-architecture, at once more than architecture and scarcely architecture at all.

Decorated has also suffered from a growing tendency to isolate aspects of it as a court style, its main formative elements appearing in works made for the king and his circle, and adopted by the wider population for their courtly connotations. This creates a false opposition between the court and the realm. Works made for the king were certainly significant in the development of the style, but they were not alone in this; and Decorated was not identifiable with the interests of monarchy, even though ideas of monarchy were expressed through it. There were undoubtedly strong secular forces within Decorated. The style appeared in castles and houses as well as churches, and one reason for its success was that it responded so well to the patrons' desire for display. In the medieval secular world display was linked to lordship and vassalage; at the highest levels chivalric display bound the leading magnates closely to the person of the king, and the king himself used display to establish the supremacy and sanctity of the monarchy. In churches at least some display was an intrusion from the secular world: lay aristocrats were buried in tombs that took to the afterlife the status and magnificence that their occupants had enjoyed on earth, and bishops, often aristocrats themselves, had equally magnificent tombs and displayed their arms all about the building. Yet the Decorated style was not devised primarily to serve the interests of humankind on this earth. Like all styles in medieval art, it was essentially the art of the Church. It was formed to express religious devotion, to enable the Church to proclaim its own power to channel earthly ambition to Christian ends, and to enforce its central position in people's lives as the instrument of their salvation.

A church building was the earthly embodiment of the Heavenly Jerusalem, and everything in it, from its decoration to its liturgy and music, reinforced the message. It was the place where the worldly life met the spiritual, where people were linked to God physically and symbolically through the act of communion, and where they prayed for salvation through the intercession of Christ and the saints, chief among them the Virgin Mary. In the western Church the use of imagery had had a long and uninterrupted history, but now, especially in Decorated England, imagery became paramount. Saints and biblical figures were depicted not only in stained glass but in sculpture, with statues deployed on walls, window embrasures, screens and altars, surrounding the congregation with three-dimensional figures, large and small, the denizens of the Heavenly Kingdom brought uncannily to life. Paradise was shown not as a remote abstraction but as a palpable presence.

This way of using imagery had implications for architecture. With so much destruction through Puritanism and neglect it can be difficult to appreciate the original prominence of the carved and painted figures that once adorned Decorated buildings. All that remains are the niches, foliage and decorative sculpture that made up the setting for the images themselves. Once these figures are mentally replaced, however, the purpose of the Decorated style is immediately clear, and the more purely architectural elements can take their place quite coherently in the wider picture.

Given that it is now fashionable to do precisely this, and to set the arts into a broader historical context, concentration on style might seem somewhat outdated. Yet style is another word for fashion, or modes of expression, which cannot exist without the people who set them. This book examines a particular mode that was devised to express both long-held and novel beliefs, and it seeks some answers to the question why the fashion took this particular form. When the style began is easy to determine. Since 1220 the monks of the royal abbey of Westminster, the burial church of its sainted founder, King Edward the Confessor (d. 1066), had been building a Lady chapel east of the eleventh-century church, but in 1246 Henry III, out of personal devotion to the Confessor, chose Westminster as his burial place, and undertook to finance the building programme. When work halted at Henry's death in 1272 the presbytery, choir, transept and one bay of the nave had been completed, and a new type of church interior had been inaugurated in Britain. Underlying continuity of taste is an essential element of English medieval architecture, and Westminster did not constitute a complete break with the past, but the choices that were made in its architecture and decoration affected all that came after it, whether through imitation or emulation, or through a more negative reaction that was itself a response to a building that could not be ignored.

The ornate quality of Westminster Abbey is apparent even today, when so much of its decoration has gone. Foliage and figure sculpture adorns arcading, vault bosses and even wall surfaces; surfaces are enriched with paint or carved rosette diaper; the elevation is enlivened by window tracery; and the dark Purbeck 'marble' shafts are a reminder that all the stone work was enhanced by gilding and colour. The novelty lay not in the ornamented interior as such, which was not new in Britain, but in the manner in which the ornament was deployed. Described by Geoffrey Webb as 'illuminated architecture', it gives the impression of a gigantic metal reliquary turned inwards to enhance the smaller reliquaries within it. This concept was taken over from the newly-built Sainte-chapelle in Paris, which was itself a reliquary-like building designed to house a famous relic, the Crown of Thorns. The relic is attended by large sculptured figures of the Apostles, like those on the outside of a reliquary casket, a comparison that was not lost on contemporary commentators. At Westminster, too, the shrine is attended by

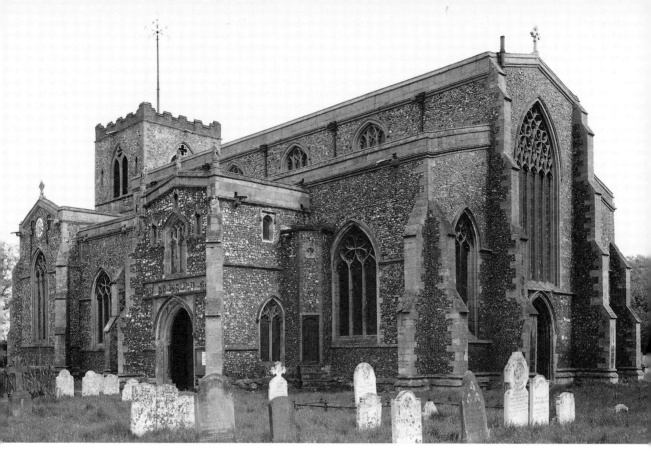

3   Attleborough church, Norfolk, built mostly in the fourteenth century. The Decorated west window, with a characteristic East Anglian petal design, was made after 1360.

large-scale interior figure sculpture, and it was the concept of the reliquary combined with imagery that was to exert so profound an influence in succeeding years.

The end of the Decorated style is much less easy to establish, for the beginnings of the Perpendicular style that followed were rooted in the same decorative principles. The new work at Gloucester began in 1332, when the quintessentially Decorated Lady chapel at Ely was unfinished and much Decorated work in the north not even begun. Some of the finest Decorated window tracery in East Anglia dates to around 1360. 3 The choice of the latter to end the period is dictated as much by politics as by art. The events of the 1340s, especially the first English victories in the Hundred Years' War and the Black Death, had strongly affected both the national outlook and the balance of power. In the 1350s new institutions were in place, a new generation was taking office; men and women were organising their material and spiritual welfare in new ways. It was a decade that looked forward to the future rather than back at the past. If occasionally, however, this book strays beyond 1360, it will be in recognition that no breaking point is either tidy or final.

Although the Decorated style does not readily submit to any single scholarly category, it does make sense if it is examined from many points of view. Decorated buildings developed in response to the social, spiritual and intellectual preoccupations of the people who used them.

In the Middle Ages all works of art except some books and small decorative pieces were made to commission, and the relation of the patron to the craftsman and their social organisation explain much about the way the style spread. It emerged in a period of booming wealth and greater social mobility, and it reflects a society composed of vertical links through lordship, from the king to the peasants, and horizontal links through the fundamental social unit, the household, the lord's family and retainers and the wider circle of his clients. It was a society at once cosmopolitan and local. Many people, the king, bishops and greater magnates, together with officials, merchants, bankers and craftsmen, travelled widely both within the country and abroad, bringing knowledge of events and developments from all over Europe and beyond. The country was not isolated. Although the forms of Decorated were unmatched on the Continent until the fourteenth century, illuminated architecture was being explored in the thirteenth, with notable examples in Notre-Dame, Paris, the great Franciscan church of San Francesco at Assisi in Italy and Naumburg Cathedral in Germany. Yet in England, beneath this outward-looking surface, was a current of extreme localism, many people never penetrating further than thirty miles from where they were born. These characteristics are reflected in buildings, some influences at their most potent only a short distance from their source, others from much farther afield.

Social divisions were as powerful as social connections. Although there is evidence of the trickle-down effect, with lower social groups adopting the decorative trappings of their superiors, there is equally strong evidence that different groups built or had made what was appropriate to them. Thus, royal patronage was preoccupied with stressing the sanctity of kingship and cementing social bonds with chivalric display; magnates ensured their salvation and looked after their castles; bishops built new residences and rebuilt their cathedrals; merchants and the gentry, the new rich, built fine new houses, endowed churches and prepared for their burial; priests rebuilt the chancels of their parish churches. While all these classes followed fashions in decoration, the uses to which the decoration was put were quite distinct.

These distinctions were part of a general increase in self-awareness, which is manifest in contemporary poetry and in such artistic developments as greater naturalism in representation. It is no coincidence that the doctrine of Transubstantiation and the Feast of Corpus Christi were both promulgated in the thirteenth century: both emphasised the actuality of Christ on earth and in the Eucharist, a favourite theme of the new mendicant preaching orders, the highly popular Franciscans and Dominicans, who also preached the personal relation of the individual to God. Personal religion was expressed in tombs, in chantry chapels founded for masses to be said for the soul of the deceased, and in private devotional books and images; but it was also seen in the encroachment of the secular world into that of the Church. The balance of power between Church and laity, always theoretically in favour of a Church that claimed total control over communication with God, was in practice always shifting, and the spread of wealth gave more people a chance to participate in the material aspects of church life and therefore to impose their tastes on both buildings and decoration. The cult of relics and of the Virgin, promulgated by the Church, became so popular that the Church was obliged to modify its buildings to accommodate them. The necessity of salvation was so powerfully preached that new altars for soul masses had to be established, again often in special new buildings.

Many aspects of life and art contributed to the Decorated style; but for the historian the picture is by no means complete. Not only have the contents of buildings been destroyed or dispersed, but so have many structures that would undoubtedly have added to our understanding of the style as a whole. Some, Vale Royal abbey in Cheshire, and the great mendicant churches of the Franciscans and Dominicans in London, were evidently architecturally magnificent; others, for example St Mary in the Newarke at Leicester, built by the earls of Lancaster, were much more austere; some people had very grand tombs, others simple slabs. Information from such buildings would have helped us to a more balanced idea of the circumstances in which luxury or plainness were deemed appropriate. Yet thanks to the work of many scholars who have discovered, and conserved or reconstructed on paper, decorative schemes on both monumental and miniature scales, it is now possible to gain much clearer insights into the thoughts and expressions of the day. Before examining the thoughts, we must look at the buildings.

CHAPTER ONE

Illuminated Architecture

Although the motifs of the Decorated style ramified into all art forms it is best seen as a style for buildings, the 'illuminated architecture' characterised by Geoffrey Webb. Its richest manifestations were in churches, for which it was primarily intended, but all the evidence indicates that palaces and seigneurial residences shared the same decorative approach. To some extent the nature of any discussion of medieval art is hindered by imbalance and gaps, which have to be borne in mind. Late thirteenth- and fourteenth-century buildings survive – if often wholly restored – in surprisingly large numbers. They are almost all ecclesiastical, as churches were more likely than houses to be built of stone and less likely to be replaced to suit changing ways of life. Of secular buildings we still have castles which, for obvious reasons, were made of stone, and some stone houses and halls. Most houses and unfortified seigneurial residences (including many royal palaces) were built of timber. They were ephemeral, often intentionally so: royal hunting lodges are known to have been dismantled and re-erected at new sites. The balance of evidence for all the arts in this period is overwhelmingly ecclesiastical and seigneurial, for if the houses have vanished so have almost all their contents. Churches, too, have lost their stained glass, liturgical furniture and objects in precious metals to Puritanism and the greed of Henry VIII. Nevertheless, the bias towards churches and aristocratic residences is not misleading. Only those at the highest social levels could afford to commission works of art and to build; and owing to the position of the Church in society and of lay people's relation to it, most creative effort was devoted to the construction and embellishment of church buildings and their furniture and fittings.

4 St Augustine's, Bristol (now Cathedral), south choir aisle, begun after 1310 (see p. 46). The aisle vaults lie transverse to the central vault, and are supported on pierced diaphragm arches, an arrangement perhaps inspired by carpentry. The tomb niches of the Berkeley family line the walls.

Antecedents

By the mid-thirteenth century English Gothic architecture had taken a highly distinctive form. It was embedded in the traditions of its Anglo-Norman past, which were inimical to the structural implications of Gothic as developed in France, and strong enough to withstand many of the influences that began to arrive from there in the later twelfth century.

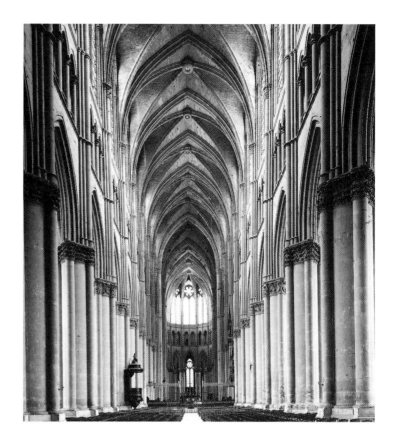

5   Reims Cathedral, France, begun *c*.1211, interior looking east. The coronation church of the French kings, the elevation of tall arcade, narrow band triforium and long clerestory represents the fashionable type of contemporary great church in France. Its design of bar tracery influenced that of Westminster Abbey.

Early Gothic great churches (abbeys and cathedrals) in England were low and solid; they had continued with the Anglo-Norman type of elevational wall, up to 4m thick and composed of two layers of ashlar masonry sandwiching a rubble fill that gave way to a passage in the top storey. The elevation usually consisted of three storeys, an arcade, a deep, high gallery opening through arches to the main vessel, and small clerestory windows pushed high into the roof, obscured from within by arcading on the inner plane of the wall. Copious mouldings alleviated the mass of masonry. The plans of these buildings were as distinctive as their elevations: the choir was usually rectangular, ending either in a sheer east wall or with an extension of low chapels built out eastwards. This preference for rectangular rather than apsed east ends may even be an Anglo-Saxon feature, suppressed at the Conquest and re-emerging about a century later; it certainly owes nothing to France, where contemporary buildings were very different.

During the twelfth century builders in the Paris area, far from abandoning the apsed Romanesque plans, had refined them to create the polygonal or semi-circular Gothic chevet with its ring of chapels. They had also devised a structure based on a thin, skeletal wall with a high arcade, a deep clerestory without a passage, and a narrow, so-called band triforium passage in the place of the gallery. This was the minimum needed to cover the otherwise blank wall fronting the aisle roof space. The elevation design was all visual logic. The quadripartite rib vaults descended to the wall shafts that apparently supported them, running down to the floor; and the thrusts exerted by the vault were carried safely to the ground through flying buttresses arched over the aisles. By 1240, when English windows were still plain lancets (sometimes, however, arranged in dramatic groups), French great churches were embellished with huge windows bearing the new patterns of bar 5 tracery. Inside, where the French stressed the vertical, the English denied it. The latter accepted the rib vault and the pointed arch, which had in any case appeared early in Anglo-Norman buildings and presented no difficulty; but the vault shafts, far from descending to the floor, were corbelled in above the arcade, individual storeys were emphasised by abundant shaftwork, foliate and geometric ornament and the use of contrasting 'marbles' to enhance colouristic effects. Wherever possible plain walls were adorned with arcading, and by 1240 even the vault, seated firmly on the thick wall without need of fliers, was adorned with a pattern of ribs.

The retention of the Anglo-Norman wall structure undoubtedly owed something to the way church buildings were altered over the years. After 1200 few great churches were built from scratch, as new monastic foundations were comparatively rare and no new dioceses were created until 1547. One result was that a campaign of construction often involved only an extension to or replacement of an existing part of a building; and there was evident pressure not only to conform to the earlier work, but also to reuse it as far as possible. This tendency persisted through the Decorated period: the ghostly presence of Anglo-Norman predecessors lurking in the dimensions and structure of Decorated buildings makes it difficult to define specifically 'Decorated' proportions or structural characteristics. At Ely Cathedral the extension 7 built on to the Anglo-Norman choir from 1236 corresponded storey for storey with the earlier work, only the ornamental details being up to date; and when in the fourteenth century the Anglo-Norman bays were themselves replaced, the new work, again up to date in detail, otherwise matched the proportions of the old. The design of Exeter Cathedral, apparently a Decorated building of the late thirteenth century and the 83 fourteenth, is largely preordained by the surviving Anglo-Norman masonry in its main walls, which dictated its height, width and the length of the nave. Despite this continuity, however, the early aesthetic clearly survived from deliberate choice. When Salisbury Cathedral was 8 built on a new site from about 1220, it still conformed wholly to tradition in both plan and elevation, its horizontality positively enhanced by the striped effects of Purbeck marble contrasting with pale limestone, its thickness emphasised by the abundant shaftwork in the upper storeys.

By the 1240s, when the main campaign began at Westminster, two great churches apart from Salisbury were establishing a powerful aesthetic principle that was to govern many of the developments of the later

6 Lincoln Cathedral, St Hugh's choir vault, late 1190s. The so-called 'crazy' vault defies structural logic by 'splitting' the diagonal ribs into a hairpin effect. All the ribs meet a longitudinal ridge rib, the junctions masked by carved foliage bosses.

thirteenth century in both positive and negative ways. The building that had most significant effect was Lincoln Cathedral, where work was more or less continuous for most of the thirteenth century, successive architects developing and clarifying the design as the structure progressed. Building had begun in the 1190s, with the replacement of the Anglo-Norman choir by St Hugh's choir, named from the bishop responsible: working within the Anglo-Norman constraints, with a kind of Gothic overlay derived from Canterbury Cathedral, the architect loaded his building with ornament, extending the decoration even to the vault. Here, the split hairpin effect of the divided ribs rising to a longitudinal ridge rib denies the arched construction implied in ordinary cross-rib vaults, and presents the vault as yet another surface to be

7 *Left* Ely Cathedral, upper levels of the choir bays. The five eastward bays were built by Bishop Northwold from 1234, their proportions corresponding to those of the Norman building. The bay on the left of the picture was built almost a century later by Bishop Hotham, in the same proportion but with contemporary decorative details.

8 *Right* Salisbury Cathedral, begun *c*.1220, the nave. The elevation with the tall, deep gallery and short clerestory follows English tradition. Dark Purbeck stone is used for piers and decorative shafts to enhance horizontality and colour contrasts.

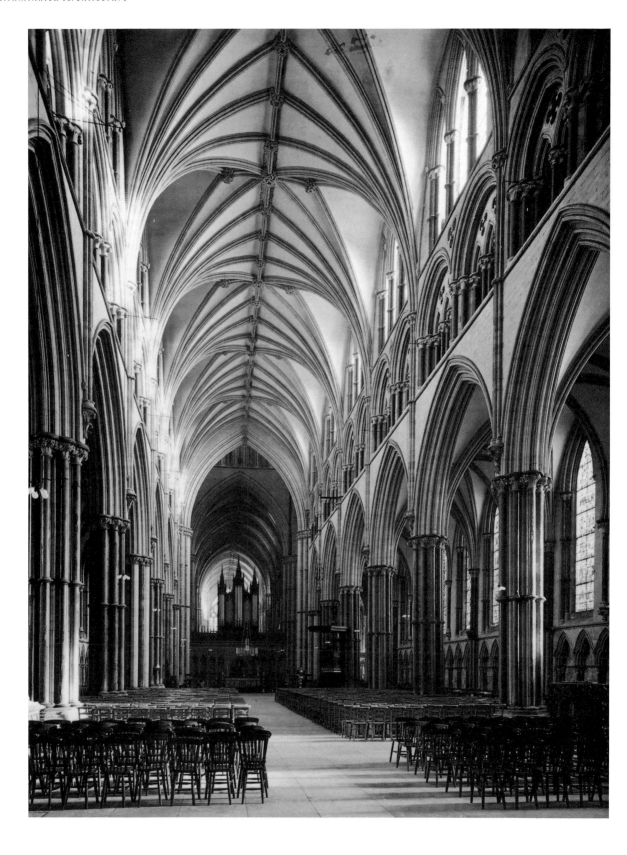

decorated. The nave, built from the 1220s, was in many ways a reworking of St Hugh's choir. The columnar main piers were now surrounded 9 by eight detached shafts, and the split hairpin vaulting was elaborated into the branch-like form in which five ribs rose from each springer, with two extra ones (tiercerons) meeting not at the ridge rib itself but further back at a short transverse rib. The lighter impression of the nave is derived from the widely spaced piers and concealment of massed masonry under sharply defined mouldings and abundant shaftwork. The ornament is crisp and delicate: shaft rings, foliage capitals at all levels and the foliate vault supports and keystones helped to produce an interior in which the carved ornament was as important as the coloured decoration of stained glass and (lost) paintwork.

The metallic quality of the ornament at Lincoln is no accident: it was almost certainly designed to resemble more precious materials. Even closer to metalwork is the choir extension built at Ely Cathedral from 1234 by Bishop Hugh Northwold. Designed to provide extra space for 7 altars and the shrine of St Etheldreda, Northwold's choir is a rectangular box with a flat east wall. Decoratively, the designer took as his starting point the nave of Lincoln. The vault is identical in pattern, but the keystones and foliate supports are more emphatic, crisper, more stylised and deeply undercut. As at Lincoln, contrasting marble, foliage and geometric ornament enhance and balance mouldings and shafts; but here there is extra applied foliage sculpture, and any plain walling is punctured by foiled openwork patterns. The flat east wall is opened up by three huge lancet windows, without tracery.

This, then, was the fashionable style of the fourth decade of the thirteenth century. Isolated from French developments, whether or not by choice, English builders remained faithful to rectangular plans and traditional elevations with thick walls, high galleries and short clerestories. Although Westminster Abbey, built from the 1240s under direct and specific French influence, made an irreversible impact on designs for windows and wall surfaces, it had no direct effect on ground-plans, and only an indirect effect on wall structure. Much of what followed in the second half of the thirteenth century can be seen as attempts to reconcile the irreconcilable.

Westminster Abbey

The Decorated period begins with Westminster Abbey. Architecturally, 1 the building is extremely odd, reflecting Henry III's desire to promote the cult of St Edward the Confessor and establish Westminster as the 10 coronation church. For these he turned to two French models: the Sainte-chapelle in the Palais in Paris, which Louis IX was rebuilding to house his newly acquired relics of the Crown of Thorns and the True 11 Cross, and Reims Cathedral, where the French kings were crowned. Westminster was specifically intended to evoke those buildings, and it is, therefore, one of the few English medieval buildings in which the

9   Lincoln Cathedral, the nave, begun in the 1220s. The decorative tierceron ribs of the vault meet at foliate bosses along the ridge rib. The elevation, of traditional proportions, is enlivened with mouldings and other ornamental carving, sharply angled to give a metallic effect.

10   Westminster Abbey, the base of St Edward the Confessor's shrine, before 1269. The shrine, which has niches for pilgrims in the sides, was the focus of Henry III's rebuilding of the church. Decorated with Italianate mosaic pattern related to the church floors (see p. 124), the base is elevated to enable the reliquary on top to be seen behind and above the retable of the high altar (see plate VIII).

French references were clearly readable.

Master Henry, the first architect of the new church, was later referred to as Henry of Reyns, which was the English name for Reims. Whether he was a Frenchman who compromised with English tastes and an English workforce or an Englishman who could build in French style is disputed. He produced a design that is very French in an English context, but not very convincing in a French one. The plan has a polygonal east end with ambulatory and radiating chapels, and the elevation a tall, narrow proportion with steeply pointed arches and a long clerestory, with no wall passage, that descends well below the springing level of the vault. The quadripartite rib vault is supported on shafts that run down to the main arcade and thence to the floor, giving the essentially French illusion of verticality and linkage of vaults and piers. The Frenchness of the Westminster elevation is, however, belied by the middle storey, which is the traditional English deep gallery. It is conceivable that Master Henry had no control over this, for the great width and interior finish of the gallery, with its finely carved head stops,

11 A tile from the chapter house floor in Westminster Abbey, 1250s. It reproduces the original pattern of the south transept rose window, which is French in origin. Architectural motifs were frequently reproduced in miniature on small objects.

indicates that it may have been built for spectators at coronations and suchlike events. It is equally possible that the English taste for galleries simply prevailed. Whatever the reason, Westminster has both a long clerestory and a gallery, an arrangement attempted nowhere else. Other aspects of the new abbey church did not find favour: the apsed ground-plan has its own history in England, where it is rather strongly associated with royal foundations, at Beaulieu Abbey in 1203/4, and after Westminster at Hailes and Vale Royal, but elsewhere the rectangular plan now prevailed. Plain rib vaulting was also now quite unacceptable; even at Westminster the design was tempered by a ridge rib, and in the eastern bay of the nave, the last to be built before work stopped at Henry's death in 1272, they reverted to the tiercerons of Lincoln and Ely.

The true significance of Westminster lies in its decoration, the ornament and the window tracery. Westminster may not have been the first building in England to be decorated with bar tracery, as Lincoln Cathedral may already have had some simple forms of tracery in the 1230s, and bar tracery of the Westminster type appeared at Binham Priory and possibly at Windsor early in the 1240s. Westminster, however, had far wider influence. The window designs are drawn from Reims and the Sainte-chapelle: like Reims are the main windows with cusped oculi, and the great rose windows in the transepts, the original pattern of which is preserved in the glazed tiles of the chapter house 11 floor; and from the Sainte-chapelle are derived the curved triangular forms on the outside walls of the gallery. For the interior decoration, however, the most potent influence was the Sainte-chapelle alone. Henry III's building is encased in ornament: the vault bosses are carved with foliage and figure sculpture; window embrasures and the blind arcading in the aisles and chapels are adorned with busts of angels, foliage and figured scenes; and all about, especially in the gallery, are head stops, many clearly taken from the life. The greater set pieces are the transept ends, across which were disposed large-scale sculptures of 12 angels and other figures set among foliage and the rosette diaper ornament that is carved into all the main surfaces. These carvings, in deep relief, were painted, as were the walls. Plain walls were lined out with the usual red imitation masonry joints, except in the transept dado, where there were monumental figures of saints; the diaper was gilt against a red background, and the arcades were gilded, with the hollows of the mouldings picked out in red, blue and green. Painted sprays of foliage surrounded the vault bosses, and the dark, burnished surfaces of the Purbeck marble piers and vault shafts stood in contrast to the paint and gilding. The rich concentration of colour was heightened by the stained glass windows, and in the candle-light of a great feast day the gilded reliefs would have sparkled and glittered like goldsmiths' work.

There was nothing new in the use of colour, nor in the metallic quality of the ornament. What was new was the sheer density of the interior decoration, together with the use of large-scale sculptured figures. The

idea for these is derived from the figures of the Apostles attached to the piers inside the Sainte-chapelle, where they witness the great relic and the events depicted in the stained glass windows. Whether, as in the Sainte-chapelle, the Westminster glass included detailed allusions to the great relics cannot now be known, but we can see the idea transposed to the transept sculptures. On the north transept façade, the main entrance from the Palace, the sculptures were related to the relic of the Holy Blood of Christ, which Henry had obtained in 1247. Inside, the figures of John the Evangelist and Edward the Confessor illustrated Henry's favourite story of the Ring and the Pilgrim, in which the Confessor gave his ring to a beggar, who later, as St John, returned it, foretelling Edward's death. This is the dramatic interior, a setting transformed into a theatre, with scenes enacted by monumental figures, both two- and three-dimensional. The deployment of such figures inside the building to stand alongside their equivalents in the stained glass is one of the defining characteristics of illuminated architecture and Westminster's great legacy to its successors.

Continuity and response

That the dramatic interior was to become one of the main preoccupations of late medieval builders was not entirely obvious at first. In the 1250s, after work had started at the royal abbey, patrons and architects found the choice of possible designs bewilderingly rich. This much is demonstrated by what they actually created. As most buildings took many years to construct the question of influence of one on another can be difficult to resolve, but the new generation of buildings in the third quarter of the century clearly shows the different attempts to come to terms with both the current of tradition and intoxicating novelty offered by the new work of Salisbury, Lincoln, Ely and Westminster.

At only three places, Lichfield, Hereford and Salisbury, was there direct acceptance of the architectural and non-figurative innovations of Westminster, and at all three there is also a strong element of English tradition. The nave of Lichfield Cathedral, begun c.1260, has a clerestory without a wall passage, its windows in the distinctive curved triangular form of the Westminster galleries; and the vaulting shafts descend uninterrupted to the floor. Galleries and aisles are alike traceried, but otherwise the Lichfield nave, with clustered piers and tierceron vault, conforms to the type established at Lincoln and Ely. The north transept of Hereford Cathedral (1240–60) developed Westminster forms with 13 fewer distractions, although the latter include a very thick elevational wall and a quadripartite rib vault corbelled in at the arcade. The striking features of Hereford are the diaper ornament covering the gallery spandrels, the curved triangular clerestory windows and the all but triangular arch form, which was adopted from various arched entrances in the abbey, in the north transept and the chapter house vestibule. The Westminster chapter house, with its huge, four-light windows, each

12 Westminster Abbey, upper levels of the interior wall of the south transept, c.1250. The first dramatic interior in England, it combined stained glass, tracery and foliage and rosette diaper carving with large-scale polychrome figure sculpture, here St John and Henry III in a scene from *The Ring and the Pilgrim*, flanked by censing angels.

14 bearing a cusped oculus, was imitated at Salisbury as late as *c*.1280; and the great expanse of glass and tracery introduced at Westminster had a permanent effect on the otherwise English design of octagonal chapter houses, as in the highly decorated versions at Southwell and York.

III At the two great cathedral works begun in the 1250s, the Angel choir of Lincoln and the New Work at Old St Paul's, London, we see distinct reactions to the new ideas, the former exploring the possibilities offered by the dramatic interior, the latter endorsing tracery by adopting the latest French fashions. Begun in 1256, the Angel choir completed the major building campaigns at Lincoln. The continuation eastwards of St Hugh's choir, it was partly intended as a setting for St Hugh's shrine, and the old east end was replaced by a rectangular box, as at Ely, of low, broad proportions. The three-storey elevation has a clerestory and passage pushed high under the vault, and a tall gallery. This was a harmonious development of both St Hugh's choir and the nave; it made no concessions to Westminster either in its general outlines or in its clustered piers, the tierceron vault corbelled in above the arcade, and the multi-shafted, crocketed gallery openings. All the wall surfaces are, however, arcaded, sculptured or traceried. The Angel choir takes its name from the angels carved in relief in the spandrels of the gallery, angels that, like the figure sculptures of Westminster, convey a specific message to the viewer. At Lincoln it is a choice between Paradise and

13 *Above, left* Hereford Cathedral, north transept, 1240–60. Built by Bishop Aigueblanche to house his tomb (see p. 40), it employs the diaper and tracery patterns of Westminster Abbey, together with the characteristic triangular arch heads, and windows shaped as curved triangles, here in the clerestory. The tomb/shrine of St Thomas Cantilupe (see p. 90) can be seen in the centre.

14 *Above* Salisbury Cathedral chapter house, *c*.1280. The octagonal form, delicate central column and design of the huge windows reflect the chapter house of Westminster Abbey.

15 Lincoln Cathedral, Angel choir, begun 1256, the south door. The theme of the Last Judgement prepared pilgrims to contemplate salvation. Christ's unusual gesture pointing to the wound in his side may be derived from Westminster Abbey.

damnation, a choice offered upon entering the choir through the great south or Judgement door. That this door is based typologically on the north transept door of Westminster is no coincidence, for the link between the message of the exterior sculpture and that of the interior is essentially the same.

Also developed from Westminster is the window tracery, here adapted for three lights in the aisles, four in the clerestory and eight in the east window. The presence of the clerestory passage meant that in order not to lose its effect the tracery had to have layers on both the inner and outer planes of the wall. The patterns are based as yet on the cusped circle, but the odd number of lights and the subdivisions allowed variations, the large oculus containing seven circles in the east window even suggesting a rose. Perhaps a little ironically, the advent of tracery sealed the victory of the flat east wall, for whereas in French churches elaborate traceried compositions had to be confined to the transept ends, in England their full glory could also be celebrated in the choir, the east window filling its entire width, with another above it under the great gable.

When the theme of tracery was explored at Old St Paul's Cathedral, however, the influence was not Westminster but a new generation of French buildings of the 1260s, related to work on the transepts of Notre-Dame in Paris. The New Work at Old St Paul's, begun probably in the 1250s and destroyed in the Great Fire of London in 1666, was the greatest building enterprise of the day. When completed, St Paul's was the longest church in England, and its wooden steeple was higher than that of Salisbury Cathedral. The New Work was the replacement of the eastern arm. It was a huge structure twelve bays long, now known only from drawings and engravings, including those made by Wenceslaus Hollar and Sir Christopher Wren; but although some details are vague, the building's general appearance is clear.

France had little influence on the structure or disposition of the main elevation. Apparently ignoring Westminster, the architect adopted the rectangular plan with a three-storey elevation that owed much to Ely and Lincoln. The elevation had clustered piers, twin traceried openings in the gallery and a tierceron vault, almost certainly with a ridge rib, that sprang from the clerestory, thus pushing the latter high into the recesses of the vault webs. The aisles were lined with blind arcading and most of the windows had three lights. Where the design differed from Lincoln was in the clerestory, which had no inner layer of tracery and perhaps no passage, and in the vaulting shafts, which were designed to give the same impression of vertical continuity as at Westminster. The piers and shaftwork were possibly of Purbeck marble, but there appears to have been no interior architectural sculpture at all, neither foliage nor diaper work. All the decorative effort was concentrated in the windows and buttresses, both far bolder than Westminster, the latter in particular assertively French. If the interior of Westminster suggested a reliquary,

16 Old St Paul's Cathedral, London, the choir, begun in the ?1250s and destroyed in 1666. This engraving by Wenceslaus Hollar shows that the building combined traditional English elevation and vault designs with the latest French tracery patterns, deployed to full effect in the great rose on the flat east wall.

17   Tintern Abbey, Gwent, begun *c*.1270. The view westwards into the nave. The style of this Cistercian abbey is plain except for the magnificent tracery designs, derived from Old St Paul's. The characteristic two-storey Cistercian elevation design can be seen in the transept (left).

so did the exterior of St Paul's. That the reliquary of the sainted bishop of London, Erkenwald, made *c*.1319, was composed of miniature tracery, buttresses and pinnacles was no coincidence: inner and outer reflected each other.

The windows, French though they were, demonstrated the English trick of improving on an outside influence even as it is absorbed. The number of lights in a window affects the arrangement of the patterns in the tracery head, and although windows with an odd number could be found in France, most French churches had a more conventional four or two. At St Paul's, as at Lincoln, the windows had three lights, the odd number not needing subdivision and allowing a greater area for the tracery itself. The main motifs of the St Paul's tracery were pointed trefoils and curved triangles, both derived from Notre-Dame and its associated buildings; and the influence of Notre-Dame is even clearer in the east window, a vast rose of twelve radiating spokes set in a square frame above seven tall lancets, and filling the entire end wall of the main vessel. The derivation directly from Paris rather than the transepts of Westminster shows in the use of curved triangles within the pattern itself, and the glazed spandrels between the rose and its square frame. The tracery of St Paul's is significant not only because it reflected more recent French thinking than Westminster, but also because of its profound influence. The use of multiple oculi in the tracery head became the basis of many later tracery patterns; and the pointed and elongated tracery shapes, together with the habit of filling interstices as well as the main pattern with tracery or cusping, was to become widespread.

The Angel choir of Lincoln was consecrated in 1280; building at Old St Paul's continued perhaps until after 1310. Up to the end of the thirteenth century the pointed trilobes of the tracery at Old St Paul's predominated 17 in window tracery as far afield as Exeter, Hereford, Tintern Abbey and St Mary's Abbey in York; and they were beginning to be developed locally, as in a pattern that alternated round and pointed trilobes, used at Lincoln, York, Howden and Ripon. In these years, too, St Paul's may also have shared in the taste for naturalistic leaf sculpture, a Europe-wide phenomenon that in England appeared on buildings, most showily in the new work at Exeter and the chapter house at Southwell, and on 18 smaller pieces such as the base for the shrine of St Frideswide in Oxford (*c*.1270s) and the tomb of St Thomas Cantilupe (d. 1282) at Hereford. Yet not surprisingly, St Paul's was out of fashion long before it was finished. Architects had already seen that its Anglo-Norman type of deep gallery diminished the effect of traceried windows, and although a galleried elevation was built at St Mary's Abbey, York, from *c*.1270, it had been abandoned for most new buildings by the turn of the century. The thick wall structure was, however, retained for most aisled buildings above a certain size; and throughout the Decorated period designers had to find

18 Southwell Minster, Notts, foliage carving on the chapter house door, ?1270s. The species of naturalistically carved leaf include buttercup, vine, oak and hawthorn.

19 Selby Abbey, N. Yorks.,
choir *c*.1315–35, looking east. The
two-storey elevation has a wide
arch to the clerestory and a wall
passage. Much of the original
sculptured decoration has been
destroyed, including most of the
small figures that sat on the
parapet. The pattern of the east
window appears in churches in
Nottinghamshire and
Lincolnshire (see p. 175).

ways of reconciling a lengthened, prominent clerestory with a massive
masonry wall. The two main solutions to the problem were either to
adopt the triforium in place of the gallery or to reduce the elevation to
two storeys.

The two-storey elevation with a clerestory passage had been a
traditional form in England for those churches where three storeys were
unnecessary or unsuitable, cathedrals of the second rank, such as Lichfield (*c*.1220) and the choir of Southwell Minster (1230s), Cistercian
abbeys (Netley, Hants, *c*.1240) or churches of other religious orders, as at
Pershore Abbey (Heref. and Worcs; 1230s). After the fashion of their
day, most had lancet windows screened on the inner plane by free-
standing colonnettes; but Netley had a wide, unscreened arch, giving
more prominence to the window itself. This design was also chosen for
the transepts of the Cistercian abbey of Tintern when it was rebuilt from
c.1270, and it continued into the fourteenth century, in Winchester
Cathedral choir (*c*.1310; traces remain) and in the north at Howden
19 Minster and Selby Abbey (*c*.1315–35).

At Exeter Cathedral there was a variant. The original extension to the
Anglo-Norman choir built from about 1280 was followed by a reconstruction of the entire building except the transept towers, which lasted
iv until the 1340s. Exeter is regarded as a showpiece of Decorated vaulting

and tracery, the ultimate attempt to combine all possible forms of decoration. Its elevation, low and stocky, was, as we have seen, partly dictated by the presence of its Anglo-Norman predecessor. The first design, still partly visible in the eastern bays of the presbytery, had two storeys, an arcade and a clerestory with no passage but a sharply sloping sill that would have given much more prominence to the windows. The design was perhaps thought to be too simple for a major cathedral church; at any rate in the next phase of building a triforium was introduced, and the earlier work altered to resemble it. In the choir the triforium 'passage' is a fake, blocked at each pier, but in the nave there are real passages in both triforium and clerestory.

Genuine superposed passages, consciously chosen rather than arrived at through compromise, seem to have been built first at St Albans and Chester (now Cathedral) in about the late 1270s, and later at Guisborough Priory, N. Yorks, c.1300. These were the first buildings of the time in Britain to adopt the French triforium, probably from Burgundy, where double passages were already popular. They provided a neat solution to the problem of the thick wall; but like many of the designs that arrived in England from abroad their history was short-lived, partly because they were rapidly superseded, and partly owing to the inconsistent, almost random manner in which French ideas were adopted. The nave of York Minster, rebuilt from 1291, demonstrates 20 how the architects, even if they had a specific French building in mind, produced a general notion rather than an identifiable copy. In an English context, the nave of York was structurally ahead of its time: it was the first great church in which Anglo-Norman elevational principles were abandoned in favour of a thinner, more skeletal wall, and it was imitated only in the later fourteenth century, first in the choir of the same building, then in the nave of Canterbury Cathedral. By English standards York nave was gigantic, wide and lofty. The arcade was surmounted by a tall triforium that was combined with the clerestory, linked to it by the downward continuation of the window mullions, and the phenomenon, unique to England, of the clerestory glass lying on the inner plane of the wall, which gives the interior elevation the flatness of a contemporary French design. The Frenchness is enhanced by the vaulting shafts, which run uninterrupted from floor to vault springers. Although the essential Englishness of the Minster is betrayed in many details, from mouldings to its wooden vault, the elevation as a whole is deliberately French. Its source, however, is a mystery – the cathedrals of Strasbourg, Clermont Ferrand, even Cologne, have all been suggested – and this exemplified the English mason's method of merging ideas from many sources to achieve the desired, specific result.

Decoration and ornament

The problem of elevation design was peculiar to basilicas, aisled buildings with a higher central vessel. The wide variety of solutions offered

might suggest that the design of the elevation was a major preoccupation; but the interests of architects and their patrons were shifting away from conventional structures towards other aspects of the building. The most immediately significant developments of the late thirteenth century were in decoration, particularly of chapels and liturgical furnishings, which were structurally simpler than before. It was in the 1280s that the idea that the sacred connotations of a church building could be enhanced by decorating it with associated forms and motifs began to be explored widely. Architecture and the other arts were growing increasingly close, architectural forms appearing in miniature as decoration on paintings, altarpieces, metalwork and tombs, reflecting the building around them while it, in turn, reflected them. With the advent of structurally simpler buildings the decoration became paramount. Much of it was concentrated on the niche. As a miniature vault, the niche designated as sacred the space that it enclosed; it also represented the greater church structure; and it could itself be reduced to an almost two-dimensional formula that yet conveyed its essence, the so-called arch-and-gable motif. This, a decorative gable set over a cusped arch, was to be a leitmotif of the Decorated style, and in reducing two important structural elements to ornament, it typifies one strand of thinking behind the style.

The arch-and-gable had a long association with metal reliquaries, which naturally had strong connotations of sanctity and on which figures and architecture had long been combined. During the thirteenth century the arch-and-gable had developed as an architectural feature in France and England, used on a monumental scale over windows, and in miniature as canopy-work over statues, particularly on church façades. From the mid-century, however, the motif had also returned to the interior, for small-scale use both on the building itself and in its furnishings. For example, it frames the miniatures in the Missal of Henry of Chichester (Manchester, John Rylands Lib., MS lat. 24; *c*.1250); it is found 21 in the window tracery of St-Urbain at Troyes and in the triforium of Clermont Ferrand Cathedral, both of the 1260s; and in the following decade it formed a setting for the painted figures on the great retable of Westminster Abbey, the coloured glass, gesso, cameos and gilding of VIII which gave the same impression of jewelled preciousness that they were intended to convey in the architecture.

This aspect of architectural decoration can be seen in St Etheldreda's, Ely Place, formerly the chapel in the London residence of the bishops of 22 Ely, which was built from 1284 to 1286 in the two-storeyed tradition of private chapels. The main, upper chapel is a wooden-roofed single space, articulated by the overall surface decoration of window tracery, wall arcades and figure sculpture. The windows, with their intersecting Y-tracery, pointed, impaled trilobes and cusped circles, reflect Old St Paul's, but the chapel otherwise represents a highly concentrated form of the Westminster type of illuminated architecture. It is much restored,

20   York Minster, nave, begun 1291, looking west. The tall, flat elevation, with continuous vaulting shafts and the clerestory glass on the inner plane of the wall, is strongly French in appearance. The wooden vault (replaced) was made *c*.1350.

21 *Left* Missal of Henry of Chichester (Manchester, John Rylands Lib., MS lat. 24, fol. 149; *c*.1250). The *Annunciation to the Virgin* is set beneath trilobed arches surmounted by triangular gables. In the spandrels are censing angels (compare Westminster Abbey, p. 26).

22 *Below* St Etheldreda's, Ely Place, London, 1284–6. The chapel of the London residence of the bishops of Ely, its interior is lined with arch-and-gable niches in which are set statues (now modern). The pattern of the east window develops motifs in Old St Paul's.

lacking the original glazing and painted colour, and the statues on foliate corbels between the windows are modern; but the interior still conveys the sense of encrusted miniaturism found on the Westminster retable. The wall arcading consists of a series of arch-and-gable motifs linking the windows and acting as niches or frames for the carved figures. Enclosing tracery patterns and crested with foliage, they are closely related to those of the retable.

With its sacred connotations the arch-and-gable had been popular for tombs: it could be a framing device round the effigy, as on the tomb of Louis of France, once at Royaumont Abbey (after 1260; now at Saint-Denis) or part of the canopy, as on three splendid free-standing episcopal tombs in England, those of Walter de Grey (d. 1255) in York, Giles de Bridport (d. 1264) at Salisbury and Peter of Aigueblanche (d. 1270) in Hereford. There they are interspersed with pinnacles, a combination that was refined to become a ubiquitous Decorated motif. On the wall tomb of Bishop John de Bradfield (d. 1283) in Rochester Cathedral the tomb chest is set in a niche under a single arch-and-gable adorned with cusping and tracery. Other forms of canopy-work were treated with the arch-and-gable, notably those over the stalls in the chapter houses of York and Southwell.

The last years of Edward I's reign, to 1307, confirmed the course that the Decorated style was to take. Architects now concentrated on shape and ornament. The only really large churches in building were Old St Paul's and York Minster, the next generation of work at Exeter, Wells, Bristol and St Albans being generally smaller in scale. In addition to the smaller types of church, castles, houses and halls were now making their contribution to stylistic change. While Gothic had developed as a style for churches that had some influence on secular buildings, in this later period influences were also moving the other way and secular motifs were lodging comfortably in an ecclesiastical context. To some extent this phenomenon reflected the increased power of the laity in the Church: as more lay people were entombed in prominent monuments they brought into the church building the insignia of their secular life, and such motifs as heraldry and miniature battlements became accepted ornamental details. In this context there appeared in the 1280s the first intimations of a preoccupation that would later produce spectacular manifestations: an interest in polygons.

Medieval architects had long been professionally interested in geometric figures for help in setting out apses; and in England the polygon had taken an overt form in octagonal chapter houses. Now it was to be exploited further. The earliest signs of a wider interest in polygons had appeared in castles as early as the twelfth century; and polygonal towers were incorporated into the designs of the castles built in Wales by Edward I. Uninhibited by demands of the terrain, the use of complex 'geometric' shapes was clearly deliberate: octagonal towers were built at Caernarfon, and the entire ground-plan of Rhuddlan Castle was

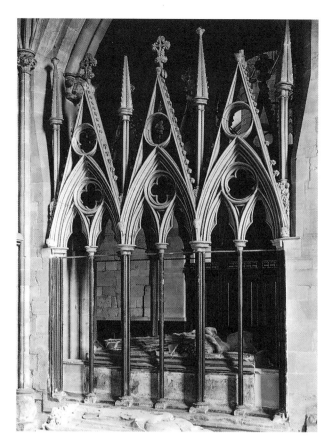

23 *Above* Hereford Cathedral, tomb of Bishop Peter of Aigueblanche, d. 1270 (see p. 28). The canopy is composed of arches with crocketed gables and tracery interspersed with pinnacles. The supporting shafts are of Purbeck stone. The structure gives an impression of metalwork.

24 *Above, right* Rochester Cathedral, tomb of Bishop John de Bradfield, d. 1283. The gable displays the earliest dated example of the Kentish motif, with long spikes and split cusps.

conceived as a rhomboid. In the next decade the Eleanor Crosses, built by Edward I to commemorate his wife, Eleanor of Castile (d. 1290), were small-scale polygons, octagonal, hexagonal or triangular.

Geometric shapes did not appear only in monumental plans but also in vaulting. Lozenge and star patterns were created by the introduction of the lierne, a short rib that does not rise from the springer but runs between the main ribs nearer the crown of the vault. A lozenge-pattern was used in the crypt of St Stephen's chapel in the Palace of Westminster, refounded by Edward I in 1292, but the idea of a compartmented vault pattern probably arose in the west country. At Exeter Cathedral such a compartmented pattern was designed solely with tiercerons in the vault of the retrochoir bay linking the presbytery and eastern chapels; but at Pershore Abbey, which is stylistically related to Exeter, the choir vault built after a fire in 1288 has a lozenge pattern using true liernes.

In the 1290s the Decorated style was consolidated not only in building programmes but in tombs and monuments. On a monumental scale the taste for complete coverage of surfaces can be seen in the chapter house of Wells Cathedral, built 1293–1307, which was a contemporary of the eastern extension at Exeter and shared its taste for emphatic mouldings and decoration. At Wells every surface is given over to arcading, tracery

25   Eleanor Cross at
Hardingstone (Northampton),
1291–4. One of twelve built to
commemorate and invite prayers
for Edward I's queen, Eleanor of
Castile, d. 1290. The hexagonal,
tiered structure shelters statues
of the queen (see p. 100). It is
decorated with arch-and-gable,
foliage, pinnacles, heraldry and
slight ogees. The cross-shaft is
broken off.

or vault ribs, the effect concentrated by the centralised, octagonal plan.

It was, however, in tombs and liturgical furnishings that many significant developments occurred, for there the miniaturist aspects of the style could be fully exploited, together with the use of mixed media to create the maximum effect of precious detail. The works associated with Edward I and those related to them demonstrate the repertory of motifs that prevailed for a generation or more. Together with the Eleanor Crosses, Edward's project to commemorate his wife included three tombs, one at Westminster, and gilt bronze effigies of Eleanor and of his father Henry III. His new work at St Stephen's chapel began at the same time, and in the rest of the decade additional family tombs were installed in the abbey church, notably those of his kinsman, William de Valence, Earl of Pembroke, and his brother, Edmund Crouchback, Earl

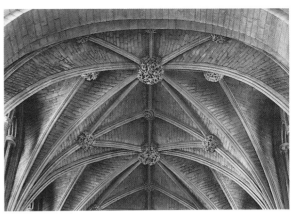

26   *Above* Pershore Abbey, Heref. and Worcs., choir vault, after 1288. An earlier example of a lierne vault, in which short ribs branch from the main diagonals to create net patterns.

27   *Left* Wells Cathedral, chapter house, 1293–1307. The interior is fully moulded; the tracery patterns are derived from London and the clergy seats are defined by arch-and-gable motifs.

of Lancaster (both d. 1296), together with a tomb to Edmund's first wife, Aveline de Forz, who had died in 1273. In these works the same motifs were deployed in different media: the obsessive covering of heraldic diaper, done in gesso and paint on the Crouchback and Aveline tombs, was chased in gilt-bronze on the tomb of Eleanor of Castile and enamelled on that of William de Valence. The number of decorative motifs was now restricted in favour of repetition – the variety of naturalistic leaves, for instance, was reduced to a type of bubbly, stylized seaweed – and it revolved to a large extent round rosette diaper, leaves and micro-architecture, which were used on everything. The Eleanor Crosses and the Westminster tombs were composed of all the motifs by which Decorated is defined, arch-and-gable arcading, pinnacles, foliage cresting and rosettes, miniature battlements, blind tracery, diaper, heraldry and figure sculpture. Arcading, in the form of arch-and-gable with pinnacles, as in Wells chapter house and York Minster, was popular both on wall surfaces and on tombs and liturgical furnishings. The decorative look is epitomised by the canopy of the prior's throne in the chapter house of Canterbury Cathedral, which is composed of identical elements, but on an even more miniature scale. It is delicate, three-dimensional and encrusted, at once a monumental structure and an enlarged metal ornament. Many of these works also display the most significant decorative innovation of the decade: the ogee arch.

28　Westminster Abbey, tomb of Edmund, earl of Lancaster, d. 1296. The tripartite, vaulted canopy and the weepers have French prototypes. The decoration exemplifies Decorated in the 1290s: arch-and-gable, delicate ogees, diaper, crockets, pinnacles, miniature battlements, seaweed foliage. Considerable traces of the original coloured decoration survive.

The S-shaped ogee curve had appeared sporadically in eastern and western art for many centuries; it was used in some thirteenth-century western manuscripts and metalwork, and is found shaping window arches in San Marco, Venice, in about 1250. England, however, was the country in which the ogee flourished and whence it influenced the rest of Europe. In England it first appeared rather covertly in the so-called wave moulding, an undulating form used first in door- and window-

29 Stanton Harcourt, shrine base of St Edburga of Bicester, before 1312. It has some of the earliest surviving nodding ogee arches, as well as seaweed foliage, pinnacles and heraldic shields.

jambs, giving a soft, pliable profile well suited to the way Decorated would develop. The earliest wave mouldings are found in the work of masons in the royal works in Wales and Cheshire in the 1280s; in the next decade the ogee arch was used modestly in the arch-and-gable work on 84 the tomb of Archbishop Pecham (d. 1292) in Canterbury Cathedral, on 28 the Northampton Eleanor Cross, and on the Crouchback tomb at Westminster. The ogee curve appeared more or less simultaneously in tracery, on the choir screen of Canterbury Cathedral, the crypt of St Stephen's chapel, Westminster, and, if Hollar's engravings can be trusted, in the rose window of Old St Paul's. Gradually the ogee became ubiquitous, and while it started as an enhancing motif, it was eventually to characterise the Decorated style.

Yet the ogee took at least a decade to become established in the south and even longer in the north. The tomb of Bishop Louth of Ely (d. 1298), which is based on the Crouchback tomb, does not have them; the combined shrine of Bishop Remigius and Tomb of Christ, set up *c*.1300 near the high altar of Lincoln Cathedral, is a gabled structure with pinnacles, figure and naturalistic foliage sculpture, decorative vaults and blind tracery, but the arches and traceries are not ogival; the tomb of Henry de Lacy, Earl of Lincoln (d. 1310) in Old St Paul's had the arch-and-gable, shields and weepers, but no ogees; nor did the canopied tomb in York Minster of Archbishop Greenfield, who died in 1315. At St 55 Albans, however, the new shrine base of *c*.1305–8 displayed the Decorated repertory of arch-and-gable, pinnacles, foliage and figure sculpture, with on its interior panels tracery in the form of linked ogival 1 quatrefoils, known as reticulated, which was to become a standard pattern. The ogival niche underwent its final refinement a few years later, when the arch was bent forward to form the nodding ogee, a form 29 adopted at once for such small-scale pieces as the shrine of St Edburga of Bicester (before 1312; now at Stanton Harcourt), and in the window embrasures of the Lady chapel at St Albans, before 1315. The ogival tomb canopy was not slow to develop, with the Alard tombs in Winchelsea 93, 101 church (E. Sussex) after 1312, the tomb of Aymer de Valence, Earl of Pembroke (d. 1324), in Westminster Abbey and one of the latest, with a frontis gigantic nodding ogee, the Percy tomb in Beverley Minster *c*.1340.

As residential buildings were now becoming more opulent Decorated motifs were used in them as much as in churches and liturgical furniture. The sumptuous town house of the bishops of Ely was not unique: also in the 1280s Robert Burnell, Bishop of Bath and Wells and Chancellor of England, built a hall for the palace at Wells with fine transomed 86 windows, and a quadrangular house at Acton Burnell, Shropshire, the hall of which boasted tracery with curved triangles. The halls of *c*.1300 that survive from the palaces of the archbishops of Canterbury at Charing and Mayfield in Kent had timber roofs supported on finely 62 carved human-head corbels, a device used thirty years later in the guest hall at Ely. Monastic patrons, too, advertised themselves: Abbot

30 St Augustine's Abbey, Canterbury, the gatehouse, built 1300–09 by Abbot Fyndon. The design is similar to recent work in London and in Canterbury Cathedral. The battlements and polygonal turrets reflect secular buildings.

Fyndon's great gate at St Augustine's Abbey, Canterbury, built 1300–9, 30 almost certainly by the makers of the screens in the Cathedral and the royal works at Westminster, is richly embellished with ogival arch-and-gable niches.

Perhaps the greatest contribution made by secular life to church buildings was the element of fantasy that now became so strong. In the Middle Ages much was conveyed through images and symbols, and the image of seigneurial rule was, to modern eyes, curiously fanciful. In their present state the castles seem grim, austere and forbidding, fitting a modern perception of authoritarianism based on the architecture of Fascist and Communist regimes; but at the time they were not like that. The castle asserted power not only through bulk and strength but through colour and ornament. The walls of Caernarfon are banded with 78 courses of coloured masonry. Conwy Castle gleamed white with lime-wash, the royal standard flew from the turrets atop the towers of the inner ward, and the battlements were adorned with decorative pinnacles. Before 1306 the battlements of Marten's tower at Chepstow Castle were topped with seated figures, and by 1317 the Eagle tower at Caernarfon had been crowned with the stone eagles that gave the tower its name. Parapet figures had quite a future in the north. Small stone soldiers stand on the battlements of the town gates at York, and the castles of Middleham and Alnwick. Heraldic beasts similar to the

Caernarfon eagles found their way on to the parapet of York chapter house, where stone bears are a pun on the name of the Treasurer, Francis Fitzurse. York Minster itself, Selby Abbey and Beverley Minster are all adorned with parapet figures; the parapets of York are themselves crenellated, an early example of the fashion that was soon to overtake many church buildings.

Fantasy was not, however, confined to decoration, although structural fantasy rarely exists unaccompanied by ornament of a similar character. The Augustinian priory of Bristol (now the cathedral), was partly rebuilt by the Berkeley family as their burial church, work starting seriously probably in the second decade of the fourteenth century. It is one of the nearest buildings we have in England to a hall church, a building in which the aisles are the same height as the main vessel, so that there is no clerestory, and the building is lit through the tall aisle windows. In a design of this kind the dado, windows and vault are of great importance. At Bristol the east wall of the projecting Lady chapel is decorated with ogival arches, pinnacles and heraldic shields; the tomb recesses in the side walls are defined by polygonal frames surrounded by reversed arches crested with foliage; the windows are filled with varieties of tracery that are just becoming ogival or curvilinear; and the main vault is a lierne pattern of cusped lozenges. The aisle vault is, however, the visually interesting one: each bay is covered by a barrel vault set at right angles to the main vessel, supported on a diaphragm arch. The vault surface is decorated with ribs, but the lower parts, and the spandrels of the diaphragm arches, are cut away to give an openwork effect, each vault appearing poised like a ballet dancer on points. This design is almost certainly derived from carpentry. Masons were discovering that the flexibility of wood could be reproduced in stone, and combined with the latter to create on a monumental scale the pliable effects offered by the wave moulding and the ogee arch.

The greatest piece of carpentry to survive from these years is the bishop's throne at Exeter, part of the set of liturgical furnishings made to the order of Bishop Stapeldon between 1316 and 1324. Soaring to just below the choir vault, the throne canopy is a series of receding stages ornamented with the full panoply of Decorated motifs – nodding ogees, gables, pinnacles, finials, tracery, seaweed foliage and figure sculpture, and its own little wooden vault. Forms overlap, boundaries are merged. The same qualities informed the stone fittings, the altar reredos and sedilia (damaged and restored) composed of receding, openwork tabernacles encrusted with foliage, pinnacles, gables and decorative vaults. The pulpitum has like forms of ornament, and its vaults develop the tierceron patterns of the earlier retrochoir. Designed by the master mason of the Cathedral, these pieces show how by 1320 the Decorated style was both monumental and miniaturist, and a design made for one context could be used in another, wholly different one.

Nowhere is this demonstrated more clearly than at Ely Cathedral

31 St Augustine's, Bristol (now Cathedral), choir, begun after 1310. The Lady chapel lies to the east. A hall church, with all three aisles the same height, it has a main vault pattern of cusped lozenges.

32 Ely Cathedral, Lady chapel, 1322–49. The epitome of Decorated, the chapel is encased in ornament at every level. The upper niches held over-life-sized carved figures. In the dado are relief sculptures depicting the *Life and Miracles of the Virgin* (see p. 177).

I *Right* Westminster Abbey, choir and transept, begun 1245. Paid for by Henry III as a setting for the shrine of St Edward the Confessor, the Anglo-French design was enhanced by rosette diaper and large- and small-scale figure sculpture.

II *Overleaf left* The Sainte-chapelle, Paris, built 1241–8 by Louis IX of France. It housed the relics of the Crown of Thorns and True Cross, and was made to resemble a metal reliquary in stone. Its decoration strongly influenced Westminster Abbey.

priory, where the building works initiated from 1321 epitomise every aspect of Decorated, from minutely detailed surface ornament through illusionism and fantasy to a spectacular *coup de théâtre*. The original intention to build a huge new Lady chapel and add a study and small private chapel to the Prior's lodging was modified by the collapse of the central tower in 1322, obliging the clergy also to rebuild that and the three Anglo-Norman bays of the choir. These works were carried out simultaneously or in rapid succession, and there are many shared motifs. Vaults and pier forms were an interest, with net vaults (developed from St Stephen's, Westminster) in the choir and Lady chapel, and moulded piers with sharp keels or hollowed-out casements in the choir and crossing. Ogival trilobe tracery designs in Prior Crauden's chapel appeared in the crossing as niches for statues, and a tripartite framing device as a mask over a difficult joint. These, however, are details. The two chapels and the crossing exemplify the dramatic interior, and despite the damage inflicted at the Reformation and later their illuminated architecture can be restored at least in the imagination. The nodding ogees, niches, diaper and foliage, once coloured and gilded, are settings for the imagery that has been damaged or destroyed: figures were painted in windows, on walls, and in the backs of niches; they were sculptured in niches and tabernacles, stalls and window embrasures, ranging in size from larger than life to a few inches. They

III *Previous page* Lincoln Cathedral, Angel choir, begun 1256, interior looking north-east. The contrasting stonework, abundant foliage decoration, window tracery and monumental relief sculpture at gallery level typify the early phase of the Decorated style.

IV *Left* Exeter Cathedral, choir and presbytery, *c.*1290–1310. The ornamental coverage of shafts, arches and foliage is echoed in the wooden bishop's throne (right), made 1312–19, and would also have characterised the stone high altar screen (destroyed).

33 Prior Crauden's chapel, Ely, *c.*1324–5, piscina niche. It is framed by a foliate ogee arch and pinnacles with miniature battlements adorned with arrow-loops. Traces of a painted figure are visible on the back wall.

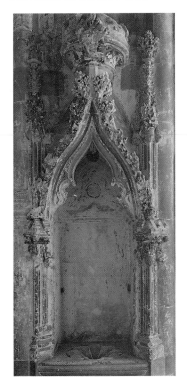

acted as congregation, witnesses and performers in narrative scenes, the sculptured figures in particular implying reality through their colour and three-dimensionality. The linkage thus created between the real and the imaginary was enhanced by the treatment of the micro-architectural settings: the miniature battlements in Prior Crauden's chapel, for instance, were finished with painted arrowloops, and the 33 vertical shafts in the Lady chapel were made to seem continuous as the ogival mouldings apparently wove among them.

Although the essence of Decorated is encapsulated in the enclosed, chapel-like space rather than the airier forms of the aisled basilica, at Ely its mood was celebrated to the utmost in the great octagonal crossing, where the effects were further enhanced by the subtle use of natural light. The irregular octagon created by the removal of the old crossing 34 piers was built in stone to vault level and surmounted by a wooden vault and central lantern. The sources lie in octagonal buildings such as chapter houses or kitchens with central roof openings, and just before the Ely Octagon was built a complex wooden vault with a central opening for bell ropes had been made for the south transept of Exeter Cathedral; but the Ely structure is nevertheless in a class by itself. Held by a huge, concealed timber frame the vault and lantern seem to float above the crossing, as the light slants in to the shadowy depths below.

If Ely celebrated the possibilities of Decorated to the full, its several themes were explored in other buildings. Formally, the preoccupation with shapes was manifest at every scale from monumental to miniature, in plans, vaults and tracery. The Ely Octagon was only one of several monumental polygons built in the 1320s: the north porch of St Mary Redcliffe in Bristol is a hexagon encrusted with nodding ogees, its 36 foliage and door shapes clearly derived from the Berkeley tombs in Bristol Cathedral; and the Lady chapel at Wells is an irregular octagon, three of its sides pulled back and merged with the adjoining retrochoir 59 in a typically Decorated manner. The Lady chapel is vaulted with a linear star pattern based on tiercerons, related to the earlier vaults at Pershore and Exeter and the slightly later one over the choir of Tewkes- 45 bury Abbey. The choir at Wells, however, a boxy, chapel-like space, has a rectilinear net vault possibly akin to Bristol; and more complex pat- 35 terns, arranged round parallel ridge ribs, were devised for the nave of Tewkesbury and the later choir of Gloucester Abbey. In the 1350s the 44 nave of York Minster was given a wooden vault with a pattern of 20 tiercerons and liernes arranged diagonally in threes.

The ogee curve scarcely appeared in vault patterns, except over the choir of Ottery St Mary in Devon in the 1330s. It swooped dramatically 54 in the monumental strainer arches of Wells Cathedral and the more delicate flying ribs at Gloucester, but its principal role was in tracery designs, where it became the basis of curvilinear or flowing tracery, in which the standard shapes of earlier tracery, the oculus, the trefoil and the quatrefoil were squashed to make figures known as *soufflets* (a

34 *Left* Ely Cathedral, the Octagon and lantern 1322–*c*.1330. The octagonal crossing was created after the Norman central tower fell in 1322, and surmounted by the great wooden vault and octagonal lantern. The trefoil niches and tripartite motifs above the arches are similar to designs used in Prior Crauden's chapel.

35 *Right* Wells Cathedral, choir and presbytery, 1330s. A chapel-like space covered in niches and settings for figure sculpture, surmounted by a net vault. In the foreground can be seen how the twelfth-century bays of the choir were adapted to correspond to the new work.

36 *Above* St Mary Redcliffe, Bristol, north door, *c*.1325. Framed by reversed arches similar to those round the Berkeley tombs in St Augustine's (see p. 16), the door jambs are filled with heavily stylised and filigree versions of seaweed foliage and diaper.

37 *Above, right* Lincoln Cathedral, 'the Bishop's Eye' in the south transept, *c*.1330. The design is the leaf-stem peculiar to eastern England.

rounded shape) and *mouchettes* (a directional shape). The dominance of tracery patterns derived from London was now over, and there is some evidence of regional preference, especially in the north and east, where a series of petal and leaf patterns was designed for the cathedrals of 37 Norwich, Lincoln and York, and for lesser churches throughout the region. Even the plainest building could be enlivened with tracery. With the niche, it became a backdrop for imagery, as on the west front of the bridge chapel at Wakefield (W. Yorks), *c*.1350. It appeared on the shrine 38 bases of St Birinus at Dorchester (Oxon) *c*.1320, and St Werburgh of Chester, *c*.1340. It was naturally taken over into other media, notably 99 embroidery, woodwork and metalwork; and at Canterbury Cathedral the diaper-like design inserted in the window of St Anselm's chapel suggests that tracery, too, was intended to evoke the sacred and the precious.

Imagery and illusionism

Imagery and illusionism were equally powerful and pervasive, although scraped walls and empty niches now convey little of their original colour, meaning or formal complexity. The images that once filled them were not made simply of painted stone. To give two 39 examples, the destroyed kings on the stone reredos of Christchurch Priory, Dorset, *c*.1350, were of gilded wood; and the great stone reredos at Exeter was both painted and gilded, with the figures of Christ and the Virgin fitted with silver-gilt crowns. Not all imagery was human: there 60 were many angels, and an abundance of small monsters and half-156 humans crawled over bosses, canopies and arch mouldings. Imagery

38   Chester Cathedral, shrine base of St Werburgh, *c.*1340. The lower tier has niches for pilgrims, and the reliquary was probably placed in the upper tier, which resembles a small chapel. The base is decorated with carved, gilded decoration and figures.

was both passive and actively involved in narrative: at Ely, for instance, the Lady chapel combined passive witnesses in niches and windows with active narrative scenes around the walls. The reredos at Christchurch combined the *Nativity* and *Adoration of the Magi* with a *Tree of Jesse*, the individual kings set in tabernacles. Figures had various roles: as witnesses they lined the walls of the choir and presbytery at Wells Cathedral and sat on the parapet and choir screen of Selby Abbey; they occupied niches on the shrine of SS Edburga and Werburgh; they 29 appeared in elegant contemporary dress as weepers on such aristocratic tombs as that of Aymer de Valence (d. 1324) in Westminster Abbey; they 93 were arrayed in niches over the prior's door into Norwich Cathedral. 114

It was, however, narrative scenes and tableaux that suffused the works of the 1320s and later. At Exeter, the tomb said to be of Richard de Stapeldon (*c.*1332) shows the effigy of the knight accompanied by 102 figures of his squire, page and horse; the minstrels' gallery in the cathedral nave is fronted by figures of angels holding the musical 40 instruments that would have been played by real people concealed within the gallery; and inside the south porch of the great image screen on the west front are fully free-standing sculptured scenes of the *Annunciation to the Virgin* and the *Adoration of the Magi*. Many sculptured set pieces such as these must have been lost to time and iconoclasm; but the *Tree of Jesse* carved in the tracery of a window at Dorchester Abbey 41 *c.*1320, as well as those at Ducklington (Oxon) and at Christchurch, shows how the architecture, at once a setting and support, could be

39　Christchurch Priory, Hants, part of the reredos, *c*.1350. The sculptures were of both wood and stone, with metal attachments. The subjects include the *Nativity of Christ*, the *Adoration of the Magi* and the *Tree of Jesse*, with the figure of Jesse at the bottom in the centre.

wittily transformed into something else, in these instances the branches of a tree. Such monumental sculptured scenes were intended to convey the reality of the event and to involve the spectator directly. The greatest survivors are perhaps the East Anglian Easter sepulchres or Tombs of Christ, associated with the ritual of Easter and Corpus Christi, and belonging to sets of chancel fittings that include heavily ornamented sedilia and tomb recesses, and elaborate flowing window tracery. Those of Hawton (Notts) and Heckington (Lincs) are large stone structures let into the wall, bearing reliefs of the sleeping soldiers and other figures. The Hawton Tomb has in its central recess monumental reliefs of Christ and the Maries.

Sculpture was essential to the displays of imagery, but, just as at Westminster many years before, not all imagery was sculptured. The imagery in the choir of Tewkesbury, representing the Lords of Tewkesbury in Paradise, combined sculptured bosses with standing figures in the stained glass windows. Similarly, the choir of Gloucester has an angelic orchestra carved in the vault, and ranks of saints and other figures in the window glass. The sculptures in the window traceries at Dorchester were related to the programme in the stained glass, as was probably once the case at Ducklington and elsewhere. It was, however, at Ely and St Stephen's, Westminster, that the complexities of decoration and imagery in an enclosed space reached their apogee.

Although the decoration of the three dramatic interiors of Ely – Prior Crauden's chapel, the Octagon and the Lady chapel – was completed over perhaps thirty years, the programmes were quite coherent. All three combined carved, painted imagery with wall painting and stained glass. In Prior Crauden's chapel the imagery extends to the floor, where, as part of a general theme of Salvation, the Fall of Man is depicted in tiles before the high altar, balanced at the opposite end of the chapel by Redemption expressed through paintings of the *Annunciation* and *Crucifixion*. There were also carved figures, probably of kings, in niches flanking the altar, a female figure painted in the back of the piscina niche, and other small figures in the east window itself. The only contemporary imagery now surviving in the Octagon is the *Life of St Etheldreda* carved on the eight corbels on the piers, and the repainted central boss of the lantern, of *Christ Displaying His Wounds*. The scheme also included carved figures of the Evangelists and (probably) the apostles, with a painted *Crucifixion*, all perhaps associated with the litany; and on the wall backing the choir stalls that ran through the Octagon were paintings of the Anglo-Saxon benefactors to the abbey, whose bones were kept in small coffins above. In the stained glass were represented St Etheldreda's husband, King Egfrith, her mentor, St Wilfrid, and a generous benefactor to the abbey, King Edgar. Thus the imagery of the Octagon was close to the interests of the monks. The Lady chapel, to which the laity were admitted, was a more public space, and its narrative sculptures of the *Life and Miracles of the Virgin* presented to 113 them a comprehensive and impressive series of scenes, attended by

40 Exeter Cathedral, minstrels' gallery in the nave, *c.*1340. Live musicians probably stood in the gallery behind the carved and painted angels, playing instruments corresponding to those 'played' by the angels.

41 Dorchester Abbey, Oxon.,
Tree of Jesse in the north window,
c.1320. The branches form the
mullions and tracery of the
window itself.

42   St Stephen's chapel, Palace of Westminster (destroyed 1834), copy of part of the painting on the altar wall, 1350s. Below scenes of the *Infancy of Christ* were depicted figures of Edward III, Queen Philippa, their children and their patron saints, in fictive architectural settings.

figures of clerics, kings representing the *Tree of Jesse*, and the large figures on the upper walls.

After a brief burst of building at St Stephen's in the 1320s, the upper chapel was finished and decoration begun from 1340, continuing until 74 1363. The interior was wholly coloured, both by such materials as Purbeck marble, and in its surface covering of paint, gilding, heraldic diapering and stencilling. Figures were everywhere, made of metal or painted sculpture, or else they were painted in a grisaille technique to imitate natural stone. The dado arcade contained painted figures of angels. Elsewhere were depicted servers and military saints, and there were sculptures of angels and kings in the tabernacles of the east wall. These were painted, and the angels were provided with real censers suspended from their hands with wire. Illusionistic devices were carried into the wall paintings, both the narrative scenes from Job and the altar wall, which bore scenes from the *Infancy of Christ* with members of the 42 royal family and their patron saints kneeling in a fictive architectural framework. As at such buildings as Dorchester and Christchurch, the artists were combining aesthetic opposites, light and shadow, three-dimensional and flat surfaces, creating ambiguity and complexity with which to underpin the mystic meeting of living and dead, the whole experience made more concentrated by the enclosed space.

Enclosure and continuously moulded surfaces were essential in this
art. The chapel of the Flemish merchants built in the 1340s at St Mary's,
Beverley, shows how mouldings could be used to merge vault and
window patterns. The tierceron vault is supported on mouldings that on
one side intersect and on the other rise without capitals to spread
umbrella-like to the ceiling, to become imperceptibly the mouldings of
the flowing tracery windows. The continuity of wall and window
decoration is seen also in the nichework that literally covered some
façades of the 1320s and 1330s, notably those of Howden and York
Minsters, which have lost most of their imagery, and Exeter Cathedral,
which has not. At Howden, as at Ely, the niches were arranged to
correspond exactly with the spacing of the window mullions, giving an
effect of vertical panelling. In the upper chapel of St Stephen's, Westminster, the painted and sculptured decoration was backed by moulded
rectilinear panels resembling those used on the exterior of the chapter
house of Old St Paul's. Similar flat, rectilinear panelling was used,
perhaps by the architect to St Stephen's, to line the south transept and
choir of Gloucester Abbey when they were refurbished from 1332 to
house the tomb and possible shrine of the murdered Edward II. There it
was deployed over all surfaces, whether masonry, glass or empty air.

This panelling, later to be used on monumental basilicas and
extended to vaulting patterns, was the basis of the last great style of
medieval architecture, the Perpendicular. Decorated and Perpendicular
have much in common, similarities missed by the nineteenth-century

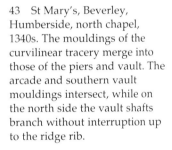

43 St Mary's, Beverley,
Humberside, north chapel,
1340s. The mouldings of the
curvilinear tracery merge into
those of the piers and vault. The
arcade and southern vault
mouldings intersect, while on
the north side the vault shafts
branch without interruption up
to the ridge rib.

44   Gloucester Abbey (now Cathedral), choir, built from 1337. The flat, rectilinear, panelled decoration is the earliest surviving example of the proto-Perpendicular style, which originated in London. Its non-structural function, combined with a net vault, sculpture and stained glass, shares the principles of Decorated.

scholars whose concern with classification caused them to see only the differences. Both were essentially settings for decoration and imagery; these proto-Perpendicular designs are as unstructural as Decorated, and the earliest occurred at least a generation before the more curvilinear and three-dimensional forms of Decorated were abandoned. The chapel of St Mary on the bridge at Wakefield (W. Yorks) was in building around 1350, such churches as Attleborough and Wilby in Norfolk even a little later than that. It was only with the strong architectural statements at York, Winchester and Canterbury in the 1360s and 1370s that the new forms prevailed over the old.

These, then, are some of the buildings and other works that constitute the Decorated and early Perpendicular styles. Many elements contributed to their making. While they can be analysed at a purely formal level as collections of architectural details, it is more rewarding to look beyond, to the people for whom they were made, those who made them, and the social and intellectual patterns of those people's lives.

CHAPTER TWO

Kingdom, Land and People

In the 1350s Simon Simeon, a leading esquire in the household of Henry of Grosmont, Duke of Lancaster, founded a chapel at Pontefract (W. Yorks), marking the place where Henry's uncle, Thomas, Earl of Lancaster, had been executed over thirty years before. It was a chantry chapel, endowed for a priest to say prayers on behalf of the dead man, who was widely seen as a martyr and revered unofficially as a saint. Simeon's act, at once pious, political and feudal, is a distillation of the web of relationships and motives that composed contemporary society and formed the context in which the Decorated style developed and flourished.

England in the century of the Decorated style was beginning to change into a society that was recognisably closer to our own, with the emergence of some of the institutions by which the country is still governed. By the mid-fourteenth century parliament had been formally divided into lords (the nobility) and commons (knights, merchants and gentry), and although parliaments themselves were not yet always held at Westminster, by then the government administration was permanently established there. While the kings were of largely French descent, and Henry III and Edward I both spoke in French, the linguistic gap that divided the French-speaking rulers from the English-speaking ruled was gradually closing. Henry III stressed his Anglo-Saxon ancestry, and his sons, the future Edward I and Edmund, Earl of Lancaster, were named after sainted Anglo-Saxon kings. At this time, too, more classes of people, in particular the merchants and gentry, were becoming involved in the king's government and administration. These developments, which were crystallised by the early fifteenth century, are already detectable in our period; the England of Edward III was not the same as that of his great-grandfather.

Yet certain fundamentals changed, if at all, only in degree. Wealth was based predominantly in agriculture and trade; trade was both local and international, with the export mainly of wool in return for a huge variety of raw materials, non-indigenous foodstuffs and luxury goods. Social and political institutions revolved around the person of the king. Power and patronage were rooted in the tenure of land, with consequently

45 Tewkesbury Abbey, Glos., the choir, refurbished from the 1320s by the Despenser family. The foliate vault and the subject-matter of the bosses and stained glass windows evoked the Lords of Tewkesbury in Paradise.

strong vertical ties between landlord and tenant. Unlike other European countries, where local barons could exercise effective independence of a nominal ruler, in England the king's writ ran everywhere, and all land was held ultimately of him, although in many localities the nobility and gentry were gaining control over the king's government, particularly in the judicial sphere, for their own purposes. Large estates, held directly by the magnates and the Church, were subdivided into the holdings of the lesser nobility and further into those of the lower social orders through the knights and gentry to freemen and peasants, making a pattern of innumerable small settlements. By this time feudalism was stronger in theory than in fact: most peasants were free and discharged their obligations in money rather than in labour, although the diminishing class of unfree peasants was a daily reminder of traditional ties. Feudal attitudes lived on in so-called 'bastard feudalism', the patronage extended by a lord to the paid retinue that supported him and wore his livery; and the concept of feudalism retained enough symbolic power to be a credible cause of friction when the king of France insisted that the king of England pay homage for his French landholdings.

Essential to the rural economy was the large number of small market towns, with populations of about five hundred, that were spread right across the country, and served their immediate localities in a radius of perhaps no more than thirty miles. The substantial cities, such as Bristol, Norwich, York and Boston (Lincs), were river- or sea-ports that handled both coastal and international trade; in 1300 the two former had perhaps ten thousand inhabitants, the latter about five thousand. London was by far the largest city, with a population as high as eighty thousand. The towns were not independent of either the king or the local lords, who derived much of their income from trading levies, and there were as yet no buildings equivalent to the civic palaces and town halls that were already beginning to be found in the cities of the Empire and Italy; but from the later thirteenth century an urban identity was established both through the growing economic power of the merchants and the activities of the emerging craft guilds and fraternities. As the monarchy came to rely increasingly on loans from merchants and bankers the towns were able to assert their claims to self-regulation, and as the merchants rose to wealth and prominence they seem to have remained detached from the old rural societies based on land tenure and arms. Unlike nowadays, a successful merchant did not automatically retire to the country when he had made his fortune. Sir John Pulteney, the builder of 46 Penshurst Place in Kent *c*.1340, is one of the very few merchants who not only invested in land but actually went to live on it. The chivalric activities of the nobility and knights held no appeal for townspeople. Even when in 1331 the tournament was held at Cheapside in London, it was attended exclusively by the aristocracy, the merchants holding aloof. At the same time craftsmen were forming their own colonies within towns: in Oxford, for example, the manuscript illuminators

46 Penshurst Place, Kent, the great hall, built *c*.1340 by the London merchant Sir John Pulteney. The wooden ceiling is supported by large wooden caryatids, and the decoration generally alluded to his knighthood, the first awarded to a merchant.

worked in Catte Street, and in London painters of all kinds lived around Cripplegate, adopting the church of St Giles as their own.

Craft guilds and fraternities are particularly associated with such new religious feasts and rituals as the celebrations of Corpus Christi and the Holy Cross, which helped to give a distinctive character to urban life. Religious life in the cities was already distinguished by the presence of the new orders, the mendicant Franciscan and Dominican friars and the Augustinian Canons, priests who lived according to a Rule, but were dedicated to working among the laity. These orders reflected the shift of interest away from enclosed monasteries that devoted themselves to praying for the world in withdrawn isolation, and they enjoyed all the moral force that had once been identified with cloistered monks. The power and prestige of the papacy in the early thirteenth century and the Fourth Lateran Council of 1215, with its provision for the proper instruction of lay congregations, had greatly enhanced the moral authority of the secular clergy, that is the bishops and priests with parochial responsibilities. The mendicants worked and preached in a non-parochial capacity; but, by the early fourteenth century, their light, open preaching churches were beginning to influence the design of parish churches: the thin walls, large windows and slender, quatrefoil piers in the parish churches of the new towns of Winchelsea, and Hull 47 and Hedon in east Yorkshire seem to be close to those of the now

47 Winchelsea church, Sussex, looking north. New Winchelsea was founded by Edward I, and the parish church, of which only the choir was built, was probably modelled on the light, spacious preaching churches of the mendicant orders. The tombs of the ancestors of the Alard family, relocated from the old town, are on the north wall.

destroyed great Dominican (Blackfriars) and Franciscan (Greyfriars) churches in London, which were themselves largely the result of aristocratic patronage. Mendicant confessors were now part of the royal circle, and by the end of the thirteenth century a Dominican, Robert Kilwardby, and a Franciscan, John Pecham, had served as Archbishops of Canterbury.

In Edward I's reign the country seemed to be growing in prosperity, with a high population, steady wages and active trade; but from early in the fourteenth century trade was disrupted by war with both France and Scotland, there were big inflationary cycles, and a brief but severe famine in 1315–17 was followed by a cattle murrain. These events, however, mainly affected the rural poor, whose difficulties were exacerbated north of the River Humber by incursions of Scottish marauders. Matters had not improved in the 1330s, when Edward III, ever in need of money, debased the coinage and instituted potentially disastrous methods of raising taxes on the wool trade upon which the economy depended. It was only in the 1340s that the economy began to pick up, to be temporarily halted once more by the first visitation of the Black Death in 1348–9, which killed up to a third of the population. This time, however, there was a delayed reaction. Vacant landholdings were taken by survivors, who quickly married and produced children, and any deep changes wrought by the plague were visible only later. Surprisingly perhaps, the 1350s have about them an air of optimism, possibly enhanced by the relative gloom of the decades around them.

Society was stratified, headed by the king and a minute class of nobility, about five hundred people in all, descending through the lesser barons, knights and gentry to the majority, the rural poor. It has been described as pyramidal, but a more apt analogy has been drawn with skyscrapers, the king and leading nobility towering over the undiscriminated mass of the population whom they so far outstripped in wealth. As a group, the higher nobility changed over the period as families died out or fell from favour, to be replaced by others. The nobility hardened into a self-conscious class only towards the middle of the fourteenth century with the emergence of the peerage, the lords who were summoned regularly to parliament, and with the introduction of a new rank in 1337, when Edward, the future Black Prince, was created Duke of Cornwall. Even then, peerage was never exactly equated with wealth. Several of the new peers created in 1337 were worth only about £1000 a year. In the previous reign a very few magnates had had annual incomes of between £6000 and £8000, but only the Lancasters (descended from Edward I's brother; see genealogical tables, p. 193), the de Valence earls of Pembroke and the Clares were exceptionally wealthy; and even among these the annual income of £11,000 enjoyed by Thomas, Earl of Lancaster, was outstanding. Few even of this class could hope to match the king's powers of display. Those with large disposable incomes did, however, include some notable women, not only successive queens of England but such powerful, longlived widows as Marie de St Pol, Countess of Pembroke, and Elizabeth de Burgh, Lady of Clare and joint heiress in 1314 to the great Clare estates, both of whom were prominent patrons of art.

Over a gap of seven centuries most figures are misleading and largely meaningless, but comparisons can demonstrate the differences in wealth between this class and those below. The lesser barons could expect an annual income of between £1000 and £500, that of a wealthy knight. The main body of knights and gentry (defined as men who bore a coat of arms), who in the mid-fourteenth century amounted to not more than three thousand people, had incomes of between £10 and £40 a year. These figures were the minimum necessary to maintain arms and a horse, the knights and gentry and those above them being expected to bear arms on the king's behalf. Church incomes were more or less the same as those of the laity: the richest episcopal sees, Winchester and Durham, were worth about £3000 a year, but most yielded just over £1000 and Lichfield, Exeter and the sees in Wales were worth less than £500. It was from the gentry and their clerical equivalents upwards that the patrons of art were largely drawn. The annual earnings of a skilled craftsman paid between 6d and 12d a day would be between £7 and £16:

a mason who worked for a lord was paid the same as the lord's squires.

Medieval theorists divided society into three: those that work, those that pray and those that fight. Like most theories, this one gained currency only when it was becoming less valid, divisions were softening and social mobility was increasing. Sir John Felton, knighted by Edward I, rose to gentry status through service in war, becoming one of the king's captains in Wales and Constable of Beaumaris Castle. William de Clinton and William Montague, who became earls of respectively Huntingdon and Salisbury in 1337, were likewise knights who had risen in royal service, and became friends of Edward III. Sir Geoffrey le Scrope, founder of the Scrope dynasty of Masham in Yorkshire, was a middle class practitioner of common law who became Chief Justice of the King's Bench. Good chances for social improvement were offered in the Church: Walter de Merton, the founder of Merton College, Oxford, who became bishop of Rochester and Chancellor of England, was the son of a poor freeholder, assisted, like others, by scholarly ability and a helpful patron. Nevertheless, as the theorists imply, society was composed of distinct entities. The Church, indeed, was in a sense a society within society. As the guardian of people's souls, it exerted great power. It claimed separate jurisdiction and therefore some independence of the Crown, and the struggle for supremacy between Crown and Church

48 Merton College, Oxford, the chapel, 1289–84. Its stylistic kinship to St Etheldreda's, Ely Place (see p. 38) may reflect the fact that the founder, Walter de Merton, had been in the household of John Kirkby, builder of Ely Place.

was a continuous political theme of the age. The martyrdom in 1170 of Thomas Becket apparently at the king's behest, and his subsequent canonisation, all in the cause of Church privilege, was like a perpetual open sore on the body politic, liable to bleed afresh at any conflict and very effective for exerting moral blackmail on the king. Another exiled archbishop of Canterbury, Edmund Rich, canonised in 1246, merely added to the burden of royal guilt, the expiation of which is a perpetual feature of the kings' acts of piety.

In practice, Church and king needed each other. The Church found it expedient to establish a working relationship with its secular overlord in such matters as taxation and papal nominations to bishoprics, although relations from time to time broke down, sometimes spectacularly. The king needed churchmen, with their training in literacy, to run the administration of government, which still conducted much of its business in Latin. Many a bishop was called in to hold a great office of state, and many top administrators were rewarded with bishoprics. Chancellors included Robert Burnell, Bishop of Bath and Wells, John Salmon of Norwich, John Hotham of Ely and John Thoresby, Archbishop of York. John Kirkby of Ely, Walter de Stapeldon of Exeter, William Melton of York and William Edington of Winchester were among the Treasurers; and Thomas Bek of St David's and Richard de Bury, Bishop of Durham, were Keepers of the Privy Seal. This involvement with the monarchy was often enhanced by friendship and personal alliance. Anthony Bek I of Durham, William Melton and John Hotham all fought on the king's behalf in the Scottish Wars. Burnell was so close to Edward I that the king gave him some timbers for building his house at Acton Burnell; 86 Hotham received Queen Philippa on her arrival in 1327; and John Grandisson of Exeter bequeathed a psalter to Philippa's daughter, Isabella. The kings for their part made political use of Church institutions. Acts of piety were an important aspect of kingship; very extensive under the fervently pious Henry III, they were more moderate under his successors, but Edward I in particular knew when to be present at important ecclesiastical events, such as the translations of St Richard of Chichester in 1276 and St William of York in 1284. He also politicised shrines by relating pilgrimage to war, visiting the main English shrines before military expeditions. Edward III, in whose reign many of these earlier tendencies became more clearly defined, made a point of touring the northern shrines before fighting the Scots; and one sign of the emerging sense of his 'Englishness' was his deliberate cultivation of all the English saints.

As an institution the Church was separate from lay society, but the lives of churchmen themselves were very similar to those of laymen. To a large extent the Church hierarchy mirrored that of the laity: its wealth, like theirs, was based on land and rights in trade, and at the lower levels the established diocesan, parochial and monastic clergy were the equivalent to the lesser nobility, knights and gentry. Even the rural poor had

counterparts in the population of clerks in minor orders and unbeneficed clergy (those without a parish). The Church's role of secular
lordship was reflected in the fourteenth century in the battlements and
corner turrets of the gatehouses to both episcopal and monastic pre-
cincts, as at St Augustine's, Canterbury (1300–09) and, later, at Wells, St
Albans and Battle (E. Sussex). Clergy and laity met as a matter of course,
even in monasteries, which gave access to their lay patrons; and they
met also across the dinner table: Bishop Hamo of Rochester in 1322
entertained at his residence at Halling abbots, priors and distinguished
local laymen, including Henry de Cobham, of the rapidly rising local
gentry family who were to found their own church at Cobham in Kent.

Such connections were further strengthened by ties of blood. Despite
the opportunities offered to such landless individuals as Walter de
Merton and John Salmon, the higher clergy were still drawn largely
from baronial families. Walter Giffard, archbishop of York (d. 1279), and
his brother Geoffrey, bishop of Worcester (d. 1302), were from a middle
ranking baronial family based in Worcestershire, and James Berkeley, of
the prominent Gloucestershire family, was briefly bishop of Exeter in
1328. Such people behaved according to their equivalent secular rank.
The prior of Worcester, for example, was socially a baron, and kept an
appropriate retinue, and Richard de Bury was accompanied on visits to
the pope by twenty clerks and thirty-six squires, all wearing his livery.
Some senior churchmen, for instance the Bek brothers, were born into
the aristocracy; Louis de Beaumont, Bishop of Salisbury then Durham,
was cousin to both Edward II and Queen Isabella; and Bogo de Clare, a
renowned pluralist and Treasurer of York, was brother to the Earl of
Gloucester. His way of life was largely indistinguishable from that of his
lay relatives. He was a keen huntsman, retained actors, a jester and a
harpist in his household, numbered a gilt saddle among his possessions,
and gave cloth of gold for the burial of his servant, John de Worteley, in
Holy Trinity Aldgate, near his London home. Other bishops became
aristocrats by holding a lucrative office of state or by virtue of the wealth
of their sees, and all bishops were expected to maintain a certain standard of living. It was for both social and political reasons that they kept
magnificent London houses, the Archbishop of Canterbury at Lambeth
opposite Westminster, the Bishop of Bath and Wells in Westminster
itself, the Archbishop of York on what is now Whitehall. The surviving
traces of Winchester House at Southwark, and Ely Place at Holborn give
some idea of the state in which they lived.

For the laity the most significant links were between families, which
formed a network of connections that balanced and reinforced the
vertical tie of landlord and tenant. Marriage was a matter of great
importance at a time when it meant property, and the value of an heiress
was judged at her value in land. The most powerful nobility held vast
estates: the earls of Pembroke held land in Wales, the borders, Kent, the
Home Counties and East Anglia; before the death in 1314 of Gilbert de

49 Winchester House, Southwark, window in the great hall, *c*.1330s. Winchester House was the London residence of the bishops of Winchester.

Clare, Earl of Gloucester, the Clare family estates covered much of south Wales, Suffolk and Kent; and by judicious marriage the inheritance of the earls of Lancaster came to include the estates of the earls of Warenne and Lincoln in north Wales, Yorkshire, the borders, the Midlands and the north-west. Through marriage the nobility were intricately related both to each other and to the king. Marriage links in the reign of Edward II included that of Thomas, Earl of Lancaster to the daughter of the Earl of Lincoln, the Earl of Arundel to the sister of the Earl of Surrey, the Earl of Cornwall to a sister of the Earl of Gloucester; while Gilbert of Gloucester himself and his sister Elizabeth both married into the family of the Earl of Ulster. Edward II was widely related to the nobility of England: his sister Joan was mother to the Earl of Gloucester; another sister married Humphrey de Bohun, Earl of Hereford and Essex; Edward's niece was Countess of Surrey; Thomas of Lancaster and Aymer de Valence, Earl of Pembroke, were his cousins.

The gentry, too, could form widely flung connections through marriage. One particular network of gentry families that exemplifies such links is of particular interest here owing to the survival of associated buildings and works of art (see genealogical tables, p. 193). A burgess of Ipswich, Gilbert de Reymes from Wherstead in Suffolk, founded two family branches: his son, Robert (d. 1295), rector of Eston Gosebeck, also in Suffolk, had a daughter, Alice (d. 1310), who married her father's executor, Robert de Reydon, and whose Book of Hours survives in Cambridge (University Lib., MS. Dd. 4. 17); Robert, the son of Gilbert's son Hugh (also dead by 1295), migrated to Northumberland, where he and his descendants built the fortified house known as Aydon Castle; and in about 1348 Robert's daughter, Joan, married William de Swynburne, with whose family is associated the beautiful eponymous silver-gilt and *basse taille* (translucent) enamel pyx in the Victoria and Albert Museum, London.

The many links formed by professional connection, kinship and marriage were strengthened by the institution that lay at the heart of all domestic, business and government organisation: the household. Every family, from peasant to king, was based on the household, as were most crafts and trades. At its simplest level it was the family unit that needed to be housed and fed. The household consisted of, as appropriate, the immediate family members, their servants and administrative officials, who formed the inner household or *domus*, while other employees and the retinue of knights and gentry formed the wider household or *familia*. The *domus* was the permanent household, while members of the *familia* came and went according to circumstances. The lord's status was both reflected and enhanced by the size of his retinue. In 1318 Edward II had more than four hundred and fifty domestic servants. Noble households reflected that of the king according to their wealth: the first Beauchamp earls of Warwick probably had a household of two hundred, as did Thomas Berkeley II (1282–1321). As the members of a noble household had retinues of their own, those of the king, leading churchmen or greater magnates could be enormous. Great households were peripatetic, travelling constantly between estates as the need arose for food, clean quarters or for hunting. Owing to the geographical spread of a magnate's estates his interest and influence were far-flung and frequently reinforced by his physical presence and that of his retinue. Furthermore, the king's household (the queen and children had their own) was the centre of government of the kingdom. Although in this period the great offices of state were gradually being detached from the *domus* and settled permanently at Westminster, the *domus* was the king's private finance office through which much money was channelled not only for his personal spending but also for government purposes, particularly in times of war. It also supplied the king's personal bodyguard and maintained the degree of magnificence required by his rank.

Household organisation and the peripatetic way of life affected the spread and nature of the Decorated style in various ways. Decorated buildings closely mirror the public and private faces of household life, every Decorated building combining to some degree a private petition with a public statement. It is seen not only in the personal nature of public government and its expression in lavish display but also in private building. At Tewkesbury Abbey, for instance, Edward II's protégés, the Despenser family, paid for a decorative programme on the theme of Paradise; it was created to celebrate and explore the relation of man to God, but although its manner of presentation was public, with the stained glass, the flowery vault pattern, the sculptured keystones and the tombs visible to all, the programme was concerned not so much with humanity in general as with the specific patron. The Despensers were interested only in their own prospects. They put on an opulent display not to assist everyone else to salvation in the next world but, in ensuring theirs, to assert their own status in this one. The household, at once both the heart of domestic organisation and the public expression of the status of its head, embodies the same public-private duality.

At more specific levels, members of households set up their own personal connections as people trained in one household left to join another or form one of their own. Awareness and influence evidently went with them. Men who became bishops had often seen service in the households of episcopal colleagues, and the resemblance between, for instance, Merton College chapel and St Etheldreda's, Ely Place, may 48, 22 well reflect Walter de Merton's service in the household of John Kirkby of Ely. Similarly, such fortified gentry houses as the Feltons' Edlingham, or Mettingham in Suffolk, with polygonal turrets and gatehouses recalling the royal castles in miniature, probably proclaim the careers of their builders in the king's retinue.

Household clerks were rewarded with benefices, often strengthened further by family links. Richard de Potesgrave, the royal chaplain entrusted with the escort of Edward II's body from Berkeley Castle to Gloucester, was rector of St Andrew's, Heckington, and probably built 79 the chancel there *c.*1330. This church is interesting for several reasons, one of which is an unusual design of pier, which otherwise appears in the choir of the collegiate church of Howden, a manor belonging to the bishopric of Durham. The manor of Heckington was held by Henry de Beaumont, a cousin and household knight to Queen Isabella and the brother of Louis, Bishop of Durham, who probably rebuilt the Howden choir. All over the country clerks used the money accrued from service in the royal household to build their burial churches in their native areas. Thomas Sibthorpe, a chancery clerk between 1317 and 1351, founded a collegiate church in his native village of Sibthorpe, near 50 Newark in Nottinghamshire, and John de Winwick, a Keeper of the Privy Seal in the 1350s, established a chantry at his home town of Huyton in the Wirral.

England at this time was strongly regional, and such men were employed as part of the Crown's deliberate policy of binding the regions closely to the centres of power. The kingdom was not, however, inward-looking. The economy was sustained on international trade; the kings themselves were financially dependent not only on the greater merchants but on such Italian bankers as the Riccardi of Lucca (bankrupted by Edward I), and the Florentine Frescobaldi, Bardi and Peruzzi. Although some people never travelled further than a day's journey from home, others – itinerant households, masons, carpenters, merchants and pilgrims – journeyed more widely, and diplomats, churchmen and crusaders might go as far as Rome, the papal court at Avignon, the Baltic

50   Sibthorpe church, Notts. A collegiate church founded for the burial of Thomas Sibthorpe, a chancery clerk between 1317–51, it has curvilinear tracery and an Easter Sepulchre.

or the Holy Land. Members of families, as we have seen with Hugh de Reymes, moved to other parts of the country. Even a century after the loss of Normandy the king and other barons had extensive landholdings in France. The kings had a legitimate interest in European power struggles, which led them into political adventures over Sicily, the Holy Land and, above all, France. In 1257 Henry III's brother Richard, Earl of Cornwall, was elected King of the Romans (i.e. Germany), although this did not succeed; and in equally controversial circumstances Henry III's son Edmund was offered the kingdom of Sicily by the Pope. The future Edward I followed Louis IX on Crusade; and his reputation for martial prowess so dazzled his contemporaries that on his accession to the throne he slipped easily into the role, vacated at the death of Louis, of leading monarch in Europe. Edward III's claim to the throne of France through his French mother had enough substance to pose a genuine threat.

Edward I, who visited France, Castile, the Holy Land and Italy, was the most widely travelled monarch in Europe; but the journeys of his father and grandson also had considerable cultural impact. The future Edward III's exile in Flanders won him a wife from a highly cultivated background that supported his own interest in chivalry and its visual expression. Eleanor of Castile, too, seems to have brought aspects of her native culture with her to England, and maintained them all her life. When she arrived in London in 1255, the chronicler Matthew Paris remarked on her Spanish propensity for adorning her lodgings with tapestries and silk hangings; a carpet maker was permanently attached to her household. The wardrobe account that survives for the year of Eleanor's death records many items bought from abroad: basins of 'Damascene work', cloths from Tripoli, Venetian vases, 'pictured cloths' from Cologne and Limoges enamels.

Edward I married three of his daughters out into continental families for political and dynastic reasons, but royal marriages also brought relatives and retinues into England, from the Languedoc, Castile, France and Flanders. Servants included Richard de Acco (Acre in Palestine), Eleanor of Castile's Spanish gardeners and grooms, and Thierry le Alemant, who served Henry III and became an esquire in the household of Edward I. Royal relatives were rapidly established in high positions. Not only did Aymer de Valence, Henry III's half-brother from Poitou, become Bishop of Winchester, but his brother William acquired the lands of the earldom of Pembroke through marriage, and established what became the new earldom. Both William and his son Aymer received privileged burial in Westminster Abbey. Under Henry III, too, the queen's uncle, Peter of Savoy, became Earl of Richmond and his brother, Boniface, the Archbishop of Canterbury. The county of Savoy provided Edward I with his military architectural supervisor, James of St George, and Count Amadeus the Great, one of the king's most trusted allies, led the English army into Wales from Chester in 1282. Edward's other great military supporter, Otto de Grandisson, was a member of a prominent Savoyard family, a branch of which settled in the west Midlands; Sir Otto's nephew John became Bishop of Exeter in 1328.

Like the kings, most of the English barons had European blood. Humphrey de Bohun, Earl of Hereford (d. 1322), had a French mother, the mother of Edmund, Earl of Arundel (d. 1326) was Piedmontese and the father of Edward II's niece Joan, Countess of Surrey, was the Count of Bar in the Empire. English knights attended tournaments and knighting ceremonies in France, Flanders and the Empire, and continental knights came to Britain, notably for the famous 'round table' held at Nefyn in 1284 to celebrate the conquest of north Wales, but also for less spectacular jousts.

The leading laity were not the only travellers, however, nor were they necessarily the most significant from our point of view. It is possible, but not demonstrated, that Italian paintings and other artefacts were brought in by the Italian banking families. Many of the scholar bishops, for example John le Romeyn, Archbishop of York, Grandisson and de Bury, had been educated abroad, and many had either worked as clerks in the papal court in Rome and, after 1308, in Avignon, or travelled there, either on their own account or as diplomats on the king's business with the Pope; bishops' wills and inventories are full of references to precious objects and textiles purchased abroad. Many of the abundant but piecemeal continental influences on English art and architecture at this time can be explained by their interests. Abbot Richard Ware of Westminster brought back with him from Rome both the materials and some of the workmen for the sanctuary floor of the abbey church.

76

People such as these, linked by rank, household and patronage, were also the political core of the country. It is perhaps not surprising that throughout the century the continuous theme in politics, alongside the struggle for supremacy between Church and king, was the power struggle between the king and the barons. In these years, for the first time since the Conquest of 1066, the English throne passed uninterrupted from father to eldest surviving son over four generations, and the succession of the legitimate heir was upheld even after the murder of Edward II in 1327. A secure succession gave the Crown some necessary strength as it veered between instability and settled supremacy while king and barons tested the fragile limits of their power.

It is impossible reliably to assess the personalities of the different kings, for they are filtered through the self-interested reactions of contemporary commentators and the bias of modern historians, who tend to assess them for their military skills and their effect on such matters as the economy or the development of the constitution. On these criteria Edward I and Edward III invariably receive higher praise that the less successful Henry III and Edward II. We, however, noting the latter's interest, knowledge and pleasure in works of art, might view them more favourably. What they evidently lacked was political instinct, a quality abundantly possessed by both Edward I and Edward III, who lost their touch only late in their respective reigns. Thus, although Edward I was as extravagant and manipulative as his father, these traits were outweighed by his ability to neutralise potential opposition by working along with it. He could control powerful barons by meeting them in terms they understood, as a fighting man on the battlefield, or its peacetime substitute, the jousting ground, where he excelled. At the same time, however, through the marriages of his daughters, he secured both baronial loyalty and even greater tracts of land to Crown control. As a Crusader, Edward was held in high regard by the Papacy, and he controlled the Church at home by paying his religious dues and rewarding bishops with high offices of state. Only in his last, disastrous decade did his gifts desert him, and his taxation policies provoke crises with both the barons and the Church. Similarly, although it is Edward II who is accused of frivolity for, among other things, rewarding his painter, John of St Albans, for dancing on a table, Edward I, throughout his marriage to Eleanor of Castile, had an annual pillow fight with her ladies-in-waiting on Easter Sunday morning to mark the end of Lenten abstinence. Yet Edward I is invariably presented as a model of *gravitas*. Edward II inherited a bankrupt exchequer (his father had died £200,000 in debt) and possessed both a tendency to show undue favouritism and less military skill; but although his father's political abilities passed him by, they reappeared in his son, who could also bind men's loyalty to himself by playing on their mutual interests.

Nevertheless, however skilful the monarch, the lay magnates used their own powers to check the king whenever he seemed to threaten them. There was a crisis of this sort in every reign. When the barons led by Simon de Montfort took power from Henry III in 1258, it was not fully restored to him until after Simon's death at the battle of Evesham in 1265. In 1297 the barons refused Edward I's demand that they should fight in Gascony, and humiliated him further the following year by forcing him to confirm Magna Carta and other charters that established the limits of royal power over the barons. In 1311 Edward II was compelled to submit to the control of the so-called Lords Ordainers, who had drawn up Ordinances under which England should be governed; and in addition to the years of crisis around the fall of Edward II in 1327, the position of Edward III was badly shaken in 1340 after his financial mismanagement of the initial stages of the Hundred Years' War. Yet the crises of the 1290s and 1340 were more in the nature of severe warnings against excessive taxation. The barons actually assumed power only when the system of royal patronage, in the form of land grants, marriages to heiresses and other privileges, worked not in their favour but in that of a perceived interloper. This was the pretext for the rebellion of 1258, when Henry III's Poitevin half-brothers were thought to be receiving more than their due, and of 1310/11, when Edward II's Gascon favourite, Piers Gaveston, had been similarly honoured. Edward's next favourites, the Despensers, were not foreigners, but in the course of sorting out his finances they arrogated vast personal wealth to themselves, and duly fell from power with the king.

Taxation and the need to finance war were behind many of the events and developments of the time. The king was often at war, and war was expensive. Both the growth of the central administration and the increased importance of parliament can be traced to the Crown's need of money. In addition to the civil strife between 1258 and 1265, and from 1310 until Edward III gained supremacy in 1330, there were wars against other powers. Edward I's Welsh wars of the 1270s and 1280s were followed by a nearly-successful Welsh rebellion in 1294; his wars with France and Scotland in the 1290s were a prelude to intermittent clashes with both (defeat for Edward II at Bannockburn in 1314, victory for Edward III at Halidon Hill in 1333), until Edward III claimed the French throne and became involved in 1336 with what developed into the Hundred Years' War. It was against this background that the barons, in alliance with the Church in the 1290s and the commons in 1340, put a check on the increasingly desperate royal efforts to raise cash. Edward III, however, was successful; despite the aftermath of the Black Death, in the 1350s Edward was more in control of his kingdom than he ever would be again, surrounded by fresh faces at court and basking in the afterglow of victories in 1346 against the Scots at Neville's Cross and the French at Crécy, and the fall of Calais the following year. The mood of lightness is symbolised in the king's new chivalric order of the Garter, which was founded to recognise his closest companions in arms and based at his new buildings at Windsor Castle. It also perfectly demonstrates Edward's instinctive understanding of the ties and patronage on which society functioned.

The political events of the time were not without their effects on art, but they were limited and almost wholly specific. When trying to assess these it is important to distinguish between the mere existence of a building, which may well be located in a particular spot because of a political event, and its appearance, which may owe nothing to that. In addition, while some works can be seen as the result of reaction to events, others were clearly an effort to control them. Reaction to events is seen more in the increased number of fortified stone houses that were built in the first half of the fourteenth century to protect against greater lawlessness and, north of the Humber, the danger of Scottish marauders. In that category, too, come the houses built from the profits of war, particularly after the campaigns of the 1340s and 1350s, among them the Savoy palace in London, built in 1349 by Henry of Grosmont, Earl of Lancaster, the Berkeley family's Beverstone Castle in Gloucestershire, and the extensions to Warwick Castle built by Thomas Beauchamp I, Earl of Warwick (d. 1369). The economic crises of the time seem to have little general effect, no doubt because they bore hardest on the absolutely poor, who would not have been building in any case. Throughout the period building was both copious and diverse, even in the beleaguered north. In York itself there were construction delays at the Minster, and in the 1330s the monks of Selby had delayed so long in finishing the new choir of their church that they were admonished by Archbishop Melton; but St Mary's Abbey, York, was completely rebuilt from about 1270. Other late thirteenth-century monastic work included Kirkham, Guisborough (twice) and Bridlington; the nave of Beverley Minster was rebuilt in the fourteenth century, and numerous parish churches were built or rebuilt in the prosperous new and established towns of south and east Yorkshire.

A personal economic crisis was, however, a different matter. The most stark effect of this was seen in 1297, when Edward I needed £5000 each week to finance the Scottish wars. The Exchequer was instructed to cease all the building operations of the Crown except the castles in Wales and 'the painting of some rooms in Westminster'. Work on St Stephen's chapel was halted at once, and it remained intermittent until the 1330s, except for a brief period in the early 1320s when Edward II had amassed enough money to pay for craftsmen and materials. This is one of the few contemporary examples of an event in the art world that can unequivocally be ascribed to political developments. Its effects were incalculable

51 Caerfili Castle, Gwent, begun 1268 by Gilbert de Clare, Earl of Gloucester and Hertford. The type of late thirteenth-century castle with defence concentrated on the twin-towered gatehouse was developed in the Clare castles.

and are still being debated. Certainly the craftsmen from St Stephen's seem to have found work elsewhere, and developed their style in other centres; how St Stephen's itself would have looked if completed by 1300 is a tantalising question.

The castles in Wales, which had been exempted in the prohibition of 1297, owed their existence entirely to the political need to subdue the recently conquered Welsh; and their appearance was naturally propagandist. Apart from their sheer strength, their supremacy was emphasised by the perfection and symmetry of their planning. Two of them were built on sites of significance to the Welsh, Conwy beside the remains of Aberconwy Abbey, the burial place of Llywelyn the Great, which was peremptorily moved elsewhere; and Caernarfon on the site 78 of the castle that had been the centre of Gwynedd. The castles controlled Wales so effectively that they were not threatened until the Civil War of the 1640s, but Beaumaris and the extensions to Caernarfon were nevertheless reactions to the Welsh uprising of 1294. The exemption of 1297 is a measure of Edward's continuing anxiety about the situation in Wales. The design of the castles, however, reveals reaction to a different threat. The scheme of concentrating strength on the gatehouse, often combined with concentric defences, was perfected in Snowdonia but it was not invented there. Probably in the 1260s Gilbert de Clare, Earl of Gloucester, had built the great twin-towered gatehouse at his castle at Tonbridge in Kent; in 1268 he had begun at Caerfili in the southern marches a magnificent castle that deployed just such a system. As a marcher lord Earl Gilbert was permitted to build strong castles (it is no accident that many of the finest surviving castles are on or around the borders); but Tonbridge and Caerfili were both tactical masterpieces and a challenge from an extremely powerful subordinate that could not be ignored.

The castles in Wales reveal the complexity of political and social motives, a complexity even more clearly visible in those artistic efforts that were undertaken to control events rather than as reactions to them. In this category come the propagandist assertions of the sanctity of kingship seen in Henry III's Westminster Abbey and the refurbishment of Gloucester Abbey to receive the body of Edward II. A similar gesture was Edward III's rebuilding of Windsor Castle as the centre for the Order of the Garter. In buildings such as these appearance was paramount. The spectator's response is dictated by the lavish gilding and emphasis on sainted kingship at Westminster Abbey, and the netted tracery of the Gloucester choir, so redolent of palace chapels in its caged seclusion, and sheltering a shrine-like tomb. Even Gloucester, which could be seen as a reaction to disaster, was not begun until Edward III had regained the initiative and was in control. Yet if the kings seem to be moved more by political considerations than by piety, it should be remembered that to them the two were not incompatible. At Westminster Abbey Henry III was moved by deep piety that was more than the expression appropriate to a king. The pilgrimages to English shrines made by Edward I and Edward III were as pious as they were political; and the Eleanor Crosses, another public display of royal splendour, were equally the expression of a husband's grief. These works, however, take us out of politics and into what was a more significant context in which to see them: the intellectual and spiritual culture of the period.

52 Gloucester Abbey (now Cathedral), tomb of Edward II, 1330s. The alabaster effigy is set among towering, delicate cages of stone, with ogee arches, pinnacles and cresting. The resemblance to a shine was deliberate. The altar screen of Exeter Cathedral (see plate IV) would have looked very like this.

53 Queen Mary's Psalter (London, BL, MS Royal 2. B. VII, fol. 112v; *c*.1310–20). The *Adoration of the Magi* is set in an architectural frame, with figures in niches. At the bottom of the page are marginal illustrations of animals from the Bestiary. The cult of the Virgin was an essential focus of medieval devotion.

CHAPTER THREE

Mind and Spirit

If the occurrence and spread of the Decorated style were influenced by the pattern of landholding and patronage – masons in particular were able to realise their ideas and designs only where the work was offered – its appearance and, indeed, what was made, were as much a response to cultural and intellectual assumptions as a purely artistic exercise. In this period art was rarely, if ever, produced for art's sake. The notion of the artist as a commentator detached from society and a free spirit striving for self-expression is comparatively recent. No medieval artist saw it as his main purpose to innovate or to push at the boundaries of what was permissible; in the Middle Ages artists worked within understood limits. This is not to say that their creative gifts were suppressed. The limits were largely of subject-matter; and in a world in which everything from shoe buckles to buildings was handmade and decorated there was no lack of objects on which craftsmen could exercise their skills. Nor were they more or less guided by fashion than artists of today. What sets them apart from their modern descendants is that everything they made had a purpose, to serve and reflect, rather than comment upon, the main tenets of contemporary life.

The Decorated style developed largely in response to and in the service of the spiritual and ritual requirements of both the religious and secular life of the time. These were based on certain assumptions that everyone held in common. It was a Christian society, driven by belief in the Kingdom of God, by the acceptance of Christ as the incarnation of God, who had died to save the world from sin, and the belief that the world would end in Judgement Day and Christ's Second Coming, for which man must be prepared. Against this moment, repentance of sin and insurance of salvation were lifelong duties. Remote though these beliefs may seem to be from the drudgery of everyday life, they were taken for granted and were the focus, however deeply submerged, of existence. To medieval people life on earth was merely a prelude to the eternal life to come. The eternal world was not an abstract concept. It existed beside and within its earthly counterpart, and it governed the ways in which the temporal world was interpreted and understood.

Everything within the latter was explained in relation to the former. Thus a garden was a place for pleasure and repose, and for growing fruit and vegetables for the household; but it was also a symbol of Paradise and the Virgin, around whom developed an elaborate garden imagery, especially the idea of the walled garden, the *hortus conclusus*. The symbol could be reduced to a single flower, a lily or a rose, by which the evocation of the Virgin would automatically be understood.

The arts were a powerful expression of this system of thought, dependent as it was on allegory and metaphor, multiple, layered meanings. It was the basis of poetry; but such poems as *Pearl* and the *Roman de la Rose* had visual counterparts in subject matter that explored the borders between the known and visionary worlds, and which was expressed both naturalistically and in illusionism, signs and representations. There was constant awareness that any object represented both itself and some deeper meaning. The church building represented the kingdom of Heaven; but, just as the lily and the rose represented the garden, the same concept could be embodied in a small, canopied niche. In the Decorated period the ritual level of life, where art became an important means of expression, was dictated by covert and overt Christian values; but the secular world was now imposing its own values on the Church, and its own motifs and images on church art. Allegory and metaphor were therefore used ever more strongly to explain the world in Christian terms.

In this chapter these themes will to some extent interlock, but the chapter as a whole is concerned with the effects of cultural and intellectual developments on buildings, their planning and their decoration: the preparation for the afterlife and insurance of salvation through the cult of saints, particularly the Virgin, relics and shrines; new doctrines; and the steady encroachment of secular and chivalric values.

Salvation of the soul was controlled by the Church as guardian of the path to the next world. While preachers averred that the kingdom of heaven lay within each individual, they also emphasised the presence in church of the images and relics of the saints to whom prayers could be addressed for intercession on the sinner's behalf. By the Council of Lyon in 1274 the traditional doctrine of Purgatory had been refined by contemporary theologians to the state of being occupied by a soul between death of the mortal body and the Last Judgement, when it could be cleansed ready for Paradise with the help of prayers by the living. This gave new emphasis to prayers for the soul, which were provided by the Church as a service, although strictly according to the ability to pay: the more you gave, the greater the number of prayers would be said on your behalf. The purpose of dividing a body so that the heart, for example, was buried elsewhere was designed to attract more prayers and masses, and a similar intention lay behind the Eleanor Crosses, each of which was to be a focus of prayers for the queen's soul. Even the poor could guarantee some respite from Purgatory through making offerings at a shrine, the rich could take out greater insurance by endowing or building churches and religious houses in return for soul masses and perhaps for burial. Some of these new buildings, convents of friars for example, were also for general worship; but others, chantry chapels and small churches served by colleges of priests, were specifically intended for the burial of the founder and his family, and for masses on their behalf. 50

The new buildings

The mendicants and Augustinian canons, endowed with the spiritual purity that had once been identified with Benedictine monks, were the recipients of much lay patronage. The wealthiest people increased their chances of salvation by patronising more than one order. Henry III largely financed the buildings of the Franciscans at Reading and the Dominicans at Canterbury, and Dominicans regularly became confessors to members of the royal family. The mendicants generally attracted the notice of all three Edwards and their wives. The Dominican church in London, the Blackfriars at Ludgate, was particularly favoured by Edward I, who gave substantial sums towards the building, and his second wife, Margaret of France, was a prominent benefactor of the Franciscan church, the Greyfriars at Newgate, when it was rebuilt from 1306. Henry of Grosmont assisted the Franciscans at Preston and the Dominicans at Thetford and Leicester.

The fashion for burial with the mendicants was not, however, set by the kings, but by the higher nobility, although the latter included three queens of England. Two generations of the Beauchamp family were buried in the Franciscan church at Worcester in the later thirteenth century. The Greyfriars at Newgate received the remains of Eleanor of Provence (d. 1291) and Queen Margaret (d. 1318); and in 1358 Edward II's widow, Isabella, who had adopted the habit of a Franciscan nun, was buried there with the heart of her murdered husband. The heart of Alphonso, son of Edward I, was buried in the Blackfriars in 1284, to be followed by that of his mother, Eleanor of Castile, who had a special chapel built off the choir. Elizabeth de Bohun, Countess of Northampton (d. 1356), was among those who came later. Elizabeth de Burgh, Lady of Clare, chose to be buried in the Minories, the house of Franciscan nuns at Aldgate, which had been founded by Edmund Crouchback, Earl of Lancaster; and Elizabeth de Bohun's brother-in-law, Humphrey, Earl of Hereford and Essex, built the church of the Augustinian friars, in which he was buried in 1361.

The merchants and gentry, too, were active benefactors to mendicant churches, and sought burial in them. Sir William Thorpe, justice, and Sir Hugh Clare, knight, followed their social superiors to the Greyfriars at Newgate. The Dominican churches in, for instance, Norwich, Scarborough and Oxford included leading townsmen among their founders, and the burial of Baldwin and Chabill de Shipling in the chancel of the Dominican church at Sudbury (Suffolk) suggests that they were

54   Ottery St Mary, Devon, collegiate church begun 1337 by Bishop John Grandisson of Exeter as a chantry for himself and his family. The net vault has a pattern of ogival lozenges.

substantial patrons. The Augustinian canons also received general lay support. The priory at Blythburgh (Suffolk) had strong links to the Harnhulles, a gentry family; but the Augustinian house (now the Cathedral) at Bristol was the burial church of the Berkeleys, and after 1320 several Augustinian houses were founded by rising families: Haltemprice .(Humberside) by the Wakes in 1325/6; Maxstoke (Warwicks) by the Clintons and Bisham (Berks) by the Montagues with the king's help in 1337; Flanesford (Heref. and Worcs) by the Talbots in 1346.

The alternative to burial or intercession with one of the established orders was to found a chantry, which need be only an endowment for a priest to say masses in an existing building but could be a complete new church served by a college of priests. That it was considered a socially appropriate act as well as a reflection of disposable income is suggested by the chantry and family burial chapel established at Winterbourne in Gloucestershire by Thomas, Lord Bradeston, in 1351, after his rise in status. The endowments stipulated the conditions of prayer, how often they should be said, through which saints and on whose behalf. A collegiate foundation could specify not only the number of clergy but detailed rules for their behaviour. Such foundations provided employment for many unbeneficed clergy, and gave the founder a measure of control denied him by the established orders. This seems to have been important to the secular clergy as well as the laity, as many chantry foundations were by bishops and senior clerics, who established them for their families although they themselves had the right of burial in their cathedrals. The Giffards built a chapel at Boyton (Wilts) in the 1280s, and *c*.1299 Bishop Bitton of Exeter built one at his birthplace, Bitton in Gloucestershire. Bishop Grandisson of Exeter, who arranged his funeral in 1328 only to survive another forty years, rebuilt Ottery St 54 Mary specifically as a chantry college for himself and his family, although he was buried in Exeter Cathedral; and from 1351 Bishop Edington of Winchester rebuilt the parish church at Edington in Wiltshire as a collegiate establishment. The earls of Lancaster added collegiate churches to their existing ecclesiastical interests: Thomas, Earl of Lancaster (d. 1322) founded at Kenilworth (Warwicks) a chapel served by thirteen secular canons; and his brother Henry founded as his burial church the college of St Mary in the Newarke in Leicester, which was to be refounded in 1354 on a grand scale by his son Henry of Grosmont. The collegiate churches at Astley (Warwicks), founded in 1343, and 98 Sibthorpe (Notts) are among many established by the gentry. With their clerical equivalents the gentry also endowed parish churches with chantries, extra clergy and new buildings, for example Heckington (Lincs), by the chancery clerk Richard de Potesgrave, *c*.1320s; Elsing (Norfolk), 79 *c*.1340s, by the lord of the manor, Hugh de Hastings; Fledborough 112 (Notts), 1343, probably by the lord of the manor, John de Lisieux; and Huyton (Lancs), by the chancery clerk John de Winwick in the 1350s.

Relics, shrines and tombs

The new mendicant buildings, chantry chapels and collegiate churches complemented the established monastic and secular churches; they did not supplant them. Many benefactors remained loyal to the enclosed orders. Roger Bigod, Earl of Norfolk, rebuilt Tintern Abbey church from 17 *c*.1270; Henry of Grosmont continued his family's support for the Cistercians at Furness and Whalley despite his enthusiasm for the mendicants; and Edward III actually founded a Cistercian house, St Mary Graces in east London, as late as 1350. Yet very few monasteries were now new-founded for burial. Rare examples are Richard, Earl of Cornwall's Hailes Abbey, founded in 1246 and Upholland (Lincs), founded by Lord Holland in 1319. Henry III's selection of Westminster for his burial did not entail a refoundation, although there was a complete rebuilding. Some patrons did, however, remain loyal to their traditional family burial churches. The earls of Oxford, who had been buried at Colne Priory in Essex since its foundation in the twelfth century, were still using it for burial in the fourteenth. Those who acquired the patronage of an existing monastery through marriage or inheritance, notably the Despensers at Tewkesbury, chose burial there to enhance their family's status.

The traditional monastic and secular churches survived because they served the general population in ways that mendicant and collegiate churches, and chantry chapels, functioning primarily on behalf of the benefactor, did not; and certain paths to salvation, particularly through the intercession of saints in their relics and shrines, were more easily exploited by the older establishments, which were not only experienced but also had accumulated relic collections of a kind that recent foundations had not had time to acquire. Relics, the physical remains of saints or objects associated with them, helped to maintain faith and belief in the reality of the Christian story, which was especially necessary in northern countries with no historical connections to Christ and the Apostles. Some relics had miraculous powers of healing, others represented the saint to whom prayers would be directed for intercession, and yet others were the object of wonder and curiosity. The last perhaps included some of those related to Christ and the Virgin, whose bodily assumption to Heaven precluded the existence of mortal remains; hence relics of the Virgin's milk, or the rock bearing Christ's footprint at the Ascension, which Henry III bought from the Dominicans and gave to Westminster Abbey. Relic collecting was a serious matter for both institutions and individuals: John de Winwick's collection included a 'ring with a beautiful sapphire', said to be the wedding ring of St Anne, mother of the Virgin. The royal collection of relics was continually augmented until, by the reign of Edward III, it was one of the largest in England. It included the armbone of St Alban's fictional companion, Amphibalus, the blood of St George and St Stephen, and Croes Neyd, the relic of the True Cross that had belonged to Llewelyn the Great, and was presented to Edward I in 1284 after the conquest of Wales. All the relics were kept in the Tower of London; some were taken on military expeditions, and Croes Neyd was brought out for great Church festivals until 1353, when it was given to Windsor to be displayed on the high altar of St George's chapel at Easter and the Garter ceremonies. Churches collected relics both to attract pilgrims and for the prestige attaching to the relics themselves. Holy bones were strongly promoted in this period, and there were many stories of the lengths to which respectable and holy clerics would go to acquire a saintly rib or finger-bone; thefts were not uncommon.

Amid the profusion of relics on display in a great church there was one particular shrine devoted to the main cult. In England many of these were of pre-Conquest saints, whose cults had not only survived the Norman invasion and reform of the Church, but had been preserved and supported by the incoming bishops: St Alban, St Edmund at Bury, St Cuthbert at Durham, St Swithun at Winchester, St Etheldreda at Ely and

St Erkenwald at St Paul's. They were further reinvigorated in the later twelfth century and the thirteenth, together with some more recent figures, St Edward the Confessor (who died in 1066, but was canonised only in 1161), and such bishops as Hugh of Lincoln (d. 1200), Richard of Chichester (d. 1253), Thomas Cantilupe of Hereford (d. 1282), and, above all, Thomas Becket, Archbishop of Canterbury, martyred in 1170 in the cause of Church supremacy and enshrined in great magnificence in Canterbury Cathedral. Edward I attended the translation of St Richard's relics in 1276 and rewarded a harpist who sang at the shrine. These and others attracted a popular following, at least for a time. Thomas Cantilupe's tomb had been converted to a shrine by 1287, but 57 his cult was already in decline by the time of his official canonisation in 1320. All such cults were located essentially in the churches with which the saints or holy ones had been associated in life. Relics of this kind were not available to the new collegiate and chantry foundations. More-over, these great shrines had additional functions: while they were a focus of prayers for the dead, they also offered comfort to the living.

The presence of these shrines did not dictate the planning of churches, but they affected it. Most of them were displayed on a tall pedestal behind the high altar. This arrangement, formalised apparently by the Norman bishops after the Conquest, was intended to associate the saint with the high altar, and allow the shrine to be seen above it by the priest as he celebrated mass, as described by Matthew Paris in *Gesta Abbatum*, the history of St Albans Abbey. The chronicler of Westminster also stressed the spiritual light shining from the elevated shrine of the Confessor. With the relatively poor circulation space afforded by Anglo-Norman church plans the public access to the shrine allowed on great feast days disrupted services and was hard to control. The great rect-angular eastern arms that were adopted from the late twelfth century and appeared in the vast majority of rebuildings and extensions from then on allowed the shrine to be displayed amid a bigger, more flexible space.

The setting of the shrine was, however, as important as accessibility. The need to provide a sumptuous setting was advanced at both Durham and St Albans as a useful way of raising money for the reconstruction. 55 The Trinity chapel of Canterbury Cathedral, in which Becket's shrine was richly housed, was strongly influential, particularly on Westmin-ster, where Henry III had political reasons to promote a cult to outshine that of the murdered archbishop. The shrine area of the building could be enhanced by architectural ornament, as in the lower church of Glas-gow Cathedral, where the site of St Kentigern's tomb is marked by a richer pattern of ribs in the vault. In the Angel choir of Lincoln the shrine of St Hugh was the pivot of the programme of imagery that conveyed III the wider meaning of the building, with the imagery of salvation in-dicating the path to Paradise around and east of the shrine, and the road to Judgement and damnation west of it. At Westminster the gilded

55 St Albans Abbey (now Cathedral), the feretory or shrine chapel behind the high altar. Part of the original eleventh-century building, the chapel was refurbished in the late thirteenth century and a Lady chapel built out eastwards, 1305–15. The shrine base, 1305–08, is of Purbeck stone, decorated with foliage and figure sculpture, and once painted. Before the altar screen (left) was built in the fifteenth century, the reliquary would have been visible from the presbytery.

metallic diaper and the imagery were a monumental reflection of the meaning of the shrine itself, and in Northwold's choir at Ely the surviving remains of the shrine base are made of the same highly polished Purbeck stone as the building, in which the sharply defined metallic mouldings of the arches and foliate decoration evoked the precious metal of the reliquary. The evocation of the casket that encased the holy bones was perhaps especially important because in the great shrine churches the reliquary was concealed for much of the time both for security and to enhance the spiritual value of the contents by rationing their display. At Durham, Canterbury and Westminster there was a painted wooden shrine cover, which was drawn up on feast days by a rope pulley, adorned at Durham by a peal of silver bells.

Like many shrine bases, the reliquaries were victims of the Reformation, but drawings, descriptions and surviving continental examples show that they resembled miniature chapels, with arches, gables and ornamental coping; and they were plated with gold, gilt bronze or silver, with added enamels, jewels and images. The shrine of St Eleutherius, finished in 1247, in Tournai Cathedral, Belgium, is in just such a form: a rectangular building with a pitched roof, decorated all over with trefoil arches under which are figures of the apostles, John the Baptist and an

Annunciation scene. Christ and the saint occupy the two gable ends, busts of angels the spandrels of the arches, and the whole is made of silver, gilt bronze, enamel, filigree and precious stones. The gold reliquary of Edward the Confessor, commissioned by Henry III in 1241, included figures of Christ in Majesty, the Virgin, SS Edmund and Peter, five kings, a queen and five angels, all of which were pawned in 1267 (but redeemed in time for the translation of the relics two years later). The destroyed shrine of St Gertrude of Nivelles (Belgium), made from 1272, was in the form of an aisled basilica with figures of Christ and the Virgin on the gable ends, and complex architectural details including a miniature rose window and an ogee arch. Hollar's engraving of the shrine of St Erkenwald of St Paul's, *c*.1320, shows a little building with gables, pinnacles, flying buttresses and traceried windows. The contract for the shrine of St John of Beverley, drawn up in 1292 with Roger de Faringdon, goldsmith, demonstrates the close relation between reliquaries and contemporary styles in masonry: Roger was to make plates and columns 'de opere cementario', and the reliquary was to have tabernacles and pinnacles front and back, and be covered in figures, a description that could well be applied to St Etheldreda's, Ely Place, which 22 had just been built, or such structures in the making as St Stephen's chapel, the Eleanor Crosses and the tombs in Westminster Abbey.

We have already seen that the stone bases on which the reliquaries stood shared many of these decorative characteristics. The exception was that of the Confessor's shrine, which was made of the same Cosmati 10 mosaic work as the sanctuary floors. Almost all extant shrine bases date 124

56 Shrine of St Eleutherius (Tournai Cathedral, Belgium, finished 1247). A typical reliquary casket, its architectural decoration and attached figures are closely related to ideas in monumental architecture.

from between *c.*1270 and *c.*1350, and many more renewals and translations are recorded from these years. Many of the surviving bases have been reconstructed, perhaps not quite accurately, but their details are clear notwithstanding, and they certainly assisted in the diffusion of the new repertory of motifs. The relation between shrine bases and tombs in general was becoming close. The shrine of St William of York (York, Yorkshire Museum) was made in the 1330s to stand over the site of his tomb in the nave of York Minster. York was among several buildings where cults were maintained at both the saint's original burial place and the shrine behind the high altar. Miracles could occur at both tomb and shrine, the tomb remaining potent even after the bones had been removed. At Canterbury the shrine of Becket in the Trinity chapel stood directly over the tomb in which his body had lain in the crypt, an arrangement reflected at Rochester and Glasgow. Beverley Minster, like York, had shrines to St John in both the nave and at the high altar. At Winchester Cathedral the site of the Anglo-Saxon shrine of St Swithun was commemorated in a chapel off the north side of the Anglo-Norman nave, while the main reliquary had been moved east of the high altar.

Depictions in the stained glass of Canterbury Cathedral of Becket's tomb and his shrine of 1220 make a clear distinction between them: the tomb, which seems to have resembled the so-called tomb of St Osmund in Salisbury Cathedral, had holes in its side into which a sick pilgrim could crawl to come as close as possible to the holy bones; the shrine base, on the other hand, was a flat slab supported on tall colonnettes.

57   Hereford Cathedral, tomb/shrine of St Thomas Cantilupe, d. 1282. The small figures of knights holding shields are the earliest surviving weepers on English tombs.

This type of shrine base seems to have been the prevalent form from the Conquest to the mid-thirteenth century, after which it gave way to a solid structure more closely resembling a tomb, but often with niches in the side to serve the same thaumaturgic purpose as the holes in Becket's sarcophagus. The Confessor's shrine, for all its unusual decoration, was of this type, as were all the surviving later examples and others known from descriptions, such as that of St Cuthbert of Durham, which was renewed only in 1372. An alternative design was that of the shrine of St Thomas Cantilupe, which had no niches but an open, arcaded upper 57 storey into which people could put their heads. The tomb of St William, which had two openwork storeys, and the shrine of St Werburgh, which 38 combined lower niches with an open upper storey, probably housed the reliquary within the latter as if in a chapel.

The shrines of Cantilupe and Edward the Confessor allowed pilgrims even nearer to the bones, for both men were interred in the shrine base itself, the Confessor in the upper part, Cantilupe in the solid lower part, with his memorial brass let into its surface and weepers dressed as knights along the sides. Cantilupe's shrine-tomb exemplifies a series of episcopal tombs that were evidently made with canonisation in mind. The canonisation of so many bishops in the thirteenth century was the direct result of their greatly enhanced moral authority. Some enjoyed popular cults but were never canonised, including Roger Niger of London (d. 1241), Robert Grosseteste of Lincoln (d. 1253), Walter Suffield of Norwich (d. 1257) and James Berkeley of Exeter (d. 1327). Berkeley's tomb attracted sufficient gifts to make a significant contribution to the cathedral building fund. Grosseteste apparently had a cast bronze effigy on a notably splendid tomb, and the shrine-like tomb set up in the south transept of Wells Cathedral to Bishop William March (d. 1302) was perhaps made *c*.1324 when the authorities campaigned for his canonisation, evidently as a fund-raising ploy, as his character was not saintly.

Bishops' tomb canopies could often suggest enshrinement. That of Walter de Grey, Archbishop of York, resembles the earlier form of shrine 72 base, a platform on columns, with above it a gabled, pinnacled structure reminiscent of a shrine cover. Others shared the micro-architecture and ornament of metal reliquaries. Giles de Bridport's tomb in Salisbury Cathedral has twin-light traceried 'windows' under gables, with scenes from the bishop's life in the spandrels and decorative foliage, pinnacles and quatrefoils. Peter of Aigueblanche's tomb is carved with metallic 23 delicacy in contrasting stones. The flat top to the canopy over the tomb of Walter de Stapeldon, the bishop of Exeter murdered in London in 1326, hints strongly that a reliquary was expected to stand there.

The cult of the Virgin

The high shrine was only one influence on the choice of plan for the eastern arm of a great church. The needs of the clergy and developing

58   Ivory triptych (H. 238 mm; London, BM; 1330s) belonging to Bishop John Grandisson of Exeter. It depicts the *Coronation of the Virgin* and the *Crucifixion*, flanked by saints in ogival niches.

liturgical practices were equally important, and a balance of interests was constantly sought. The arrangements in the new rectangular choirs at Ely, Lincoln and Old St Paul's all emphasised the shrine; but they also clarified other functions and spaces, with altars and lesser shrines at the extreme east and clearly defined paths to direct pilgrims through the building. The most powerful intercessor in any church was not the main saint but the Virgin Mary, and during the thirteenth century it became increasingly necessary to make adequate provision for her cult.

The Virgin was needed in ways that other saints were not. She was universal, free from the specific associations attaching to most saints, and could be revered at all levels from simplicity to sophistication. The Virgin could be reinterpreted as attitudes changed, and it was this freedom and adaptability that kept her cult flourishing and growing. She was invested with many meanings: the vessel of the Incarnation, the Bride of Christ and symbol of the Church, a shield against the Devil, the new Eve, conceived without sin. She was both a comfort and a warning, particularly to women, who were morally defined and culturally conditioned by the polarities of the sinful Eve and the sinless Virgin. Expected to model themselves on the latter's virtues, women also bore responsibility for Eve's original error, and thus became convenient scapegoats for everyday social sins. It is no accident that the people featured in the images of gossip and scandalmongering that were depicted in so many parish churches (for example, at Peakirk in Cambridgeshire) should invariably be female. Equally, it is no accident that many of the miracles of the Virgin should refer to the succour and rescue of women.

The first systematic collections of miracles of the Virgin were assembled in England. The English had been devotees of both Mary and Joseph even in Anglo-Saxon times, but in the twelfth century they played a leading part in the development of the Virgin's cult, with the revival of the Feast of the Immaculate Conception and the earliest known representation of her Coronation. The English were known on the Continent not only as collectors of the Virgin's miracles but also as originators of them, some even then being regarded as the product of misty and watery imaginations cultivated on a misty and watery island. Stories of a saint's miracle workings establish the nature of that saint and indicate which kinds of people can expect help. The power of the saint both to help and not to help was taken seriously, and some shrines attracted particular groups of people. It is possible, for instance, that the large number of women who visited the shrine of Godric of Finchale were avoiding nearby Durham and St Cuthbert's well publicised antipathy to their sex. The Virgin, on the other hand, assisted everyone. Her miracles reveal her as the intercessor for all mankind, whether humble or exalted, ecclesiastic or lay. The message is that if you do wrong but pray to her, she will come to the rescue however bizarre the circum- 113 stances might be. The miracles were combined with the apocryphal accounts of her birth, infancy, old age and death, which had arisen very early on to remedy the absence of canonical information about her, and they were all illustrated in extensive cycles of pictures, not only in such luxury manuscripts as Queen Mary's Psalter (London, BL, MS Royal 2.B.VII) and in the Lady chapels of Ely and Bury St Edmunds, but painted on the walls of parish churches such as Brook in Kent and Croughton in Northamptonshire. As the cult of the Virgin's mother, St Anne, began to flourish in the fourteenth century so did suitable iconography develop, with the English again to the fore, inventing among other delightful scenes that of St Anne teaching the Virgin to read, which appears on the Dominican altarfrontal now in the Musée de Cluny, x Paris. Another scene, known from the texts but rare in art, is that of the Virgin weaving in the temple, which was embroidered in the late thirteenth century on the English cope now at St Maximin in Provence.

By the mid-thirteenth century, partly in response to the intentions of the fourth Lateran Council of 1215 that the laity should receive proper religious instruction, the bishops had established the main liturgical

offices of the Virgin in their cathedrals, and these continued to be elaborated into the fourteenth century. The separate Lady chapel, dedicated to the Virgin, emerged with the developing liturgy, when a simple altar no longer sufficed. The need for more space was acknowledged in nearly every one of the eastern extensions and rebuildings, with obligation to the main shrine balanced by that due to the Virgin. The consequences of failure to do so are manifest at Ely, where Northwold's extension was given over entirely to the Ely saints, the Lady chapel remaining in the old south choir aisle until the 1320s when the monks were forced to build the new chapel out on the north side of the church. A separate lady chapel in that position was favoured in East Anglia, examples having previously been built at Peterborough and Bury St Edmunds; and a Lady chapel could also be an attached extension, open to the main church, as at Bristol and Oxford in the thirteenth century. In churches where an eastern arm was completely rebuilt, however, the Lady chapel tended to be the easternmost feature. In rectangular plans, as at Lincoln and Old St Paul's, it occupied the end bays, with the altar III against the east wall; one bay of the building acted as procession path between the Lady chapel and the feretory (shrine chapel) behind the high altar.

The other main plan type actually expressed the Lady chapel in the structure, the low, projecting eastern termination being instantly comprehensible from the outside and forming a distinct space inside that was devoted to the rapidly increasing number of Lady masses. St Albans, Exeter and Wells show the different ways in which such a plan could be adapted. At St Albans the shrine is contained within the bounds of the original Anglo-Norman church, with beyond it the low, spacious hall leading to the projecting Lady chapel, allowing room for pilgrims, clergy and extra altars. There could be provision for a Lady chapel even where there was no main shrine, as at Norwich, where Bishop Suffield had begun, but did not finish, what seems to have been an arrangement similar to St Albans. The same clear, logical right-angles IV of thirteenth-century planning can also be seen at Exeter; at Wells, by contrast, the elongated octagon of the Lady chapel fused with the spaces 59 of the retrochoir expresses all the ambiguity beloved of the 1320s.

59 Wells Cathedral, the Lady chapel seen from the retrochoir, 1320s. The octagonal Lady chapel is pulled back into and fused with the retrochoir space.

The Resurrection and the Passion

In this period the cult of the Virgin was essentially the elaboration of an established devotional focus; but at the same time new cults were emerging, the most significant of which was that devoted to the Passion of Christ. The doctrine of Transubstantiation, that in communion the bread and wine become the body and blood of Christ, was promulgated in the thirteenth century, and the celebration of the real presence of Christ in the Eucharist gave new prominence to the sacraments, with more elaborate and costly receptacles for keeping and displaying the host, and devotion directed towards Christ's suffering and Resurrection. Many relics of the Passion appeared in the West after the sack of Constantinople in 1204, and considerable prestige was attached to their possession. The standard was set by the Crown of Thorns and piece of the True Cross acquired by Louis IX and placed in the Sainte-chapelle. A share in the Sainte-chapelle relics became a mark of distinction. Fragments of the True Cross relic were given to each of the Saintes-chapelles that were built in France in imitation of the Parisian model, and other relics were conferred on individuals as a personal honour: in 1352, after a notorious chivalric adventure in Paris, Henry of Grosmont was presented by the French king with a thorn from the Crown, which he passed to his new foundation of St Mary in the Newarke at Leicester. The fashion also grew for combining the two relics in a single holder, like Elizabeth de Burgh's relic of the True Cross enclosing a relic of the Crown of Thorns.

That Henry III's acquisition of a relic of the Holy Blood of Christ in 1247 was prompted by admiration and envy of Louis IX's new possessions and their ceremonious reception into Paris is made clear by Matthew Paris's description of the procession from St Paul's to Westminster, in which the king himself carried the precious vessel and the officiating bishop, Walter Suffield, drew favourable comparisons with the event in France. Yet England had its own history of interest in relics of the Passion. As early as 1200 a depiction of the Veronica, the cloth bearing an imprint of Christ's face, was shown in a manuscript illumination (another Veronica picture was left by Queen Isabella at her death in 1358); and a relic of the True Cross, the 'rood of Bromholm', was already at Bromholm Priory in Norfolk in 1220, attracting Henry III's attention and support until its eclipse by the relic of the Holy Blood at Westminster.

General devotion to the wounds of Christ had been concentrated by their appearance as the stigmata on St Francis, but the Holy Blood, with its Eucharistic connotations, had special significance, emphasised in England by the unusual iconography on the north transept door of Westminster of Christ pointing to his wound. The cult had great popular appeal, and a second phial of the Blood, presented to Hailes Abbey in 1270 by Edmund, Earl of Cornwall, attracted pilgrims so successfully that the east end of the church was rebuilt to a 'royal' plan of ambulatory and radiating chapels, and the relic was enshrined in splendour behind the high altar.

More important than Christ's sufferings, however, was His Resurrection. The devout were helped to see this as an event both in and outside time by the feast of Corpus Christi, established in 1264 and promulgated in 1311 and 1317, which was centred on His physical body after the Resurrection. The feast had strong affiliations to the laity, being popular in towns and a favourite dedication of guilds and lay fraternities. Its more lasting artistic manifestations, however, are associated with the clergy, who evoked the risen Christ on their tombs. Two fourteenth-century bishops of Exeter are entombed beneath such images, one painted on the underside of the canopy over the effigy of Walter de Stapeldon, the other carved in the vault of John Grandisson's burial v chapel. The Tombs of Christ placed in some churches in Lincolnshire and the east Midlands in the first half of the fourteenth century, which focus on Christ risen from the tomb, have been linked to the interests of 109 the clerical patrons whose tombs lie alongside. With the Tombs of Christ, however, we move away from reliquaries to the other strong focus of devotion, the image.

Image and Reality

Imagery, whether devotional, didactic or moralising, was far more in evidence than relics, for where relics maintained their power through veils and secrecy, imagery was pervasive, in the form of single figures, set-piece tableaux and narrative series, any of which could be used as appropriate. Imagery of the Virgin, for instance, might comprise a figure 116 of the Virgin and Child, sequences of narrative scenes, or, on the west front of York Minster, a programme of devotional imagery focused on the Virgin that encompassed both the stained glass and the sculpture. Portable images complemented those in architectural ornament and liturgical furnishings. As early as the sixth century Pope Gregory the Great had opined that images were useful for instructing the unlettered, and although there was a continuous undercurrent of clerical anxiety about the dangers of idolatry, images were in general approved, because 'since they arouse from vain and wordly thoughts to more intent and frequent meditation on unseen things and the desire for them' images could focus the mind upon matters spiritual. To think of Christ on the cross was held to be the best weapon against sin, and the great rood in the church nave, the figures of the Virgin and St John mourning the crucified Christ, was there to help the faithful to imagine the episode and to contemplate its meaning. The dangers of too close an identification were sounded by, among others, Bishop Ralph of Armagh, who in a sermon preached in 1356 worried that people worshipped images named for those whom they were intended to represent, speaking of St Mary of Walsingham or St Mary of the Newarke as if the Virgin was actually present in the statue. This, of course, made such people idolaters, because the Virgin was not at Walsingham or Leicester but in Heaven.

There were vast numbers of devotional images. Quite modest parish churches had an 'ymago beate Mariae cum tabernaculo', and statuettes were donated to shrines and altars in piety, gratitude and perhaps expiation, as is suggested by the gifts to Canterbury from Edward I and Edward III of images of Thomas Becket. Henry III gave many individual images to Westminster Abbey, among them figures of St Edward and the Pilgrim to stand beside the shrine, and a banner embroidered with the Virgin and John the Baptist. Devotional images were also among the regular furnishings of the home: John de Winwick owned an image of John the Baptist, as did Elizabeth de Burgh, who bequeathed hers to the Countess of Warenne. Bishop Grandisson's ivory triptychs (London, BM), hinged, folding panels *c*.24 cm high, which could travel with their owner like a modern photograph frame, represent a whole class of images that has almost vanished. They were evidently for his own use, the subjects his personal choice – the Crucifixion, his favourite saints, and, most particularly, the Virgin. Grandisson's devotion to the latter was such that his ring (Exeter, City Museum) bearing an exquisite enamel depicting the Virgin and Child was buried with him, and an *Annunciation* scene was carved on the image screen around his burial chapel at the west end of Exeter Cathedral.

Imagery was essential for the relation of the temporal world to the world outside time, the domain of the saints, angels and devils, who linked the two worlds and demonstrated that the afterlife was worth the preparation. 'Horrybull fendes' lurked everywhere to trap the sinner, but the saints and the angels, the messengers of God, would help the penitent and convey praises to the Lord. Henry III gave statuettes of angels to stand beside the crucifix on the nave altar at Westminster Abbey, and eight censing angels stood on Edward II's funeral hearse. There is scarcely a work of art surviving from this period that does not include them. In their choir at Lincoln they indicate Paradise and

60 Salisbury Cathedral, tomb of Bishop Roger de Mortival, d.1330, detail showing the angels seated on the canopy. The tomb is built into the choir screen; it was in this period that bishops began to incorporate their tombs into the liturgical furnishings.

Judgement; at Ely they adorn the arch over the entrance to the Lady 113 chapel and accompany the Virgin in every narrative scene of the *Life and Miracles*; they lounge gracefully on the arched canopy of Bishop 60 Mortival's tomb in Salisbury Cathedral; at Gloucester they appear on the door from the south transept to the choir aisle, and an angelic orchestra plays in the vault above the high altar, a theme prominent at Exeter, where the angel musicians fronting the minstrel's gallery in the 40 nave would have been brought to life by real musicians concealed in the gallery itself.

The meaning of such imagery, poised between the temporal and the spiritual, was underscored by the ambiguities and layering of its architectural setting. In St Stephen's chapel the *sacra conversazione* on the altar 42 wall between living people, saints and biblical figures was set amid illusionistic space, fictive architecture, sculptured figures coloured to look live and painted figures executed in grisaille to resemble stone. Enamel, marble and textile hangings were simulated in other materials as a matter of course. The visual surroundings were backed by words, as the clergy urged appropriate behaviour on the faithful through stories that linked the inner and outer worlds. John Myrc, the late fourteenth-century compiler of homilies, demonstrated the essential truth of the miracle of the Ring and the Pilgrim by saying that the ring, having spent seven years in Paradise, was now at Westminster, where it could be seen. A similar method was employed to illustrate the benefits of prayer and penitence, and what would happen if you did not comply: when a woman refused to confess a sin Jesus took her hand and put it to the wound in His side; it came out covered in blood and remained so until she confessed. Like modern urban myths, such stories were told of people not personally known to the narrator, but at a slight though plausible remove – a distant relative or someone in a nearby town.

These exempla were not intended to deceive, but to be understood as distinct levels of truth, just as in the Eucharist itself the bread and wine 'became' the body and blood of Christ while apparently remaining true to themselves. The workings of the medieval imagination are seen at their most sophisticated in the revelations to the growing number of mystics, such people as Richard Rolle (d. 1349) or the slightly later anonymous author of *The Cloud of Unknowing*, but they were subtle even at a more mundane level. A form of song popular in the thirteenth century illustrates the recognition that the nature of truth is many sided: two sets of lyrics were sung against each other to different themes, each telling the same story but from its own point of view, and leading to no resolution. That the differences were unresolved was the point of the song. Either view was 'true'.

Where everything existed only in relation to God, and every object was a representation or symbol of God's plan, objective reality had lesser value. Poets and clergy alike moved among metaphor, a favourite clerical metaphor being the castle, sometimes invoked as the devil that

61   Hardingstone
(Northampton), statue of Queen
Eleanor carved by ?John of Battle
on the Eleanor Cross, 1291–4 (see
p. 41). The withdrawn nobility of
the figure was intended to evoke
favourable comparison with the
Virgin Mary.

repels faith, but more often as Faith itself. John Bromyard, the mid-fourteenth-century Dominican, wrote that the foundation of the castle was Faith, the outer wall Charity, the donjon Hope, the gates the five senses, the postern the thoughts of the heart, the janitor the Will and the castellan Reason. In *Le Livre des Seyntes Medecines* (the Book of Holy Cures), a work of penitential mysticism written in 1354, the author, Henry of Grosmont, used the castle as a metaphor for the body. The castle, its outer walls and towers reflecting its inner strength, was an apt image, just as the walled garden aptly stood for virginity. In all representations the outward appearance was understood to be analogous to the inner state. The surviving descriptions of, for example, Henry III and Edward I mention such characteristic details of their appearance as height, colour of hair, the drooping eyelid, but what they intend to convey is less a wholly identifiable picture than the subject's perceived moral condition. This attitude to the appearance of things had a direct bearing on the style in which they were portrayed.

Naturalism and signs

Medieval art is essentially idealising. This much it has in common with classical styles of antiquity that preceded it and the Renaissance that followed, but what distinguishes the medieval period is its comparative lack of preoccupation with idealising the human form. As the sinful earthly body was not meant to be celebrated the human form was not studied for itself; and the other-worldliness of the spirit was better rendered through abstraction and stylisation. Beauty of form should reflect the soul within. There was always the danger, warned of in sermons, that a beautiful exterior might conceal a sinful spirit, but beauty was above all the attribute of those without sin, Christ and the Virgin. It was equated with light, common epithets being 'bright' and 'shining'. The delicate serenity of such tomb effigies as those of Bishops Northwold, Kilkenny and Bronescombe were intended to convey not ephemeral likeness but the eternal sanctity of their souls. The same is true of the statues of Queen Eleanor, whose fine features and graceful, withdrawn demeanour are comparable to contemporary statues of the Virgin. We have no idea what the queen actually looked like, but we can echo the sentiments of Master Rypon, a contemporary of Chaucer writing *c*.1400, who said that were SS Peter and Paul to stand beside their statues they would not look in the least like them. The studied elegance of the Eleanor figures and others was itself a conscious means of expression: just as in literature high-quality emotion was expressed in the best Latin, so in the visual arts did elevated subject-matter call forth a 'high' style. Concerned only with the purity of the soul, sculptors did not aim to produce a physical likeness, nor to explore personality and the development of character.

Yet, for the period covered by this book, that is by no means the whole story. Careful, exact representations of nature do occur. Already in the thirteenth century the figures of benefactors in Naumburg Cathedral in Germany were apparently modelled from the life – only they were not taken from the benefactors themselves, all of whom were long dead. By the fourteenth century, however, portraits in the sense that the term is now understood were starting to be made. Simone Martini's icon of *St Louis of Toulouse* (Naples, Galleria Nazionale), painted in 1317, includes an apparent likeness of Robert of Anjou, and Simone is said later to have made a portrait of Petrarch's Laura. We cannot know whether the depictions of Edward III and his family in St Stephen's were true like- 55 nesses (almost certainly they were not) but at around the same time Henry of Grosmont described himself in *Le Livre des Seyntes Medecines* as tall, fair, slim and fond of rings, but with legs that at feasts were 'neither so good nor so ready to bring me away as they were to get me there'. He does not explore his own character, but his objective self-awareness is betrayed in a self-mocking sense of humour that also appears in *Philo-biblon* (The Love of Books), written in 1345 by Richard of Bury. The same objectivity is revealed in Philippa of Hainault's far from idealising tomb effigy (Westminster Abbey), made in the 1360s.

Change, therefore, was under way, and in the non-monumental 'low' art that is not necessarily either official or weighty with meaning, naturalism flourished. Salisbury Cathedral has a large selection of very lifelike head corbels, an idea probably derived from Reims Cathedral, which are commonly thought to follow a system of 'types' rather than being specific portraits. Sets or sometimes pairs of finely carved, often grimacing heads can be found in both ecclesiastical and secular build-ings, for example the galleries of Westminster Abbey and the gatehouse of Tonbridge castle. Early fourteenth-century corbels supporting wooden rafter roofs may also be 'types', although they do not survive in sufficient numbers to be sure; but the former guest hall of Ely has several 62 that vary from normal stylisation to renderings so vivid that the pos-sibility of genuine portraiture is not to be dismissed. Another branch of sculpture was the wax image – parts of the body offered at shrines in gratitude for cures. How realistic they were and what effect they may have had on other art forms cannot now be known, but the possibility of influence remains.

Some tomb effigies show vivid naturalism, notably the knight at Aldworth (Berks), a figure strongly *al vif* and accompanied by a small 63 page. The drapery of Blanche, Lady Grandisson, at Much Marcle near Hereford is carved as if trailing gently down over the sarcophagus. 64 Non-human naturalistic renderings occur in all art forms but particu-larly in the marginal decorations to privately owned manuscripts such as Books of Hours and Psalters, and in the foliage ornament of churches and liturgical furnishings. From around the 1270s, when a pheasant was painted on an opening page of the so-called Windmill Psalter (New XI York, Pierpont Morgan Lib., MS M.102), luxury books for private patrons were adorned with careful depictions of birds, rabbits, squir-

62 *Right* Corbel supporting the wooden roof in the guest hall (now the Bishop's House), Ely, *c.*1330. It is so naturalistic that it may have been carved from the life.

63 Aldworth church, Berks., effigy of a knight, *c.*?1320. He represents a member of the de la Beche family, and is shown in the 'lively martial attitude', rising and (probably) in the act of drawing his sword, as a knight for Christ.

64   Much Marcle church, Heref. and Worcs., tomb of Blanche, Lady Grandisson, d. 1347. The drapery is carved to hang naturalistically over the sarcophagus.

rels, monkeys and other animals. Foliage sculpture, most spectacular at Southwell Minster and Exeter Cathedral, which was derived from France or perhaps Germany in the 1270s, is specific and in some instances – the maple and the ivy – purely ornamental. Again, the verbal record provides parallels for the visual one. Intensely realistic detail was used in sermons and homilies to underscore the general point and relate the demands of religion to everyday life. Homely accounts of the Virgin's infancy made her more accessible, while its obvious difference from common experience emphasised her sanctity. By giving vivid descriptions of Thomas Becket's houses, his clothes and the food served in his hall before and after he became Archbishop, the speaker was able to make the desired point about the future saint's conversion to holiness.

65 Christchurch, Oxford, remains of the shrine base of St Frideswide, *c.*1270. The decoration includes naturalistic foliage.

Naturalistic rendition, either verbal or visual, was a conscious choice. Artists could make one if required. Edward I was apparently sent a likeness of Margaret of France when he was considering his second marriage (although this may have been a written description). The figure ordered to be painted at Westminster for Eleanor of Provence was to be so vivid that its 'sad look and miserable appearance may properly be likened to winter'. Some plants – the rose symbolising the Virgin, the vine the Eucharistic wine – had to be immediately recognisable, or the whole point would be nullified. Even after stylised seaweed foliage had generally superseded the lifelike varieties, the rose was carved in the Lady chapel at Ely, the vine on the Swinfield tomb in Hereford Cathedral. Such naturalism, whether verbal or visual, is highly particular. It was included in recognition that observed natural phenomena were aspects of God's creation and as such worthy of representation, but as precisely distinct details in a still-stylised scheme. This was not a move towards the overall realistic representation of objects within a credible light and airy space, but the admittance of identifiable birds, animals and plants to a legitimate place alongside the monsters and fantastic foliage that expressed the tortures of the soul.

It is, however, easy to overemphasise the importance of naturalism in an art that conveyed identity through representations and signs. Saints, for instance, were recognised through univerally understood attributes – St Catherine with the wheel upon which she was martyred, St Peter with the keys – or by certain iconographically 'correct' physical attributes – St Peter's curly grey hair, St Paul's domed forehead. Just as the lily and the rose stood for the Virgin, in many aspects of life people were represented not by a recognisable image but by an object that stood in for them. Thrones of Henry III and Edward III were painted with images of kings that symbolised royal authority in the absence of the real monarch, and the images of themselves that Henry III and Edward I sent to Bromholm and Walsingham respectively substituted for their actual presence and invited prayers on their behalf. A popular way of receiving the benefit of a shrine without actually visiting it was to be 'measured' by the gift of a candle encasing a wick the exact height of the donor. In business and ceremonial life people were represented and identified not by portraits or even signatures, but by personal devices on seals and rings and by their coats of arms, heraldic charges on shields which, like symbolic flowers, had to be accurately drawn or the point of their existence was lost. When Edward II was in Amiens in 1320 his arms were posted outside the lodging houses of his retinue, and coats of arms performed a similar function on countless works of art, where their

66   Kirkham Priory, N. Yorks., the gatehouse, early 1290s. It is dated by the shields of arms set between the gables. There is Kentish tracery in the windows.

necessary accuracy can incidentally help with dating. The gatehouse of
Kirkham Priory in north Yorkshire, for example, can be almost certainly
dated to the early 1290s, for it displays the sculptured arms of Ros, Clare
and England: the Ros family, the benefactors of the priory, held the land
of Gilbert de Clare, who married Joan, daughter of Edward I, in 1290 and
died in 1295. The date and ownership of many manuscripts can be
traced through the arms painted therein; the ivories, textiles and books
associated with Bishop Grandisson are attributed to him from their
prominent display of his arms. Shields of arms were attached to tombs
and memorial brasses to identify the deceased and often also the weepers; and the arms of León, Castile, England and Ponthieu on the Eleanor
Crosses are the true indicators of who was commemorated there.

Heraldry and colour

Heraldry was also used to honour and uphold social position. Not only
royalty but leading magnates, both lay and ecclesiastical, displayed the
arms of England: Bogo de Clare, the pluralist Treasurer of York Minster
and Chancellor of Llandaff Cathedral, possessed a tapestry decorated
with shields of arms of England, and in 1361 Humphrey de Bohun, Earl
of Hereford, bequeathed to his niece a set of bed hangings similarly
adorned. The shields decorating the aisle arcading of Westminster
Abbey begin nearest the crossing with the arms of the royal houses to
which Henry III was related by marriage and continue with those of the
great families, some of whom – Bigod (earl marshal), Bohun (constable)
and Montfort (steward) – also held the high offices of state. The gatehouse of Butley Priory, Suffolk, built in the 1320s, displays the arms of
the Holy Roman Emperor; most of the other shields there, however, as at
Kirkham, York Minster and Guisborough Priory, were those of prominent local families.

Heraldic devices ran deep into the art of the period. The influence of
heraldry shows most clearly in the insistent repetition of motifs and in
colour, on which it depends. Both were present in church art before the
invention of heraldry, and the latter cannot be said to have offered
innovations; yet the proliferation of motifs together with their deployment in repetitive patterns, as in the arch-and-gable, pinnacles, foliage
designs and, for example, the use of alternating foliage and heads in
cornices and stringcourses, are not simply present in Decorated but
actually define it. Westminster Abbey set the fashion for overall coverage in squares of rosette diaper; the north transept of Hereford
Cathedral, the portal of Higham Ferrers church (Northants), the pulpitum at Lincoln, the parapet of Beverley Minster and the gilt background
to the miniatures of the Barlow Psalter (Oxford, Bodleian Lib. MS.
Barlow 22; 1321–38) show how pervasive it became in both large- and
small-scale works. Yet not all diaper was rosette. The squares were
infiltrated by heraldic devices, single motifs of, for instance, eagles,
leopards (heraldic lions; as on the plate and cushion of the effigy of

67 Westminster Abbey, gilt-bronze effigy of Henry III, made 1291–3 by William Torel, detail of head. The idealising features are not intended as a portrait. The plate and cushion are powdered with heraldic devices.

Henry III), or fleurs-de-lis, as in the Peterborough Psalter (Brussels, Bibl. VI Royale MS 9961–2, fol. 10; *c*.1300). Motifs often alternate: one of the painted colonnettes supporting the tomb canopy of Aveline of Lancaster, bears a checky pattern with alternate leopards and eagles. The backgrounds to the Dominican retable (Thornham Parva) and frontal (Musée de Cluny, Paris) are decorated with both repeated single designs IX,X and alternating motifs; the niches in the shrine base of St Alban were powdered with stars and pellets bearing leopards and fleurs-de-lis; powdered backgrounds adorn the Camoys group of brasses, for example that of Ralph de Hengham of *c*.1311 in Old St Paul's Cathedral, 68 which was powdered with stars and sheep.

Patterns of this type were deployed in the same fashion in secular contexts. In the Musée de Cluny *Nativity* the bed hangings of the Virgin are decorated with a repeating pattern of stencilled quadrilobes alternated with trilobes, and stars and crescents adorned the mantle of the statue of Edward the Confessor in the south transept at Westminster. 12 These accord with contemporary descriptions of textiles and dress. All forms of textile were powdered with repeating ornament. Edward III

68 Memorial brass of Ralph de Hengham, *c.*1311, formerly in Old St Paul's, London (drawn for William Dugdale). The background is powdered with stars and sheep, and the setting is an arch-and-gable.

had a tent lined with red buckram, powdered with appliqué yellow eagles; Sir John Pulteney owned a wall hanging spangled with butterflies and white stars, and others with lions' heads, eagles and fleurs-de-lis. In 1318 Edward II gave five pieces of silk powdered with birds to lay on the body of Beatrix, Countess of Pembroke, and at his own funeral in 1327 the horses' harness and trappings were decorated with leopards (heraldic lions) in gold leaf. The trousseau of Edward III's daughter Joan included chapel vestments in cloth of gold powdered with serpents and dragons. Clothes were adorned with pearls and sewn-on gold leaf, as well as attached three-dimensional motifs in metal, which must have resembled the lead stars fastened to the wainscots at Clarendon Palace and the gold-studded wainscots in the King's house at Geddington. The general impression of textured patterns and mixed media evokes such VIII monumental works as the Westminster retable and the interior decoration of St Stephen's chapel.

Textiles were not only decorated but also strongly coloured. Bogo de Clare owned taffetas shot with red, green and blue, and the hangings recorded in the royal Wardrobe accounts shimmered with colours and gilding. Medieval life was not in the least drab: it was suffused in colour. Unfortunately, the colour has largely disappeared, so its wider significance can be overlooked amid vague notions of decorative enhancement: Eleanor of Castile possessed coloured candles, and the rose- and violet-coloured sugar bought by Bogo de Clare must have embellished his dinner table most agreeably. Yet the gift of rose-coloured sugar sent thirty years later by Edward II to the king of France suggests that there was a mark of status in it as well. Together with signs, colour conveyed meaning. Heraldry depended upon it, for the metals and tinctures used for the devices were as important for identification as the devices themselves, and the rules were both clear and strict. In literature a description of a coat of arms bearing a combination of tinctures that was against the rules signalled the same message of moral taint as a report that a body stank at a funeral. Both the moral message and the formality of the rules of heraldry influenced medieval colour schemes, and the contrasts and alternations in paintings, manuscripts and stained glass owe much to the discipline of heraldic colour patterns. The architectural diaper, the retable and the sedilia in Westminster Abbey were painted in heraldic reds, blues and green; the Dominican retable and altar frontal alternate the colours of the background squares, gold with red or green, and the niches in the shrine base of St Alban were red and blue. The flint flushwork background to the shields on the gatehouse at Butley Priory 94 is a black-and-white checky pattern, which occurs also on the gatehouse of Denbigh Castle.

Gemstones were also prized for their colour, the colour of rare stones being endowed with greater properties of 'virtue'. Individual colours were, therefore, equated with the value of the gemstones to which they approximated; but they were also priced according to their rarity. Blue

made from lapis lazuli was expensive and used for the robe of the Virgin
Mary, the only being worthy of such honour. Any notion of medieval
colour theory cannot, however, be demonstrated beyond a certain point.
The colour codes drawn up by different writers contradict each other,
and there was clearly a gulf between theory and practice. Yet there is
evidence that even if colour codes had limited application outside
heraldry, choices of colour were not random. The design of liveries was
taken seriously. Striped liveries were worn by the abbey servants at
Westminster, the retinue of Bishop Swinfield and Edward III's falconers.
The colour of the dress to be worn by the chaplains at St Mary in the
Newarke was carefully prescribed: brown, blue-grey and russet, with a
badge of a white crescent moon and a star. The livery chosen for tournaments was thematic. That for the joust in Stepney in 1331 consisted of
green mantles embroidered with golden arrows representing love's
darts and love's hope. Dress for the tournament at Lichfield in 1338 was
a blue robe and white hood, with the same colours worn by the ladies.

Colour themes were a feature of other ceremonial events. The funeral
vestments for Edward II in 1327 and the infant William of Windsor in
1348 were black with gold; Henry III dictated the colours to be worn at
major feasts in Westminster Abbey and both he and Edward III chose the
colour themes for court ceremonies. Henry chose green for the main
hangings of his bed of estate at Westminster, perhaps in reference to the
green colour of Solomon's bed as described in the Song of Songs (1:xvi),
to which Henry's bed was symbolically compared. For the betrothal of
Edward III's son Lionel in 1342 the colours were red, green and white;
Lionel's bed of estate was hung in red decorated with lovers' knots and
leaves, and powdered and fretted with other motifs including roses. The
king's bed of estate and the room hangings were ornamented with
dragons, circles and lozenges. At the churching of Queen Philippa after
the birth of the short-lived William of Windsor the colour theme for the
beds of estate was red and green, which may have been continued in
the tournament that accompanied the ceremony. The colour theme for
the Order of the Garter was blue, with gold embroidery and silver-gilt
buckles and pendants. Another ceremonial garment made for Edward
III for a feast of St George bore a pattern of silver clouds alternating with
eagles, 'under every alternate cloud an eagle of pearls, and under every
other cloud an eagle having in its beak a garter embroidered with the
words of the king's motto *hony soit qui mal y pense* [shame on he who
thinks evil of it]'. It is clear from this description that not only was the
decoration close-knit, repetitive and alternating, but the imagery, as on
the costumes for the Stepney joust, was intentionally symbolic. Alleg-
orical meaning and moral interpretation were the stuff of chivalry.

Chivalry

Chivalry and the Church were profoundly interdependent. The only
way for the Church to assert control in God's plan for Creation was to

69 Longthorpe Tower, Peterborough, wall painting, 1320s, showing the *Wheel of the Five Senses*, a moralising theme.

interpret everything within it, and as the non-religious activities of the laity often threatened the Church's control, they had to be interpreted with particular vigour. Warfare especially, although practised by the Church, had to be rationalised. In peacetime the warlike instinct was chanelled through chivalry, which at its simplest was the art of training for mounted combat; but as knighthood presupposed sufficient wealth to maintain a horse, it also demanded appropriate obligations and display, on to which were imposed the values of a Church determined to control a potentially unruly class. At the same time the knightly ranks, although obliged by their position to contribute materially to the Church, were sufficiently powerful to do so at least to some extent on their own terms. The impact of chivalry on the art of the time went far beyond the adoption of heraldic devices. The war against Satan may have been conducted with spiritual weapons, but its imagery, of soldiers, shields and miniature battlements with functioning arrow loops, was that of the lay world. The Church supported chivalric activity in the form of crusades against the infidel, and the fighting classes used the Church to justify their activities. The visual record might suggest that Christian imagery was pervasive, for it dominated the domestic as well as the ecclesiastical interior. Bishop Grandisson had in his hall a hanging embroidered with the *Apostles Creed*, and the Apostles likewise adorned a wall hanging in the hall of Sir John Pulteney. Queen Isabella possessed a painted hanging of the *Apocalypse* and a bench cover depicting the *Nativity*. The latter was among the themes in Longthorpe Tower, painted probably in the 1320s for the Thorpe family, hereditary stewards of Peterborough Abbey (now Cathedral): here, in what seems to have been a representation of a spiritual journey, were shown, along with naturalistic marsh birds, a selection of Christian, heraldic and moralising themes, including the popular *memento mori* of the *Three Living and the Three Dead* and the *Wheel of the Five Senses*. 69

Yet the world of the Church met its secular counterpart in the idea of the Christian knight, the knight as soldier of Christ, internalised as the individual's war against sin. The crusading element in funerary art is vividly encapsulated in the figure of Sir Otto de Grandisson painted below the tomb of Eleanor of Castile, and in the effigies in the London Temple church of knights who sought burial there as if at Jerusalem. It was at the Temple, too, that the aspirants to knighthood in the great ceremony of 1306, at which the future Edward II was knighted, prepared themselves beforehand. The theme of the Christian knight encompassed such ancient and biblical heroes as Alexander and Judas Maccabeus, which were painted for Henry III and Edward I. The Arthurian cycle offered much nourishment and justification of warlike activities, providing the ideal context of Christian knighthood. Edward III may have had the symbolism of the Temple in mind when he commissioned the circular jousting house for 'round tables' at Windsor, thus bringing together several strands of thought. Court cultures were steeped in Arthurian stories. Edward I encouraged and took part in tournaments and Arthurian 'round tables', Edward II and Isabella both owned romances, Isabella's collection including *Tristan*.

As we shall see in more detail later, Edward I undoubtedly used the Arthurian cycle for political reasons; here we may note that the 'round table' held at Nefyn in 1284 to celebrate his conquest of Wales, where people played the roles of Arthurian characters while making a strong political point, is a vivid illustration of the way in which medieval consciousness functioned simultaneously at different levels. Yet that Edward was interested in chivalric romance in general rather than Arthur in particular is suggested by the so-called Feast of the Swans held for the knighting of 1306. The centrepiece of the occasion was a pair of roast swans, upon which the company swore to fight the Scots and go on crusade. This ceremony was based on the legend of the Swan Knight, which had been known in England at least since the twelfth century and was not Arthurian in origin. Indeed, the Arthurian stories cannot be identified too exclusively with court cultures, for not only were non-Arthurian romances favoured by the nobility, but Arthurian stories were enjoyed by other classes. Queen Isabella also possessed stories of the *Trojan War* and *Parsifal*, and Sir John Pulteney owned a wall hanging that depicted the story of Tristan.

The choice of theme, or the reasons for it, reflected literature, in that deeds of knightly combat from which a moral could be drawn were both acceptable to the Church and satisfied the lay taste for stories of violence and derring-do. There were other ways in which the laity could turn the demands of the Church to its advantage. Edward I regularly visited the great East Anglian shrines before going to war, partly at least to stifle clerical opposition to his tax demands; and Edward III associated the Church in his victory at Sluys by presenting ships modelled in silver to Walsingham, Old St Paul's and Canterbury, and also to Gloucester, where his gift later adorned his father's tomb. Tournaments and jousts were often linked to specific Church ceremonies, as for example those held for the churching of Queen Philippa in 1332, 1341 and 1348. All this endorsed the theme of the Christian knight while allowing the knightly classes their fun. In discharging their obligations to charity and alms, and in their endowments for their own souls, the same people could impose some of their values back on the Church in the form of tomb and other decoration, some overt, some less obvious.

The series of effigies shown with crossed legs and drawing their swords has been plausibly interpreted as representing knights for Christ; but knightly weapons had very specific imagery in the heraldic arms of Christ, the Shield of the Soul and the Shield of Faith. These were drawn by Matthew Paris in the *Chronica Maiora*, but the concept was being developed in the 1230s, and he may have found the Shield of Faith in the work of Robert Grosseteste. Roundels at the three corners of the shield are linked to each other and to a central roundel: in the Shield of Faith, an emblem of the Trinity, this is marked 'deus', surrounded by 'pater', 'filius' and 'spiritus'. In 1246 Pope Innocent IV instigated, as part of the devotion to the Passion, the cult of the *arma Christi*, the instruments of the Passion as heraldic devices, which were seen as Christ's mystical weapons against Satan.

The most obvious manifestations of chivalry are nevertheless on tombs. The soldier-weepers on the tomb of Thomas Cantilupe have been interpreted as the Knights Hospitaller as Virtues, their shields combating vice. Yet other details reveal chivalric intrusions into Church art, in particular parapet figures, which were dependent on their equivalent in castles; and the Decorated leitmotif of miniature battlements complete with arrowloops. Perhaps as a compliment to the ruler, the Virtues depicted in the window splays of the Painted Chamber in the Palace of Westminster in the 1260s were accompanied by the arms of England, the Empire and SS Edmund and Edward, the arms of England being borne by *Debonerete* (Tranquillity). Late thirteenth-century troubadour songs suggest that the histories and romances in which this culture was steeped came in their turn to reflect the very culture they had helped to create. In ways both obvious and subtle, heraldry and chivalry played their part in the formulation of the Decorated style.

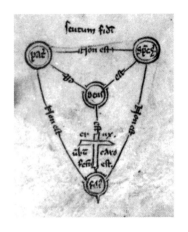

70   The *Shield of Faith*, drawn by Matthew Paris (*Chronica Maiora*, Corpus Christi College, Cambridge, MS 16, fol. 45v; *c*.1240–53). The central roundel, inscribed 'deus', is linked to the three angles, with 'pater', 'filius' and 'spiritus'.

71   *Right Debonerete* and *Largesse*, from the cycle of Virtues, 1260s, formerly in the Painted Chamber (destroyed 1834), in the Palace of Westminster. Note the heraldry and the architectural settings including miniature battlements (drawn by C.A. Stothard).

CHAPTER FOUR

The Patrons

Although by this period small objects, possibly including memorial brasses, were being made for sale on the open market, most artists worked to commission, with a particular recipient in mind. All building work was done exclusively to order. Thus, the patrons of these works assume great significance, for as there was no state subsidy to the arts it was the money of private patrons that ensured artistic production. If the money ran out the work stopped. This occurred on countless building sites, but even small works could be affected, as can be seen in illuminated manuscripts that were begun for one patron and completed for another. The very presence or absence of a patron could cause a sudden migration of artists and their designs, as in the 1270s and 1280s, when royal building interests shifted from Westminster to north Wales. The production of some luxury manuscripts around 1300 has been located in York, on the grounds that the Exchequer and its officials were present in the city at the time. Patrons were significant also at a less material level, for the essentially ritualistic Decorated style was devised in response to the need for pious expression and for social and political display. Degrees of display corresponded closely to status. We have already witnessed the behaviour of William de Clinton and Thomas Bradeston, both of whom adopted the attitudes of the social classes to which they were promoted. The king, at the top of the secular hierarchy, and wishing to dominate that of the Church, needed forms of display that uniquely reflected his unique position. Royal patronage is therefore set apart; it is also better documented, and before looking at the patrons we need to consider some aspects of the available evidence so as to be aware of the limitations.

The patronage of art is very poorly documented in the conventional sense before the middle of the fourteenth century. Household inventories and wills are rare before then, and records of purchases and financial accounting survive only for the king's works and in the accounts (fabric rolls) of some major buildings, notably the cathedrals of Exeter, Ely and York. The reason that there is any documentary evidence at all lies in the proliferation in the thirteenth century of written house-

72   York Minster, tomb of Archbishop Walter de Grey, d. 1255. The gabled, pinnacled canopy deliberately recalls metal reliquaries.

hold accounting. The royal household accounts survive because they were also those of government, but the accounts of great baronial households, although apparently modelled on those of the king, survive patchily and by accident, as a family could last only a few generations. There are also some records of religious foundations, chronicles of specific building events, and records of licences to crenellate, which show an approximate date for work on a fortified house. Heraldry, ubiquitous though it became, is not an indicator of patronage so much as ownership, which may not be the same thing, or of an event, such as the arms in the Alphonso Psalter (London, BL, Add. MS 24686), indicating the marriage (which never took place) between Edward I's son, Alphonso, and Margaret of Holland.

The documentation of patronage is not only patchy, but biased. The scholarly emphasis on royal patronage produced by the survival of such detailed royal records is inevitable in the circumstances, but it also impedes wider understanding. Royal patronage was, as we shall see, both prominent and showy, but it was also inconstant, as many monasteries, such as Netley and Vale Royal, discovered from experience. It also reflected to some extent the state of the royal finances. Immense landed wealth did not always translate into cash. Henry III was obliged to pawn the metal figures prepared for the Confessor's shrine; Edward I abandoned all non-essential building work in 1297 and died heavily in debt, leaving his heir seriously short of money until about 1320. It is clear that from the point of view of providing opportunities for artists and encouraging their work the Church was a rather more reliable institution than the monarchy. Other classes of patron have fared less well in the records in that the artistic activities of the nobility, gentry, merchants and lesser clergy have left fewer, less accessible traces, many of their buildings and tombs having been destroyed. Those who have suffered most, however, are women. As women did not normally lead the sort of independent political existence that was recorded, signs of their activities, autonomy and self-image had until recently disappeared from modern perceptions, and it is only lately that scholars have begun to bring women into the centre of consciousness, where it is becoming increasingly clear that they belong.

The surviving documentary evidence not only excludes nearly everyone except high-ranking men; it excludes almost everything about the process of patronage except the fact of a commission or ownership. We cannot find out from the written sources what most patrons wanted from works of art, nor how far their personal taste was reflected in what they had made. As so much had to be appropriate either to status or to an occasion, there was little room for individual taste to be expressed and no record of any general concept of it. In any case, a financial contribution may enable a work to be made and a stylistic development to take place, but it may have been given without conditions and as a small part of a much larger funding operation, and therefore will not necessarily reflect the taste of the particular donor. Many patrons of the day, if they resembled their successors in later centuries, will have needed the guidance of artists and advisers. The role of the latter will be examined later on, but here it is enough to point out that most conclusions to be drawn about the taste of patrons in this period can only be inferences, for what is generally lacking above all is any sense of individual say in the choice of work or ornament. Even the few who left a more personal record, such as Elizabeth de Burgh, Richard de Bury, John Grandisson and Henry of Grosmont, leave no real clues to their personal aesthetic preferences. Only the kings can be seen to exercise choice, particularly Henry III, on the occasion that he acknowledged the advice of his clerk of the works in selecting cast bronze instead of marble for the leopards that were to adorn the throne in Westminster Hall. The reason he gave was that bronze was 'more magnificent', which suggests that appropriateness was his main preoccupation.

If the documents are unhelpful, the buildings and their decoration provide more insights, at least into the kinds of building and smaller works that particular social groups expected to have made. The undoubted hierarchy of art, reflecting that of society, should not, however, be confused with artistic originality or innovation. As we shall see, these were quite distinct.

Royal Patrons

Among patrons of art the king was a special figure, and not only because we know more about him. Although he, like all noblemen, used art in service of the display of his grandeur, piety and largesse, and to meet the obligations imposed by his rank, he was more than simply a higher form of nobleman. Monarchy brought additional obligations, which set the king apart not only from the rest of society but even from immediate members of his family, including his wife. The patronage of the queens of England will be mentioned here, but it properly belongs with that of the nobility.

The use of architecture and the visual arts to expound ideas about the sanctity and power of monarchy was not a new phenomenon in the thirteenth century. The Byzantine Emperors had continued the traditions of imperial Rome that had been adopted without interruption by the successors to Constantine, and early medieval rulers in western Europe with sufficient prestige had done the same. From the twelfth century an image of royalty had been promoted in the kingdom of Sicily, under the influence of both the Byzantine and the Arab worlds. Nevertheless, it is in the thirteenth century that the visual expression of monarchy can be seen developing quite systematically in such western rulers as Emperor Frederick II (d. 1250) and Louis IX, who promoted the idea of monarchy with all the splendour that they could achieve, perhaps partly in response to the growing strength and identity of the papacy and papal court, which reached its zenith under Innocent IV (*reg*

1243–54). While in their fortified buildings they continued to address the problems of this world, and in their burial churches those of the next, rulers were now also building and decorating solely for the purpose of self-aggrandisement, beginning the process that became fully established by the middle of the fourteenth century, of erecting houses and palaces of ever increasing magnificence, in which the notion of the Christian prince, expressed in lavish private chapels, was combined with that of the secular ruler in the proliferation of state rooms. At the beginning of the period discussed here this can be seen in Emperor Frederick II's buildings in Italy, in Louis IX's Palais in Paris and in the houses and palaces of Henry III. Henry's patronage of art and architecture was not only extensive; it was clearly a personal passion. It also shows the development of an underlying purpose, as various themes on the idea of monarchy were presented with increasing focus. It was in the following reign, that of his son Edward I, that a particular splendour engulfed what might be termed the show buildings of royalty. It was not so much that Edward built a lot – he did not – but that his buildings possess a kind of concentrated magnificence that was to remain characteristic throughout the period, the culmination being the decoration of St Stephen's chapel and Edward III's buildings at Windsor Castle, where military considerations were subsumed in royal display.

The artistic patronage of Henry III is by far the best documented, owing to his habit of issuing his orders through chancery writs, which were formally copied and preserved. The activity of his successors is less discernible simply because they used a different, more personal method that was less closely linked to the official functions of the Exchequer and left fewer traces. Nevertheless, even allowing for this bias, Henry was an outstanding patron, perhaps equal in knowledge and discernment to Charles I and George IV, who, whatever their political shortcomings, were the greatest royal art patrons in English history. Although most of his buildings have disappeared, Henry's extant writs offer glimpses of his deep involvement and obsessive attention to detail. The latter was not confined to art; it extended to careful instructions for the disposal of the bones of the elephant given to him by Louis IX, after it died at the Tower of London. Henry himself had informed opinions on architecture, often specifying such details as the shape of a window or the number of its lights, and he was, naturally, concerned with building materials. Despite, or perhaps owing to, his great profligacy, he sometimes ordered cheaper substitutes: wood to be painted to resemble marble for columns in the hall at Guildford, a wooden vault to simulate stone 'after the manner of the new [transept vault] at Lichfield' for St Edward's chapel at Windsor. The characteristic type of inner window or doorway arch, with a segmental curve rising from vertical springers, which recurred often in his buildings and was imitated at Hereford Cathedral, may reflect his own taste.

There are hints that Edward II may have shared his grandfather's

73 Westminster Abbey, gilt-bronze effigy of Eleanor of Castile, made 1291–3 by William Torel. The style of quiet, vertical drapery folds with a break over the instep seems to have been developed by this artist.

interest in architectural detail. His contemporaries greatly despised his taste for the 'base and mechanical' arts of thatching and carpentry, but the occurrence in the building records of the phrase 'per proprium divisamentum Regis' shows that on occasion he, too, would specify a design. This sort of evidence does not survive for Edward I or Edward III, but the castles in Wales are presumed by all modern commentators to have been planned by Edward I in conjunction with James of St George, and given the importance and symbolism of the project as well as its cost, it is inconceivable that the king would have restricted himself only to approving the designs. Unlike Henry III, however, Edward probably had little interest in the daily business of church building: for Vale Royal Abbey he seems merely to have supplied the money, until he abruptly stopped the payments, possibly owing to fraud. Whether he chose the design of Henry III's tomb is a moot point, although the gilt bronze effigies of Henry and Eleanor of Castile must have been his choice, and he must also have decreed the relative lavishness of the various Eleanor Crosses. The paintings of fifty-four shields and 'four knights seeking a tournament' made in the hall at Langley (Berks) in 1292 conform to what is known of Edward's tastes in general, and the new iconographic themes in the redecorated Painted Chamber at Westminster were certainly put in with his approval even if he did not devise the programme himself. Much of our knowledge of Edward III's interest in what things looked like is derived from his orders for furnishings and clothes for great ceremonial occasions. These demonstrate the close resemblance of interior decorations to those on costume and textiles, and are further evidence of the increasing splendour of court ceremonial. The choir of Gloucester, however, insofar as it reflects St Stephen's chapel, might also reflect Edward's taste in architecture.

To a large extent royal works, whether commissioned or bought ready made, conformed to the general spiritual and cultural requirements of the day. Acts of piety – pilgrimage, endowments and alms-giving – were a necessary part of the rituals of kingship. All three Edwards made a point of honouring their fathers. Edward I, who was personally close to Henry III, and was said to have grieved for him more deeply than at the deaths of his own infant children, interred his father in a magnificent new tomb. Edward II, who was less estranged from Edward I than is sometimes said, had the lesser hall in the Palace of Westminster decorated with scenes from his father's life, which, if they were based on those recorded in the bishop's palace at Lichfield, depicted Edward I as a chivalric hero. He also continued the work at St Stephen's chapel and Caernarfon Castle in the manner laid down in the 1290s. Edward III finished St Stephen's, honoured Edward II's vow to found a house for Dominican nuns at Dartford, and, most significantly, arranged the grandiose funeral procession of the murdered king, perhaps also contributing to the costs of the tomb at Gloucester.

Patronage associated with such acts of piety as visiting shrines con-

74 St Stephen's chapel, Palace
of Westminster, founded 1292,
(destroyed 1834), dado of the
upper chapel. This part,
designed in the ?1290s, was built
in the ?1320s. Its architectural
decoration included, along with
the ogee-headed stalls, ogival
quadrilobes and miniature
battlements, proto-Perpendicular
rectilinear panelling that
appeared in more monumental
form in the upper walls. The
entire chapel was embellished
with wall paintings (see p. 57),
figure sculpture, gilding and
stencilling.

formed to expectations. Despite royal support for the mendicant orders,
some aspects of the kings' religion even seem to be a little old-fashioned.
Edward I's Vale Royal and Edward III's St Mary Graces were both
founded after vows made during a perilous sea crossing, and both the
choice of the Cistercian Order and the motive for the foundation recall
the habits of an earlier period, as does Edward III's persistent devotion to
the Virgin in the face of the newly emerging rival cults. The shrine of St
Thomas Becket at Canterbury enjoyed sustained placatory interest in
the form of royal gifts as well as pilgrimage. Edward I presented images
of St George, and St Edward and the Pilgrim, together with adornments
to the reliquary. Edward II commissioned a painting of the martyrdom
for a chapel in Chester castle; and Edward III gave a gold statue of St
Thomas.

Against this background of conventional piety, however, the kings
pursued a programme in their buildings and decoration that was
peculiarly theirs, centred on the theme of monarchy. This emerged
under Henry III and was consolidated, with some changes of emphasis,
under his successors. Where Henry stressed the sanctity of kingship
through his patron saint, his descendants explored the notion of the
monarch as Christian knight and chivalric prince, with less emphasis on
Edward the Confessor. Nevertheless, they developed other aspects that
had already been adumbrated under Henry, and despite the differences
in character and rule of the four men concerned the various strands can
be traced throughout the period, even though it lasted for more than a
hundred years.

The beginnings of deliberate thematic content emerged after the somewhat incoherent middle years of Henry's reign. It is likely that the actual decoration of his buildings was always as important to him as their architectural style, and his orders for this were always quite specific, a typical instruction being that for the chapel built in the 1250s at his manor of Havering in Essex, which required an image of the *Virgin and Child*, a painting of the *Annunciation*, wall paintings of the *Evangelists* and Henry's coat of arms in the stained glass. His earlier decorative programmes, from the 1230s, seem to have comprised such generally moralising, popular themes as biblical cycles, the *Evangelists*, the *Virgin and Child* and the *Tree of Jesse*, the *Mappa Mundi*, the *Wheel of Fortune*, *Dives and Lazarus* and the *Twelve Months*. These were depicted in his various residences, including Westminster, Clarendon, Guildford and Winchester. Devotion to the Crucifixion becomes evident, and the presence of the Holy Blood at Westminster possibly produced a specific reference in the iconography of the north transept sculpture. After Henry took the cross in 1250 he ordered themes befitting a Christian knight: the story of Antioch, based on events in the Third Crusade (1189–92), was painted at Clarendon as well as Westminster, and the duel of Richard I and Salah al'Din was portrayed in the floor tiles at Clarendon.

The romance of Alexander also appealed to Henry; this was an extension of the idea that gradually came to underlie many of his pictorial schemes: the concept of the wise and saintly ruler, and an expression of his belief in the sanctity of kingship, to which his cult of Edward the Confessor gave support. Henry hoped that the anointing of the ruler at the Coronation elevated him above the priesthood, and when this idea was refuted by Bishop Grosseteste Henry pursued it in the imagery of his houses and churches with determined thoroughness, but mainly centred on the abbey and palace complex at Westminster. Edward the Confessor had been canonised for political reasons in 1161, but the monks of Westminster had done little to promote his cult; it was only in the continuing battle for supremacy between Church and King that his sainted ancestor also became a useful political ally for Henry. The Confessor provided, too, a counterweight to the moral authority of St Thomas Becket at Canterbury. In the architecture and decoration of his new church, with its emphasis on the coronation rite and the cult of a sainted king, Henry built his reply to Grosseteste, underscoring his identification with his predecessor by choosing to be buried not only in the same church but in the Confessor's vacant grave.

The imagery surrounding the setting of St Edward's shrine was positioned with care. Those entering the abbey church through the royal entrance in the north transept were greeted by the scene of the Ring and the Pilgrim on the south transept wall, and the story was repeated in the tiles of the chapter house floor. It was also depicted over and over again in Henry's residences: the Painted Chamber, the Tower, Guildford,

75   Windsor Castle, Berks., painted head of a king in the former St Edward's cloister, *c.*1250 (after restoration). Figures of kings represented the absent monarch.

Winchester, Nottingham and Clavering. A copy of *La Estoire de Seint Aedward le Rei* (Cambridge, University Lib., MS. Ee. 3. 59), dedicated to Queen Eleanor, was illustrated, perhaps at Westminster, by sixty-four tinted drawings of the life and miracles of the saint; scenes (now destroyed) of his life were ordered to be painted in 1252 in the chapel that temporarily contained his shrine. Whether any such scenes appeared in the glazing of the church (as did those of Becket at Canterbury) is not known; there are surviving shields of arms and hints that there may have been standing figures of kings. These could have been Old Testament kings or, like those in *La Estoire*, some Anglo-Saxon forerunners of the Confessor. There is a little more evidence that kings were significant in Henry's imagery: the remnant of a royal genealogy may survive in the head of a king painted in St Edward's cloister at Windsor; and the image 75 could, like the shield of arms that was frequently ordered for windows, represent the monarch in absence, as in the figures of a king and queen painted at Guildford and in Dublin Castle, and the single figures depicted in the glass at his manor of Geddington (Northants) and on the throne at Windsor.

Other decoration at Westminster indicates Henry's wider preoccupations. For his throne in the abbey, Henry ordered a different theme: as well as sanctity, his conception of monarchy included wisdom and justice, the most common medieval symbol of which was Solomon, with whom Henry equated the Confessor. With the iconography of the Confessor, that of Solomon was carried over into Henry's palaces. The beds of estate at Winchester and in the Painted Chamber were flanked by painted figures of the Guardians of Solomon's bed (from the Song of Songs, 3:vii–x), on the theme of the bed as the *lit de justice*, of which the king was the ultimate source. The possible Solomonic allusion in the green colour of the bed hangings at Westminster has already been mentioned. The coronation of St Edward was painted above the bed and linked to Solomon by the presence of the Guardians. There was already (and still is) a symbolic link between Solomon and the English monarchs, for since the tenth century the Coronation Order has included the antiphon 'Unxerunt Solomonis', in reference to the anointing of Solomon by Zadok the priest. The imagery of the throne ordered for Westminster in 1245 included lions and steps, both integral to the iconography of Solomon, the lions, themselves symbols of magnanimity and justice, also representing the Old and New Testaments, the steps the Virtues. Further Solomonic allusions may lie in the shields of arms in the aisles of the abbey church: 'The tower of David, builded for an armoury, whereon there hang a thousand bucklers, all the shields of mighty men' (Song of Songs, 4:iv). It has long been postulated that the middle-storey galleries were built deliberately deep to accommodate spectators to the public moments of the coronation ceremony, and the slender crossing piers and spacious transept may also have been devised with coronations and other ceremonial in mind.

WESTMINSTER ABBEY. PLAN OF THE PRESBYTERY PAVEMENT — PAVEMENT OF PURBECK MARBLE INLAID WITH PATTERNS OF COLOURED MARBLE AND VITREOUS MOSAICS AND WITH REMAINS AND INDENTS OF BRASS INSCRIPTIONS.

Scale of — Feet ~ South side ~ Royal Commission on Historical Monuments (England). 1924

76 Westminster Abbey, the sanctuary floor (drawing). The inscription in brass letters seems to date it to 1268. The makers and many of the materials, which included porphyry, serpentine and glass tesserae, were brought from Rome. The meaning and symbolism of the pattern are much debated, but may be related to coronation rituals.

The paved floors of the shrine chapel behind the high altar and the
76 sanctuary are, even in their present worn condition, a striking contrast to the Anglo-French architecture and sculptural decoration that surrounds them. The sanctuary pavement is composed of a 'mosaic' pattern in the style of the Roman Cosmati workers, some of whom were brought from Rome by Abbot Richard de Ware, together with some of the materials, porphyry, serpentine and glass tesserae. The pattern is of linked circles that in an Italian context could have a liturgical function indicating where the clergy should stand, but here the roundels have been associated with the prostration ceremonies of the coronation. The damaged inscription implies that the central roundel represents the world, linking the pavement with the iconography of the great retable,
VIII almost certainly that of the high altar, on which St Peter is depicted holding a globe. The scenes in *La Estoire de Seint Aedward le Rei* include several devoted to the Confessor's building of the church and its consecration by St Peter in person. Henry III's father, King John, had for political reasons made England a papal fief, and the presence of St Peter in the abbey now also represented papal protection. The sanctuary was possibly the site of the Confessor's grave, although its exact location

'near the high altar' is unknown. The sanctuary brought together all the strands of thought that composed the imagery of the abbey church, Henry's identification with St Edward, the link with Solomon and St Peter and through them with the coronation.

Henry's successors undoubtedly changed the emphasis of the notion of kingship, but they introduced nothing that had not been inherent in Henry's imagery. Nor did they neglect the Confessor and abandon Westminster. Royal works at the abbey church were completed under Edward I, for the nave was no concern of theirs and they did not need to do any more building there; and although fire rendered parts of the palace uninhabitable in 1298, Edward II instituted a huge programme of repair and rebuilding for his coronation ten years later, and he frequently resided at Westminster for the great feasts of the Church. It was not that Westminster Abbey and the Confessor were neglected but that Henry's successors promoted their ideas of kingship in different buildings. The Palace of Westminster was used for this purpose by Edward I as well as his son, and St Stephen's chapel gained new significance under Edward III. Edward I in addition expressed his ideas through his great castles in Wales and the funerary works, and his grandson opposed Westminster with his great new buildings at Windsor. It is true that their attitude to St Edward appears dutiful rather than enthusiastic, but that is only in comparison to the rather overwrought devotion of Henry III. Edward I extended the function of the Confessor's chapel by converting it into a family mausoleum. Edward II owned a *Life* of St Edward, and at his coronation he presented to the shrine gold images of the Confessor and the Pilgrim.

Henry III's cult of the coronation flourished under his successors: Edward II's was particularly significant in that, contrary to Canon law, he was anointed with the chrism of holy oil that effectively consecrated the ruler, and thus achieved what had eluded his grandfather. The splendour of the occasion, with the staging lofty enough for the armed men to ride underneath it without bending, was matched by continuing emphasis on the symbolism and imagery of coronation and kingship. The theme of Solomon and other themes of kingship were now being disseminated beyond the abbey and palace. The world of Henry III had been essentially private, the visual expression of his ideas reaching only the restricted circles of his court. Edward I engaged the attention of the wider world, his castles and wayside crosses, whatever their other functions, being integral to royal display. His successors, by giving far greater access to their halls and palaces, allowed the world in. Under Edward II the Painted Chamber and the lesser hall at Westminster were routinely used for almsgiving and public feasts, a policy continued by Edward III, who also ensured in other ways that he and his entourage were highly visible. His tours of the shrines of England in 1333, 1343, 1355 and 1359 were well publicised, and such family events as marriages, baptisms and churchings were turned into general celebrations.

77 Westminster Abbey, effigy
of William de Valence, d. 1296.
The wooden core is plated in
enamel powdered with heraldic
decorations.

Thus the meaning of monarchy was before people's eyes not only in the person of the king but in his buildings and their imagery. Edward I had apparently been equated with Solomon in the opening pages of the Windmill Psalter, a manuscript illuminated in the late thirteenth century, probably in his honour. Images of kings remained persistent. Kings and their associated heraldry in the stained glass of York Minster and the late thirteenth-century *Genealogy of the Kings of Britain* (divided between the British Library and the Bodleian Library), have been linked to Edward I's Scottish wars and the presence of the Exchequer at York between 1298 and 1305. Kingly imagery, however, became particularly prominent from the time of Edward II: a copper-gilt figure of a king stood beneath an arch over the throne in the temporary enthronement hall built for the coronation in the Palace of Westminster, and another was placed in the upper part of the King's Gate at Caernarfon Castle in 1320; in 1317–18 a wool hanging with images of the king and his earls was brought to Westminster for great festivals. An image of a Solomonic king, with his feet resting on a lion, was added probably in the reign of Edward III to the back of St Edward's chair (now the Coronation chair), which had been made to the orders of Edward I to house the Stone of Destiny that he brought from Scotland in 1296; and it was Edward III who brought the cult of the king to a new intensity with the painting of the royal family on the altar wall of St Stephen's chapel.

Under the first three Edwards the image of the sainted king, the superior of the Church, yielded to that of the Christian knight, its servant and champion, but also the reflection of an increasingly secular court culture. By the time of Edward III the ideal of a crusade to the Holy Land was fading in favour of Arthurian jousts and crusades and wars nearer home. The Christian knight had featured in the works of Henry III after he took the cross in 1250, but for him it was an idea among many, whereas for his son it became the main focus. Almost all Edward I's surviving imagery is touched by chivalry and some works are imbued with it. The chivalric imagery in Westminster Abbey was enhanced by the effigies of William de Valence and Edmund Crouchback, which are accompanied on the tomb proper by conspicuous shields of arms and heraldic detailing; and although the effigy of Henry III is in ceremonial robes, its base, and that of Queen Eleanor, are powdered with heraldic motifs. On Eleanor's tomb the imagery is further extended by the painting of Sir Otto de Grandisson as a crusader at the Holy Places, praying for her soul.

In the Painted Chamber the battle scenes from the Book of Kings and the Maccabees emphasised the biblical hero and deliverer; the exploits of Judas Maccabeus, who was regarded as an honorary Christian knight, were intended to reflect those of Edward himself. Eleanor of Castile was the dedicatee of Girart d'Amiens' *Escanor*, a story from the French Arthurian cycle, here used to flatter the king through his wife. Yet

Edward's use of Arthur shows that he was interested in him less as the romantic legend than the historical figure, whose past deeds could be used to illuminate the present and justify certain acts. This use of past events to underline the message of the present sharply differentiates Edward's visual propaganda from that of his father, his son or even his grandson.

This is already hinted in the Maccabees paintings, for Judas Maccabeus was associated with Arthur as one of the Nine Worthies, and Arthur, like Judas, was equated with Edward himself by contemporary writers. Among Edward's justifications of his claim to Scotland was that Arthur had at one time been its overlord. During the Welsh wars Edward and Eleanor attended the great ceremony in Glastonbury Abbey at Easter 1278, when the bones of Arthur and Guinevere were solemnly reburied before the high altar, in order to suppress the Welsh tradition that Arthur was not dead, but would rise from the cave in which he slept and lead them to victory. Just as Edward later removed the stone of Scone on which the Scottish kings had been crowned, so in 1284 after the conquest of Wales did he remove the Crown of Arthur, which had been presented to him along with Llewelyn the Great's Croes Neyd. Edward, therefore, drew both on Arthur the legendary chivalric hero and Arthur the historical figure. To the medieval mind the two aspects of Arthur were perfectly compatible, and there is no reason to suppose that Edward did not believe in Arthur's existence, for which the chronicles provided evidence, just as the Bible gave evidence of Solomon and Judas Maccabeus.

The idea of Arthur may have lingered more lastingly in Edward's tomb in Westminster Abbey. This, a plain Purbeck marble sarcophagus, with no effigy or adornment other than a canopy (destroyed), has always puzzled later commentators; but two other tombs may help to explain it. The tomb of the ascetic Louis IX was originally a plain, uninscribed slab with no effigy, laid over his remains in the later 1270s, and knowledge of this tomb may have influenced the choice of a plain sarcophagus, without effigies and adorned only with small lions at the corners, to which the bones of Arthur and Guinevere were translated in 1278. Although a silver-gilt effigy was added to Louis' tomb about ten years later, Edward may have sought a double identification of himself, with Arthur (as Henry III had identified himself with the Confessor), but also with Louis, whom Edward enormously admired and whose original tomb design was so close to that chosen for Arthur.

Arthur was not the only past figure to be used by Edward to justify present behaviour. Caernarfon castle differs from all Edward's castles in [78] Wales in having polygonal towers, bands of coloured masonry threaded in its walls, and a huge imperial tribune arch over the main gateway. The castle was built at the site associated in Welsh legend with Magnus Maximus, the supposed father of Constantine; and the polygonal towers

and banded masonry may deliberately evoke the walls of Constantinople, with the tribune as an additional imperial image.

Edward II and Edward III seem not to have used historical references in this way. What seems to have interested them much more was the general splendour of Edward I's official works. Despite a reputation for meanness, Edward II well knew how to be magnificent, as this quality was noted by two Irish monks, Simon and Hugo, who saw the Painted Chamber in the 1320s. His financial difficulties meant that after refurbishing the palace, most of his building effort went to strengthening defences, with work at St Stephen's resumed only in 1320. Yet Edward's official gifts were clearly appropriate to their occasions. After the accession of Pope John XXII in 1316 Edward and Isabella sent him two *opus anglicanum* copes, one embroidered with large pearls; Edward gave copes, 'Lucca' cloths and goldsmiths' work for ceremonial events such as baptisms, churchings and funerals. In the main, however, monarchy continued to be expressed through heraldry and chivalry free from ulterior connotations. There was a deliberately chivalric element in the Coronation Order, in which the sword, delivered after the anointing as part of the regalia, maintained a link between the regal ceremonial and the knightly vigils and girding. Heraldry and heraldic motifs were consistently employed. Edward possessed a living heraldic motif in the form of a lion, which accompanied the king with its own keeper and attached to a collar and chain. In 1301 Edward's war tents were embroidered with the 'leopard' of the arms of England; and after the coronation the gables of the lesser hall were adorned with wooden leopards holding latten banners displaying his arms. A fireplace in the new White Chamber was painted with 'divers figures and arms', and Edward presented his sister Mary with a heraldic tapestry. It was in his reign, too, that the stone heraldic eagles were placed on the battlements of the tower that bears their name at Caernarfon castle. All of this was intensified by Edward III. The leopard imagery in particular was of the utmost importance to him: its appearance on the funeral trappings of Edward II may well have implied a reference to the living king as well as the dead one. Edward III introduced a leopard image into his coinage, and his epitaph refers to him as 'invictus pardus', the unconquered leopard. Edward III's love of shining splendour is exemplified not only at Windsor and in the interior decoration of St Stephen's chapel, but also in St Edward's chair in Westminster Abbey. Edward I originally ordered the chair to be made in bronze, but after the financial crisis of 1297 it was built of wood and painted in red, green and gold, with gilt leopards on the arms. It was probably in Edward III's reign that the chair was redecorated, with punched gilding, bright metallic tin coated with translucent paint, and inlays of enamel and glass.

The enhanced luxury discernible from the reign of Edward I may have been partly due to the habits and expectations brought by Queen Eleanor from her native Castile; and the chivalric element in the court life of

78 Caernarfon Castle, Gwynedd, 1282–1323, seen from the west. Figures of eagles sit on the battlements of the Eagle Tower in the foreground. The striped masonry and polygonal towers have been interpreted as symbols of Roman imperialism.

Edward III may have been additionally influenced by the court culture of Hainault in which Queen Philippa was reared. The stylistic sources of the royal show buildings, however, are more generally derived from France: Westminster Abbey, based on Reims Cathedral, the French coronation church, and the Sainte-chapelle in Paris, shelter of the Crown of Thorns; the Eleanor Crosses based on the *montjoies*, the crosses erected to mark the passage of the funeral cortèges of Louis IX and, before him, Philip II Augustus (d. 1223). The bronze effigies of Eleanor of Castile and Henry III may themselves have been influenced by the recently-made silver-gilt effigies of Philip Augustus, Louis VIII and Louis IX. Edward I's monumental works were created at a time when English and French painting styles in particular were so close that scholars are divided over the directions of influence, especially in such manuscripts illuminated for Edward and Eleanor as the Douce Apocalypse (Oxford, Bodleian Lib., MS Douce 180) and the Alphonso Psalter. The theme of the Judas Maccabeus paintings, however, seems to have been drawn from French prototypes; and the paintings help to encourage the current idea, which may not reflect actuality, that royal patronage was the main conduit of French styles and motifs into England as a whole.

Works that reflected purely royal preoccupations would be inappropriate to other levels of society, and would not find general acceptance. The cult of relics and the manner of their presentation, however, was a different matter, and it was Westminster as a reliquary church, disregarding the wider implications, that exerted such a strong decorative and iconographic influence. The illuminated interior and much of its ornamental expression, together with the shrine, was absorbed into the general current. The status of the king more or less obliged him to be in the forefront of stylistic fashion, and even in hard times he could find the money to employ leading craftsmen. It comes as no surprise to find Edward II sending to the Pope a basin and ewer decorated in the newly developed technique of *basse taille* (translucent) enamel. Many of the ornamental characteristics that became general in the Decorated style appeared early in the royal works, from repeated motifs to window tracery designs, heraldry and the dominating presence of angels. The sunk chamfer and wave mouldings, and the ogee curve, were developed by masons who worked for, among others, Edward I, just as the rectilinear designs that were to develop into the Perpendicular style were refined by masons who worked for Edward III. Yet not surprisingly perhaps, the kings seem to have employed artists with established reputations. The master masons and such carpenters as William Hurley were all senior figures before they entered royal service, and research into the Heyroun and Settere families of embroiderers indicates that although members of both families were prominent early in the fourteenth century, it is only in the late 1320s that Johanna Heyroun and Matilda la Settere are found working for the king. Edward I in particular was not an originator. As in other aspects of his life, in art he consolid-

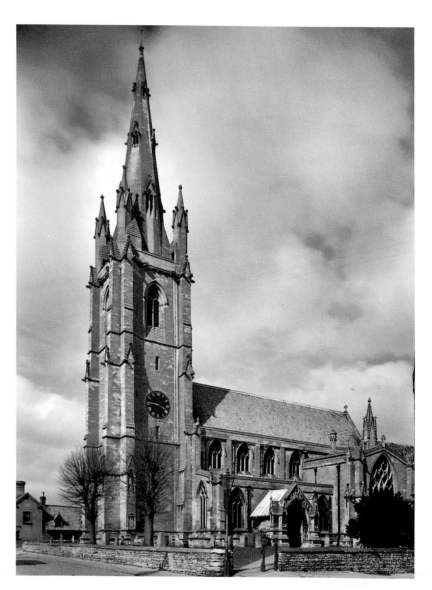

79 Heckington church, Lincs. It was built *c.*1330 by the priest, Richard de Potesgrave, a chancery clerk, and the chief lay benefactor, Isabella de Vesci.

ated and finished ideas that had been adumbrated elsewhere: the castles in Wales were anticipated at Tonbridge and Caerfili, the funerary works in French and Italian prototypes, and St Stephen's was in an established tradition of private chapels. What distinguished these works was their intentional magnificence. That they are set apart as works of royal display is shown by their relative isolation within the king's works as a whole. Where Edward's motive was purely functional, as in the *bastides*, the fortified towns of south-west France, which had a part to play in royal spheres of influence but not in the imagery of the king of England, this magnificence is lacking. The show buildings of Britain, on the other hand, transcend their models even as they depend on them. It was their deliberate splendour, together with the touch of genius added by Edward's craftsmen, that passed into future developments. Such castles as Caerlaverock and Kildrummy in Scotland and Goodrich on the Welsh marches were inspired not by Caerfili but by the geometry and fortification of Rhuddlan and Harlech; what Edward lacked in originality he made up for in consistency and ostentation, qualities that were enhanced by his son and grandson, and which found their way into the later Decorated style.

Church and laity

Non-royal patrons did not share the king's desire to realise the abstract idea of monarchy, and if royal iconography appeared in the imagery of their works, in the form of heraldry, or the scenes of Edward I at Lichfield, it was to flatter and to gain lustre by association. Like the king, however, other patrons had obligations of display and needed to seek salvation, and both the Church and lay people were concerned with realising the greatest abstract concept of all, that of God. This was expressed through patronage of the Church: in church buildings, therefore, the contributions of lay and ecclesiastical benefactors can be confused and difficult to distinguish. Lay and ecclesiastical patrons combined to build and decorate the new parish church at Heckington, and at Harlestone in Northamptonshire the rector, Richard le Het, built the chancel in 1320 while two local squires, Henry de Bray and John Dyve gave stone, timber and wages for a carpenter, to complete the church within five years. Non-monastic churches in particular were public buildings. Contributions came from many people, from the offerings of pilgrims and those granted indulgence to substantial gifts from the nobility. While the former influenced the style of the building not at all, we know that the latter did on occasions have a say in its embellishment; and amid a large group of interested persons, the taste of an individual cleric may be hard to discern. Only in collegiate foundations, chantry chapels and some parish churches can we confidently presume that the patron's taste prevailed; but even there care is necessary, for there may be more than one patron. The decoration of Heckington church has been shown to represent the tastes of both the lay patron, Isabella de Vesci, and the priest, Richard de Potesgrave, each of whom made specific contributions to its appearance and iconography. Heckington is a rare example of a building that can be made to yield that kind of information, but it may represent many for which the evidence no longer survives.

Church fittings present another aspect of the problem. In the absence of such identifying marks as heraldry, their iconography or style will not necessarily reveal the source of patronage. The retable and altar frontal associated with Thetford Priory are purely Dominican in iconography, hence the attribution; but they may well be the gift of a lay benefactor. The floor tiles from Hailes Abbey, which display the heraldry of Richard, Earl of Cornwall and his son, Edmund, can be interpreted either way, as a gift from the benefactors or as an acknowledgement of

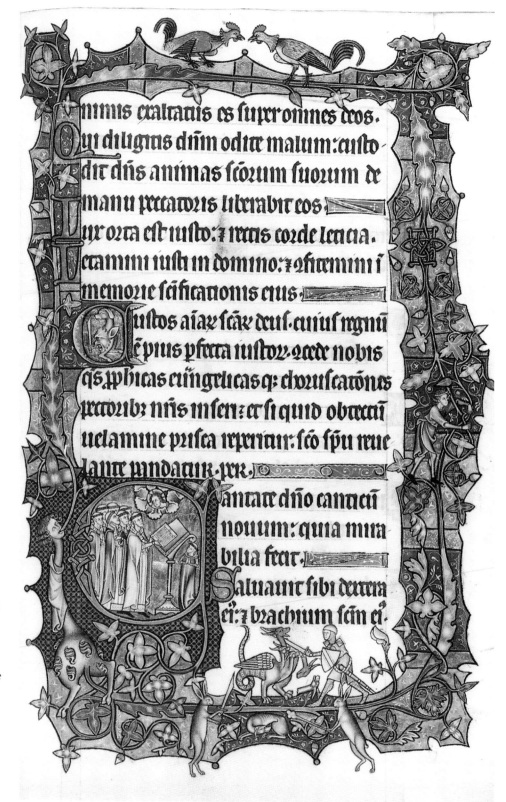

80 The Ormesby Psalter (Oxford, Bodleian Lib., MS Douce 366, fol. 128). It was given to Norwich Cathedral Priory in the 1320s. This illustration to Psalm 97 shows many characteristics of contemporary art: strong contrasting colours, diaper patterns, stylised foliage, naturalistic animals, grotesque figures, and chivalric heroes fighting demons.

their general patronage by grateful monks. The Ormesby Psalter (Oxford, Bodleian Lib., MS Douce 366) and other manuscripts associated with Norwich Cathedral priory could have been commissioned by clerics, but their decoration is indistinguishable from that made for secular owners. The building of cathedral and monastic churches was in practice supervised by committees of clergy, and the evidence offers no clear solutions. The lavish work at Tintern and Tewkesbury Abbey churches, for example, was actually paid for by the lay benefactors, but whether according to the tastes of the monks is impossible to say. This question is acute at Tintern, which as a Cistercian house perhaps ought not to have such elaborately traceried windows. Henry de Lacy, Earl of Lincoln (d. 1310) gave enough money to the building of Old St Paul's to earn himself burial in the choir; but despite his evident appreciation of good architecture, as witnessed by Denbigh Castle, it has never been suggested that he influenced the style of St Paul's. Did Bishop Baldock, buried in the Lady chapel in 1313, and the three canons buried in the choir between 1311 and 1325, who must also have given generously, have a say in the choice of pier form or tracery pattern? Although such questions cannot yet be answered satisfactorily, some aspects of clerical and lay patronage can be distinguished.

The clergy

Clerical patrons played a crucial role in the evolution of the Decorated style. Their sheer spending power, drawn both from their own wealth and from the stream of lay benefactions, as well as the number of projects on which they were engaged, enabled them to compete on equal terms with the king. The higher clergy in particular, bishops, senior cathedral clerics, leading abbots and priors, were among the leaders of fashion, doing much to promote development, and they often became significant innovators in types of works as well as their style.

The Bishops

As men of the world who commanded considerable wealth, the bishops could employ the leading craftsmen of the day for both personal commissions and public gifts to their cathedrals in the form of liturgical fittings, books and altar vessels. They indulged the forms of display considered appropriate to their office and status, and some episcopal buildings even seem to reflect the closeness of their owners to the king: the polygonal towers of Caernarfon Castle may well have influenced those in the episcopal palaces of Edward I's Treasurer Walter Langton at Lichfield and Eccleshall; and Robert Burnell's mock-castle at Acton Burnell could almost be regarded as a joint effort of the bishop and the king; the domical vaults in the towers have again been derived by scholars from Caernarfon.

If friendship and posts in the household kept the bishops in touch

81 Second seal of Richard de Bury, Bishop of Durham (H. 87 mm; Dean and Chapter of Durham; 1334–5). Possibly made in France, the extreme three-dimensionality of the canopy-work is unusual, and recalls such polygonal structures as the Eleanor Crosses (p. 41) and the niches flanking the doorway in the north choir aisle of Ely Cathedral.

82 Bishop Grandisson's ring (D. 20.5 mm; Exeter City Museum; 1324–40). It was buried with the bishop. The enamel depicting the *Virgin and Child* was made in Paris.

with the king, and their professional links in touch with each other, their strong international connections enabled the artistically sensitive among them to see the work of continental artists, particularly in Italy and France. Bishops' wills in general reveal a taste for small precious objects purchased from abroad that may have contributed to the *mélange* of French and Italian stylistic influences that appear especially in English painting in the late thirteenth century and the early fourteenth. Richard de Bury, who focused his patronage on books and small objects rather than buildings, recorded his passion for the former in his own entertaining book, *Philobiblon*; and the French design of his second seal (Durham Cathedral Library) probably reflects his periods as clerk and emissary at the papal court at Avignon. The silver crosier head bequeathed by Richard Gravesend was Parisian; Walter de Stapeldon owned metalwork from Tours; and Grandisson, whose gifts to Exeter cathedral included eighty-three textiles and twenty-two items in precious metal, left a mitre, a pastoral staff and a gilt cross, set with gems and images of the Virgin and St John, all bought in Paris. The scene of the *Virgin and Child* on the ring that was buried with him is a Parisian enamel made *c*.1320–40. Grandisson, however, is more interesting for the strongly Italianate element in his taste. He owned embroideries 'of Roman work', which he either bought in Italy or imported: an altar frontal of Florentine manufacture now in Baltimore was purchased by him and his arms were added to it. His interest in Italian subject matter is manifest in his ivories, in his orphreys for a chasuble (London, V&A Museum) and in a *Madonna of Mercy* depicted in the twelfth-century copy of St Augustine's *City of God* (Oxford, Bodleian Lib., MS Bodl. 691), to which Grandisson added extra decoration.

If the bishops were a channel for continental influences on the smaller arts, they perhaps also had a similar effect on architecture; it does not seem unreasonable to suppose that the French influences on the nave of York Minster owe something to John le Romeyn's sojourn in Paris. Yet it is in cathedrals that we have to be most wary of misreading the evidence. The bishop was present in his diocese, but the daily administration of the cathedral building was the jealously guarded responsibility of the dean and chapter. The bishop himself was expected to be personally generous and to help with fund-raising: bishops routinely issued general indulgences towards building costs, Walter de Merton being noted for his assiduity in this at Durham. They also gave large individual sums. The extent of John le Romeyn's financial help with the nave of York Minster is unknown, but a successor, William Melton, gave the west window, and paid for an extension to the chapel of St Sepulchre on the north side. Bishop Swinfield of Hereford (d. 1317) left money for building the new chapter house there, and at Ely John Hotham paid for the new choir bays that were built after the catastrophe of 1322, his workforce being carefully distinguished in the fabric accounts. The outstanding example of episcopal involvement in cathedral building is

Exeter, where the bishops took on responsibility for the fabric from the 83
inauguration of the new building *c.*1270; and from *c.*1300 Bishop Bitton
and his successors endowed the fabric with an assured income that
enabled the building work to go ahead to a prepared plan. The consistent style of Exeter cathedral owes much to the bishops' generosity, for
although construction took many years there was usually enough
money to prepare materials in advance, and work seldom halted completely. Yet even there, although Walter de Stapeldon was allowed to
involve himself to the extent of buying paints for the building when he
was in London, there is little evidence that the bishop was ever consulted on detailed building matters. It might be more accurate to see the
bishops, in their role as cathedral patrons, not as influencing taste so
much as enabling the work to be done.

Where bishops could exert stylistic influence in their cathedrals was
in their tombs, which set fashions in tomb design generally. Such a
conclusion may be biased in favour of bishops owing to the greater
survival rate of their tombs over those of the equivalent nobility.
Bishops had the right of burial in their cathedrals, and their tombs were
protected from the later destruction wrought on those of the laity in
monastic churches. Lost tombs of the laity include that of Richard de
Clare, Earl of Gloucester (d. 1262), at Tewkesbury, which was said to be
set with gems, silver and gold, and clearly rivalled in magnificence
anything the contemporary bishops could offer. Nevertheless, the
bishops were pursuing funerary magnificence well before the
mid-thirteenth century. In the period covered by this book more than
one hundred men enjoyed episcopal office, and they treated questions of
burial and the afterlife very seriously. It is not an exaggeration to say that
under their patronage the materials and design of English tombs were
transformed, the marbles, gesso, wood, inlays and paint all finding a
counterpart in monumental building, just as the details of the latter were
reproduced in miniature on tombs. There is evidence that Grosseteste
and Jocelin and Bitton I of Bath and Wells had cast bronze effigies, thirty
to forty years before those at Westminster. Walter de Merton's effigy
was of Limoges enamel over a wooden core, like the later surviving
effigy of William de Valence in Westminster Abbey. Archbishop 77
Pecham's effigy was of painted wood, probably with metal attachments.
The first known weepers in England are the knights on Cantilupe's tomb
at Hereford, which also has early heraldic decoration in a funerary 57
context. The canopy, by the late thirteenth century a symbol of power
and authority, had appeared first as a sign of sanctity over bishops'
tombs, which also established the designs of the canopies themselves,
both generally and in detail. The French type of architectural canopy
may have appeared over Grosseteste's tomb in the 1250s, and it survives
on those of Grey at York, Bridport at Salisbury and Aigueblanche at 23, 72
Hereford; later tombs, including those at Westminster, merely brought
the details up to date. Grosseteste's canopy was supported on the

83 Exeter Cathedral, the nave,
built mostly from 1328. Owing to
the strong financial backing
given by successive bishops, the
authorities at Exeter were able to
plan the building campaigns
well in advance. The elevation
design, heavy mouldings and
elaborate vault and tracery are
often said to typify the aesthetic
of the Decorated style; but the
proportions were dictated by
surviving Norman masonry.

84 Canterbury Cathedral, tomb of Archbishop John Pecham, d. 1292. An early example of the so-called Court series (see frontispiece and p. 43), with arch-and-gable, weepers and early ogees.

clusters of triple colonnettes that would become commonplace; the canopy over the wall tomb of Bradfield at Rochester has the earliest example of the Kentish tracery motif; and Pecham's tomb, with its arch-and-gable, pinnacles and weepers, was the first in the series of so-called Court tombs that were made for the next fifty years.

It was at this time, however, when the architectural tomb with an effigy had become an important symbol of secular power, that some of the bishops rediscovered humility, and chose to be commemorated by a brass plate rather than an effigy. Indeed, the emergence of the large-scale figured memorial brass as a significant art form has been closely associated with the higher clergy of the late thirteenth century, particularly Cantilupe, Louth and the abbots of Waltham and St Albans. Brasses were still often set on a tomb chest under a canopy; but just as often the brass was set in the floor, its design including a canopy in two dimensions. A brass plate set in the floor allowed burial right in front of the high altar, and, trodden by the feet of the officiating clergy, suggested suitable humility. This virtue, however, was somewhat nullified by the size and elaboration of the brass itself. That of Louis de Beaumont at Durham was over 5m long, and its design included a towering canopy with pinnacles and flying buttresses, censing angels, apostles and much heraldry. Patterns on brasses exploited the repertory of Decorated motifs to the full, and found a response in stained glass as well as in the monuments; and their coloured inlays made them gleam as richly as their surroundings.

Bishops, too, were the first to incorporate their tombs into liturgical fittings, which they also frequently gave to the cathedral. The screens, sedilia, altars and shrines given by the bishops did much to dictate how Decorated was to develop. Walter de Stapeldon, who furnished the choir of Exeter cathedral, had his tomb attached to the high altar reredos; the tomb of Archbishop Meopham at Canterbury acts as a screen across the entrance to St Anselm's chapel; and at Salisbury the tombs of Mortival and Ghent are integral to the choir screen. At St David's Henry 60 Gower refitted the choir, donated a new roodscreen, and provided a tomb with a deep ogee arch for his predecessor, David Martyn. He also revived the cult of St David. Bishops were notably active in renewing or repairing shrines: Northwold included the shrine of St Etheldreda in his works at Ely; Antony Bek I gave a new shrine for St William of York in 1284, and the saint's tomb in the nave was remade by Melton fifty years later. The liturgical vessels and hangings also given by the bishops cannot be separated from the fittings; Stapeldon's high altar reredos, for instance, was made of silver and contained images. Grandisson's surviving works show that the altar vessels, crosses and book covers given by him to Exeter would have shared and reflected the stylistic characteristics of the monumental structures around them. The orphreys for the chasuble have embroidered spiked quatrefoils, the altar frontal has figures under delicate arcades, with busts in the spandrels. Grandisson's copy of Aristotle's *Metaphysica* and *Meteora* (Paris, BN, MS lat. 6299) is decorated with all the types of marginal figure appropriate to a manuscript of its time, *c*.1310. Thus, whoever ultimately controlled the building programme, the bishops directly or indirectly made a substantial contribution to the cathedral's appearance.

The bishops' personal tastes and wider influence perhaps show best in their private building. Many episcopal residences were rebuilt in this period, from palaces – Wells, Norwich, St David's – to houses, such as Ely Place and Winchester House in London, the Archbishop of Canterbury's residences at Charing and Mayfield and Bishop Burnell's fine mock-castle at Acton Burnell. Bishop Hamo of Rochester, which was not 86 a rich see, managed during the 1320s and 1330s to rebuild or repair at least three of his residences in Kent, and gave a window to the chancel of Dartford church. The significance to the Decorated style of John Kirkby's chapel of St Etheldreda has already been discussed, but other 22 buildings also helped to disseminate it. Burnell's residences at Acton Burnell and Wells, also dating from the 1280s, have tracery patterns of sexfoils and curved triangles; a curved, cusped quatrefoil survives in the former hall, now a barn, at Charing, ogival trilobes at Mayfield, and a form of star in the gable wall of Winchester House. In the halls at 49 Charing and Mayfield the head corbels supporting the timber roof were

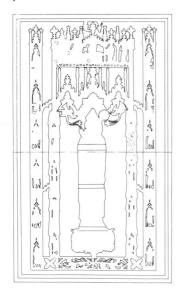

85 Durham Cathedral, matrix of the memorial brass of Bishop Louis de Beaumont, *c*.1333. Over 5 m long, the brass had a complex design of gables, pinnacles and buttresses.

86 Acton Burnell, Salop., built in the 1280s by Robert Burnell, Chancellor to Edward I and Bishop of Bath and Wells. A quadrangular house, its large windows and small towers were never seriously defensible. Many of its stylistic details are akin to those in the king's castles in Wales.

carved from life studies. Chequered masonry patterns and arcaded parapets decorate Bishop Gower's halls at St David's and Lamphey. Details in the porch of Bishop Salmon's hall of 1318 at Norwich, ogee-headed windows with continuous mouldings, nodding ogees and ogival mouldings, were widely influential in East Anglia; and the surviving chapel of his Carnary college, founded in 1318, has mouldings and traceries that anticipate early Perpendicular designs. Grandisson's great collegiate church at Ottery St Mary was adorned with the latest pattern of net vaulting. The prebendal church at Howden (E. Yorks), which belonged to the bishops of Durham, shows what could happen when a bishop took over a building project. The plain, rather simple church begun by a local canon was transformed by Antony Bek I and later probably by Louis de Beaumont into one of the richest examples of Decorated architecture in the north.

In both monumental building and the smaller works that were crucial to the development of the Decorated style the bishops were, therefore, at the forefront. For cathedral buildings they could act as enablers, raising and supplying the money for the building work. Their architectural contribution was made in their private churches and houses. In liturgical fittings, tombs and the smaller arts they were unequivocally leaders in the directions the style was to take.

The lesser clergy

The non-episcopal clergy encompassed everyone from poor, unbeneficed priests to senior monastic and cathedral officials, some of whom commanded wealth close to that of the bishops. The aristocratic Bogo de Clare even behaved like one. In general, however, few individuals could afford monumental stone buildings, and the clergy tended to act collectively in their monastic or secular chapters. Those who did build their own chantry chapels or colleges were almost all chancery clerks or chaplains to the royal household, well connected men with handsome endowments. Most individual clerics concentrated their patronage on their own tombs or such small portable luxuries as books, paintings and liturgical vessels. Whether indulging in monumental or miniature arts, however, the non-episcopal clergy were among the leaders of contemporary taste. Henry of Chichester, precentor of Crediton, employed a painter who worked in an original, futuristic style for the missal he presented to Exeter Cathedral *c*.1250; and the Peterborough, Ramsey (Holkham Hall, Earl of Leicester MS 26) and Gorleston (London, BL, Add. MS 49622) psalters, all made for church use, were illuminated by members of the so-called East Anglian group, whose advanced style was also in favour with royal patrons. The archdeacon of Exeter's seal

50, 79

21

VI

88

87 Howden Minster, Humberside, choir, east façade, *c*.1320. Howden was a manor of the bishops of Durham, who probably paid for the church. The niches and overlapping tracery have much in common with proto-Perpendicular buildings.

88 The Gorleston Psalter (London, BL, Add. MS 49622, fol. 69; *c.*1310–20). The illuminations were by members of the so-called East Anglian group, whose work combines complex border patterns with foliate and interlace designs, heraldry, animals, grotesques and marginal drolleries, here two men fighting.

(London, BL) of the 1330s is as innovatory and grand in conception as its larger fellows made for more senior clerics.

The building works financed by monastic and cathedral chapters independent of extensive lay or episcopal involvement included many of the most significant Decorated buildings, none of which merely aped fashion but explored new ideas in contemporary idiom. The choir of Gloucester Abbey in particular shows a monastic community unafraid of new ideas: although a royal architect may have designed it, there is no evidence that the king was himself involved, and the skeletal, traceried wall-covering, which developed themes adumbrated at St Stephen's and St Paul's, was probably the choice of the monks themselves. At St Albans and Chester they tried an elevation of superposed wall-passages; at St Mary's, York, they experimented with alternating tracery patterns; at Selby they adopted the two-storey elevation of Howden, but added copious figure sculpture both inside and out. The entire rebuilding at Wells, from the chapter house to the Lady chapel and the strainer arches of the crossing, was an enterprise of consummate originality, in geometric layout, elevational design and details of vaults and mould-

ings. The masons who built the monastic gatehouses at Kirkham, Bury 66
St Edmunds and St Augustine's, Canterbury, exploited the latest motifs 30
in mouldings and surface ornament. The work at Canterbury is particularly revealing, for it was done, together with the new works in the
cathedral, by the local masons who had been summoned to Westminster
in the 1290s.

Henry Eastry, prior of Christ Church, Canterbury, from 1285 to his
death in 1331, is one of the few clerics about whose individual patronage
we can be reasonably sure, although others left traces of identification,
partly as a way of ensuring eternal salvation by attaching a name or an
image to the object concerned: the Peterborough Psalter, for instance, vi
was made for Geoffrey of Crowland, Abbot of Peterborough; and Roger
of Waltham, a canon of St Paul's, had himself depicted several times in a
book of devotional texts (Glasgow UL, MS Hunter 231). Henry de
Mamesfield, who paid for the glazing of Merton College chapel *c*.1294, 89
appeared in the glass no fewer than twenty-four times. A boss portray-
ing an abbot from the nave vault at Abbey Dore indicates that he probably paid for the vaulting; and the carved stone bears on the parapet of
York chapter house are the signature of the Minster Treasurer, Francis
Fitzurse. When the records are solely in the form of written documents,
however, there can be a degree of uncertainty. Abbot Richard de Ware
arranged both men and materials for making the sanctuary floor at Westminster, but we cannot be sure that this was on his own initiative. At Ely
the question is confused by romanticism. As well as the bishop, three
monks are associated with the new work: Prior Crauden, for whom the
chapel and study were made, the sacrist, Alan of Walsingham, who,
according to later tradition, designed the Octagon, and John of Wisbech,
who is said to have discovered a pot of coins which he put towards
building the Lady chapel. The stylistic unity of the works at Ely suggests
strong, central control on design. The bold handling of space and wall
surfaces, and such details as the lifelike corbel heads in the abbey guest
hall and the strongly Italianate paintings in Prior Crauden's chapel all
show a ready awareness of new ideas, which may have characterised any
or all of the three. The evidence does not permit a definite conclusion.

Henry Eastry, on the other hand, has always been held personally
responsible for the works associated with his name at Christ Church,
Canterbury. He was wealthy and therefore could have been the benefactor rather than simply the driving force behind the building. It was he
who extended the chapter house and put in the prior's throne, and built 90
the screens and choir stalls in the cathedral. He also gave vestments,
jewels and gold to the high altar and the shrine, and enlarged the prior's
lodging. The men he employed, called back to Canterbury around the
time that work stopped at Westminster in 1297, did not merely repro-
duce the decorative ideas that they had been exploring in London, but
developed them on into a new stylistic phase.

Henry Eastry had a tomb made in the choir aisle, with a canted tomb

89 Merton College, Oxford, stained glass in the chapel, showing Henry de Mamesfield, donor of the glazing *c*.1294. He is depicted under a cusped and traceried arch-and-gable, flanked by pinnacles ornamented with architectural motifs, as on a reliquary or tomb.

chest, reticulated tracery and images. Senior clergy could have tombs that rivalled those of the bishops in both position and splendour. William de Langton, Dean of York (d. 1279) had a tomb that was not only near that of Archbishop Gray in the south transept of the Minster, but was adorned with a bronze effigy, at that date still otherwise associated only with bishops. Parish priests, too, could afford the luxury of a good tomb: that of the priest at Welwick (Yorks), made *c*.1350, follows fashion in its diaper and figures of angels, and anticipates it in the low swoop of its ogee arch. The memorial brass of Laurence de St Maur (d. 1337) at Higham Ferrers, which has figures of saints in tabernacles, miniature quatrefoils and battlements, has given its name (Seymour) to a whole group of brasses.

Some time between 1335 and his death in 1380 William de Luffwyk, rector of Aldwincle, also in Northamptonshire, had himself depicted in the glass of the east window of his church. Other priests went so far as to fit out or even rebuild their chancels, but they, however, tended to be out of the ordinary. The builders of such churches as Heckington, Sibthorpe

90 Canterbury Cathedral chapter house, prior's throne, *c*.1300. Put in by Prior Henry Eastry, it is encrusted with diaper, gables, tracery, pinnacles and crockets, exemplifying the precious, miniaturistic quality of Decorated works.

91 Higham Ferrers church, Northants., memorial brass of Laurence de St Maur, *c*.1337. Set beneath a crocketed ogee, the figure of the deceased is flanked by figures in niches (compare pp. 38, 80 and 92).

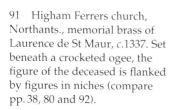

and Huyton were all senior clerics or attached to the royal household. The first two in particular were locally influential on tracery patterns and figure styles, just as the effects of the work at Ely can be seen nearby at Sutton-in-the-Isle, and further away at Mildenhall, Suffolk, where the 92 tracery of the east window resembles that of Prior Crauden's chapel. The clergy, then, were pivotal. Able to give leading craftsmen the chance to experiment, they were also in a position to encourage the spread of a style and its influence over a wide area.

The laity

While royal patronage is relatively easy to isolate, the general laity are much more elusive. Their patronage was either in the form of small contributions that were subsumed into Church projects, or, if they were rich enough to build their own castles, houses and churches, the evidence has been lost to decay or changing historical circumstances. Houses have been altered or rebuilt to meet new standards of comfort and rituals in private and public life. The monastic and collegiate churches founded or adopted by the aristocracy survived the Reformation only if they could be absorbed into parochial use, as at Tewkesbury, or were 45 sufficiently remote not to be plundered for building stone, as at Tintern. 17 Many aristocratic tombs have been lost with the buildings. The same is true of the mendicant churches patronised not only by the aristocracy but by the lesser nobility, gentry and merchants. Nevertheless, it is the works of the latter groups that have survived best on the whole, for they tend to be in the parish churches, which did come through the Reforma-

92 Mildenhall church, Suffolk, east window, *c*.1330. The outer ring of quadrilobes recalls the squashed trilobes similarly placed in the east window of Prior Crauden's chapel, Ely.

tion. In these buildings, bereft of many fittings though they are, something at least remains.

Differences in the patronage of the various groups in lay society were based not so much on class as we would understand the term, but on wealth. It was their greater disposable income that separated the higher nobility from the other landed classes. Although the obligation of display increased higher up the social scale, they all shared certain attitudes and forms of expression, particularly those of heraldry and chivalry – male lay effigies, for instance, are invariably knights, be they aristocrats or gentry. A particularly striking phenomenon is the force and originality of works commissioned by women. Perhaps women could be innovatory precisely because they were less affected by the conventions and rituals of the male-dominated society from which they were largely excluded. That women had their own cultural networks is suggested not only by the friendship between Elizabeth de Burgh and Marie de St Pol, but also, in the mid-thirteenth century, by the circle of female literary patrons that included Isabella, Countess of Arundel and the Countess of Winchester.

The higher nobility

This very small group was closest to the king in wealth and in religious and social outlook, having similar obligations in works of piety and display, but without the connotations of royalty that were peculiar to the person of the king. As the latter extended neither to his closest blood relatives nor to his wife, the queens of England are also being treated here, as leading aristocrats rather than royal ladies. The identification of power with wealth obliged aristocrats to build, and build they did; but only a fraction of their building works survives. The extent of architectural losses cannot be too strongly emphasised. The earls of Lancaster, for example, who were to become the richest landholders after the king himself, over three generations built probably more than any other family, undertaking major works in London, Leicester, Kenilworth, Warwick, Whalley, Pontefract, Pickering, Dunstanburgh and Kidwelly: only at the last four does anything survive, and the tomb of Edmund 28 Crouchback at Westminster is their only extant memorial.

Nevertheless, despite destruction, some consistency can be observed. That the distinguishing marks of aristocracy included grandiose works of piety is shown by the speed with which they were pursued by the newly enriched or ennobled: once married to Eleanor de Clare, Hugh Despenser the Younger lost no time in replanning the Clare family mausoleum at Tewkesbury as the Despenser burial church; and almost 45 the first acts of William de Montague and William de Clinton on being created earls in 1337 were to found Augustinian houses at, respectively, Bisham and Maxstoke. Clinton also built a house with such symbols of lordship as a gatehouse, octagonal corner turrets and battlements. Chivalry was naturally a strong theme in aristocratic art; it was where royal and noble artistic interests merged. In addition to knightly effigies, aristocrats had equestrian seals, the motif of the knight mounted on a galloping charger even finding its way on to the gables of the Valence 93 and Crouchback tombs at Westminster. The fantastic aspects of chivalry – the costumes and other ephemera of jousts and 'ludi' – had counterparts not only in the battlements of essentially unfortified houses, but also in the parapet figures which, if dates can be trusted, appeared in aristocratic buildings before those of the king, as at the Ros family's gatehouse for Kirkham Abbey, and Marten's Tower at Chepstow castle, 66 built before 1306 by Roger Bigod, Earl of Norfolk. This exchange of ideas occurred also in the designs of serious castles, where the type of gatehouse built by the Clares at Caerfili and Tonbridge was adapted and 51 perfected by Edward I in Wales and elsewhere, then built by earls and sons of earls at Denbigh, Kidwelly, Dunstanburgh and Goodrich. 94

Roger Bigod was equally adventurous in his church building, for he it was who paid for the exquisite patterns of window tracery at Tintern Abbey, which are among the earliest examples of the type outside 17 London. Other patrons were open to new decorative ideas: the flowerlike vault pattern at Tewkesbury was the choice of the Despensers, who are also associated with the north chapel added to the parish church at Winterbourne Basset (Wilts.), which has intersecting mouldings on its connecting pier and, under a window with enhanced reticulated tracery, a moulded tomb recess with a delicate ogival framework for statues. The most imaginative of all lay patrons, however, were the Berkeley family, who accepted a design for St Augustine's, Bristol, that included 4 a unique, boxlike hall elevation, a series of highly unusual vault and tracery patterns, and touches of decorative fantasy including the reversed curves framing the tomb niches. We take this building for

94 *Above* Denbigh Castle, Clwyd, the gatehouse, from 1282. It was built by Henry de Lacy, Earl of Lincoln, as a 'lordship' castle under the auspices of Edward I. The gatehouse is composed of three polygonal towers in a triangular plan following designs perfected by the king's architects.

93 *Left* Westminster Abbey, tombs in the sanctuary of Aveline de Forz, Countess of Lancaster, d. 1273 (left) and Aymer de Valence, Earl of Pembroke, d. 1324 (right). Aveline's tomb was made probably in the 1290s with that of her husband (see p. 43). Aymer's tomb has ogival cusps and elaborate pinnacles; the motif of the charging mounted knight in the gable resembles devices on seals.

granted as a manifestation of mature Decorated; but at the time it was almost unprecedented, and required considerable courage on the part of both the canons and the patron.

With hindsight, although it would not have seemed so obvious at the time, we can see that among the most widely influential patrons of architecture were Eleanor of Castile and Margaret of France, the wives of Edward I. Their support for the London mendicant churches, the Blackfriars and the Greyfriars, ultimately helped to set the pattern of the late medieval parish church throughout the land. The light, thin-walled structure was immediately reflected in the new town churches of St Thomas, Winchelsea and Holy Trinity, Hull, perhaps not surprisingly, as both towns were Edwardian foundations; but thence the type spread rapidly. Holy Trinity also took over the distinctive pier form of the Greyfriars, a quatrefoil with sunk chamfers, which, with the simple quatrefoils of Blackfriars, was to be the dominant pier type until the end of the Middle Ages.

The tombs of the queens and others in the mendicant churches are lost, but we know that Queen Isabella's was supplied by Agnes de Ramsey, daughter of the master mason William Ramsey; it possibly resembled that of Sir William de Kerdiston at Reepham in Norfolk, which may have been made by the Ramsey workshop. Surviving aristocratic tombs elsewhere show that in burial, too, the higher nobility liked to be progressive. The most significant tomb was that of Edmund Crouchback, Earl of Lancaster, in Westminster Abbey, which introduced the latest French type of freestanding, tripartite, gabled canopy. This tomb, and that of Aveline of Lancaster, are usually associated with Edward I, but although he would certainly have granted permission for them, neither is recorded in Edward's works. Edmund, who had lived many years in France married to Blanche of Artois, the mother-in-law of the future Philip IV, was a more likely sponsor of so overtly French a design. It was the type for a succession of variants, including those of Bishop Louth of Ely, Aymer de Valence (d. 1324), and John of Eltham (d. 1336) at Westminster, and the Percy tomb at Beverley Minster, *c*.1340. The tomb of John of Eltham made early use of alabaster for effigy and weepers, but the others originally had statues on the pedestals attached to the gables; those on the Percy tomb survive together with figures in relief holding shields of arms that identify the deceased probably as Lady Eleanor Percy (d. 1328).

The iconographic themes of salvation and humility on the Percy tomb are entirely appropriate, but they contrast with the increasingly elaborate structure that generally affected tombs in the mid-century. The lost tomb of Elizabeth de Burgh (d. 1360) in the Franciscan nuns' church in London was so striking that John Hastings, Earl of Pembroke, specified one like it for himself in Old St Paul's. The tomb attributed to Peter, Lord Grandisson (d. 1352), in Hereford Cathedral is surmounted by figures of saints and a *Coronation of the Virgin*, probably carved by the same sculptors who created the naturalistic fall of drapery over the effigy of his wife, Blanche, at Much Marcle.

Whether these tombs were commissioned jointly, separately or by one spouse (probably Grandisson himself, as Blanche died five years earlier) we do not know. The evidence of women's patronage is, in any case, buried deeper than that of men, as we can see from such royal ladies as Eleanor of Provence and Margaret of France, who, in decided contrast to their husbands, scarcely feature in the records at all. Eleanor especially is known primarily through the filter of Henry III's orders for work done on her behalf, although we know a little about her personal tastes. She owned books and liked romances, but she also enjoyed stories based on real events. It was for her that the first Antioch chamber was painted after she had borrowed a copy of the *Gestes d'Antioch* from the Master of the Temple; and it was for her also that the naturalistic personification of winter was painted on a mantelpiece at Westminster. Apart from her interest in Greyfriars we know little about Margaret of France and not much more about Queen Isabella, except that she gave appropriately lavish presents and, interestingly for us, owned three north Italian panel paintings at the time of her death. Her widowhood lasted more than

95 Hereford Cathedral, tomb of Peter, Lord Grandisson, d. 1252. The *Coronation of the Virgin* takes place in an elaborate setting. The tomb of Grandisson's wife, Blanche, at Much Marcle (see p. 103) may be the work of the same masons.

thirty years and the artistic commissions of several notable women reveal the advantages of being a wealthy widow, even if their patronage was often exercised on behalf of their dead husbands. Marie de St Pol, Countess of Pembroke, organised and paid for the great tomb of Aymer de Valence at Westminster, with its ogival cusping, and had a lasting 93 influence on British cultural history by founding, again in Aymer's memory, Pembroke College, Cambridge, there imitating her friend Elizabeth de Burgh, who had recently founded Clare College. Beatrix von Valkenburg (d. 1277), widow of Richard, Earl of Cornwall, was one 96 of the earliest known patrons to be depicted in stained glass. Isabella de Vesci (d. 1334), widow of Edward I's confidant John de Vesci, devised for her church at Heckington a scheme of imagery that attested her humility in an ostentatious celebration of the vanity and weakness of women; while its sentiments were commonplace, the manner of their expression was unparalleled.

The lesser nobility, knights and gentry
Owing to the social mobility conferred by wealth, political patronage and judicious marriages, the lesser nobility, knights and gentry had much in common, and as patrons of art they are largely indistinguishable. Like other aspects of their behaviour, their art patronage was

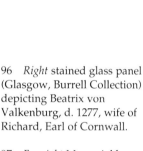

96 *Right* stained glass panel (Glasgow, Burrell Collection) depicting Beatrix von Valkenburg, d. 1277, wife of Richard, Earl of Cornwall.

97 *Far right* Memorial brass of Sir Hugh Hastings, *c.*1347, Elsing, Norfolk (see p. 176). It has elaborate gable- and niche-work and has traces of its original gilding, coloured pastes and glass inlays.

governed by social aspiration, consciousness of status and the ability to pay. The need to maintain rank is exemplified in Edward III's grant of the custody of Gloucester Castle to the newly knighted Thomas Bradeston in 1330 'for his better maintenance of the knightly rank lately conferred on him'. Their patronage shows more overt signs of social climbing than that of the established nobility, sharing with such newly ennobled families as the Montagues and Clintons the desire to display suitable status symbols. Bradeston himself, at the appropriate time, founded a family chantry at Winterbourne. The son of John Felton, the knight who became Constable of Beaumaris and builder of Edlingham Castle (Northumberland) with its open references to royalty, added a gate-house, which was not needed for defence and was intended as a recog-nisable symbol of lordship. The Cobham family, whose steady rise to baronial status through generations of public service is well docu-mented, celebrated their achievements by building their fine collegiate burial church with its handsome fittings. Heraldry was prominent on brasses and tombs, shields often placed along the sides of the sarcophagus where weepers might otherwise be: at Edenham in Lincolnshire the chivalric element is stressed by the addition of miniature battlements. Heraldry was, however, also used to establish ancestral legitimacy, and it may be a sign of the rapid rise of new men in these years that some families, notably the de la Beches at Aldworth and the Alards at Winchelsea, emphasised their family line by resetting effigies of their 47 ancestors in new tomb niches.

An advantageous marriage could likewise enhance a man's self-image. Although it is usually said that women adopted the social class of their husbands, whether higher or lower, some visual evidence suggests the opposite. The style of the Hastings brass at Elsing, Norfolk, a two- 97 dimensional evocation of Aymer de Valence's tomb at Westminster, may reflect a wish by Sir Hugh Hastings to demonstrate his connection to the earls of Pembroke through his father's first wife, Aymer's sister; and the high quality of the collegiate church at Astley in Warwickshire, with its complex alternations of flowing tracery, is perhaps a reminder 98 that Sir Thomas Astley was married to a daughter of the Earl of Warwick.

Apart from genuine seigneurial castles (as distinct from fortified houses), which the lower classes were forbidden to build even if they could afford to, no art form was denied them as long as they could pay, and works that can unequivocally be linked with gentry owners show

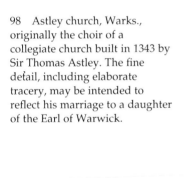

98   Astley church, Warks., originally the choir of a collegiate church built in 1343 by Sir Thomas Astley. The fine detail, including elaborate tracery, may be intended to reflect his marriage to a daughter of the Earl of Warwick.

99 The Swynburne pyx
(D. 57 mm; London, Victoria and Albert Museum; *c.*1310–25). A container for the consecrated host, made of engraved silver, partly gilt and with traces of translucent enamel. The *Virgin and Child* on the lid are stylistically linked to East Anglian manuscripts.

that they were as bold as their social superiors. Already by 1307 at Carlton Scroop church in Lincolnshire Sir John de Newmarch had himself depicted in the stained glass as patron, in the company of the priest whom he had presented to the living: this was a very short time after the appearance of Henry de Mamesfield in the glass at Merton College. The paintings in Longthorpe Tower were commissioned by the hereditary stewards of Peterborough Abbey, and a steward of the royal household, John, lord Grey, was responsible for the north chapel of Cogges church (Oxon) which he built in about the 1340s, probably as his mother's burial place, with lavish figure sculpture and a handsome heraldic tomb. The north chapel of the nearby church of Ducklington, with twin tomb recesses carved with a *Jesse*, reliefs of the *Infancy of Christ* and elaborate flowing tracery, is also probably a gentry foundation.

The main identifiable concentrations of gentry patronage, however, survive in manuscripts, tombs and brasses. Gentry ownership of the few extant liturgical objects can rarely be demonstrated, and such pieces as the embroidered orphrey for a chasuble (London, V&A Museum) associated with Joan de Wokyndon (d. 1322) and the Swynburne pyx have to represent many items in embroidery, metalwork, enamel and ivory that the gentry bought both for themselves and as gifts. Although some works show little artistic talent and poor workmanship, most manuscripts, tombs and brasses show that the gentry preferred to spend what money they had on small, luxury items rather than on monumental buildings that they could not afford to decorate. Manuscripts in particular were bought from the workshops that also supplied the king, and they display the same inventiveness and high quality. The Hours of Alice de Reydon was painted by one of the artists of Queen Mary's Psalter; the same artist also helped to illuminate the combined Psalter and Book of Hours (Downside Abbey, MS 26533) made for the Harnhulle family, a small book for private devotion typical of gentry patronage. Many 'East Anglian' manuscripts were bought by gentry families, including the Madresfield Hours (Madresfield Court, Earl Beauchamp MS M), which belonged to Maud de Tilliol of Scaleby in Cumberland,

100 *Right* St Omer Psalter (London, BL, Add. MS 39810, fol. 57v; 1320s). It was made for the St Omer family of Mulbarton, Norfolk. Its decoration has all the intense miniaturism of the East Anglian manuscripts, combining narrative scenes, foliate sprays, diaper, interlace and drolleries.

Ego autem sicut oliua fructifera in domo dei.
speraui in mia dei ineternum et in seculum seculi.
Confitebor tibi in scdm quia fecisti: expectabo no
men tuum qm bonu e in conspectu sctorum tuoru.
uit insipiens in corde
suo: non est deus.
Corrupti sut et ab
hominabiles fci sut
in iniquitatibz: non
est qui faciat bonum
Dns de celo prspexit super filios hoium: ut uide
at si est intelligens aut requirens deum.
Omnes declinauerut simul inutiles fci sunt:
non est qui faciat bonu no est usq; ad unum.
Nonne scient oms qui operatur iniquitatem:
qui deuorat plebe meam ut cibum panis.
deum non inuocauerut: illic trepidauerunt
timore ubi non erat timor.

101 *Left* Winchelsea church, E. Sussex, tomb of Gervase Alard, *c.*1322. The tripartite scheme of the Lancaster tomb in Westminster Abbey (p. 43) has been adapted to a canted design, elaborately diapered and with a monumental ogival, spiked trilobe in the gable.

102 Exeter Cathedral, tomb of Richard de Stapeldon, *c.*1332. The effigy is accompanied by small figures of the knight's squire, page and horse.

and the illustrious psalters associated with the St Omer family (London, 100 BL, MS Add. 39810) of Mulbarton, Norfolk, and the Luttrells (London, BL, MS Add. 42130) of Irnham in Lincolnshire. The Howard Psalter (London, BL, MS Arundel 83 I) was bought by Sir John Fitton, who also built a chapel at Wiggenhall St Germans in Norfolk. Although the Ormesby Psalter ended up in the hands of clerics, the Bardolf and Foliot families were involved in one stage of its production.

The gentry were equally bold in the decoration of their tombs and memorials, although structurally their tombs tended to follow fashion, adopting the wall-canopies favoured by the bishops and higher laity. At Winchelsea *c.*1322 the maker of Gervase Alard's tomb adapted the tripartite canopy of the Crouchback tomb and canted it against the wall, 101 embellishing the whole with pinnacles, battlements, diaper, foliage and ogival cusping and tracery. Ornament was often inventive: the tomb of Sir Geoffrey de Luttrell at Irnham has reticulated tracery carved in the form of twining foliage, and the weepers on a tomb at Howden represent minstrels. The most interesting aspect of gentry tombs, however, is the treatment of certain effigies where the desire seems to be to commemorate the dead not in a formal manner that implies eternity but in a way that suggests life. The living person, moreover, is captured at a fleeting moment, rather like baroque sculptures some three centuries later. The obvious examples of this are the effigies of knights in the so-called 'lively martial attitude', figures carved almost fully in the round, with their legs crossed but caught in the act of rising and drawing

103   Memorial brass of Lady
Margaret de Camoys (d. *c*.1310;
Trotton church, W. Sussex).
Memorial brasses were popular
with the gentry, who are
associated with innovatory
designs such as this.

63 their swords, as at Dorchester and in the later, more lively and supple
example at Aldworth. Added dramatic realism is given both to the
Aldworth effigy and that attributed to Sir Robert de Stapeldon at Exeter
102 by the accompanying small figure of a page (and at Exeter the esquire
and horse).

The drama and elaboration of the sculpture is not in itself surprising.
It occurs on tombs and memorials with more conventional imagery,
such as the Harrington chantry (*c*.1340) at Cartmel Priory in Lancashire,
which has a *Coronation of the Virgin*; it demonstrates that in the fourteenth century the gentry shared the taste of the clergy and higher
nobility for increased decoration on tombs. The sense of realism conferred by such anecdotal touches, however, could perhaps have been
explored only at this social level. The gentry were rich enough to afford
competent sculptors but not bound by the rules of display that beset the
higher nobility. They needed fewer marks of status to maintain their
position. They were thus freer to introduce informality and able to
employ the craftsmen who could realise it for them.

The gentry were also significant in the evolution of the funerary brass,
to which they had taken by the early fourteenth century. The emergence
of the type depicting a knight under a canopy, with shields and his feet
on a lion, which flourished in the second quarter of the century, is
particularly associated with gentry brasses, now most memorably
exemplified in those at Trumpington (Cambs.) and Stoke d'Abernon
(Surrey). Two styles of brass are named by modern scholars from
103 examples made for the gentry, Margaret de Camoys (d. *c*.1310; Trotton,
Sussex) and Sir William de Setvans (d. 1323; Chartham, Kent), sheriff of
Kent. The Camoys type, which based its designs closely on monumental
tomb sculpture, confirms documentary evidence that masons were
closely involved in the making and setting of brasses; and it also shows
that, just as with manuscripts, the gentry ordered work of the highest
quality. The canopy design of the Camoys brass is close to that of
93 Aveline of Lancaster, and the effigy's drapery follows the style associ-
73 ated with that of the effigy of Eleanor of Castile. Whether this reflects the
aspirations of the gentry or the professional connections of the artists
involved will be discussed in the next chapter, but some reflection of the
royal abbey must have been seen in parish churches and private chapels
glowing with coloured, burnished monumental brasses. It has been
argued that all these brasses emanated from a single large workshop,
that of Adam of Corfe, in London, which, if true, shows how mass
demand was creating a market for ready-made works that could be
adapted to the individual purchaser.

The urban patriciate

Although in the late Middle Ages merchants and other leading townspeople were a significant social force, in our period the most we can find
is hints of what was to come. Solid urban prosperity and the will to act

collectively were manifest in stone bridges, town walls and public buildings, but such expressions of civic consciousness as guildhalls did not yet exist. Civic religious festivals were in process of development, and all town churches received attention, not only those of the mendicants but the parish churches and the cathedral if there was one. In the 1320s, for instance, John de Triple, fishmonger of London, and John Rotenherynge of Hull prepared for burial in their local parish churches, while William Bauchun, a Norwich merchant who worked on behalf of the cathedral priory, was a benefactor of the chapels added to the choir.

Merchants' wills do not survive in numbers before the mid-fourteenth century and material evidence of their personal lives has all but vanished under the continuous rebuilding of towns up to modern times.

104 Stained glass panel (York, St Denys Walmgate; 1350s) depicting ?Robert de Skelton. In this period townspeople were emerging as the active and prominent patrons that they were to become a few decades later.

The wooden roof supported by caryatids and the ogival tracery of the
46 hall at Sir John Pulteney's country house at Penshurst in Kent were
probably by London craftsmen and must represent what is now lost
from the capital. Most of the extant material indicates that as a class the
merchants of this period were close followers of fashion, but not necessarily innovators. The earliest surviving appearance of a citizen in
stained glass dates only from the 1350s in the person of Robert de
104 Skelton, a leading citizen of York, who is depicted together with his wife
and son in the glass of St Denys, Walmgate. Yet motifs on objects that can
be associated with merchants are right up to date. The first seal of the
mayors of London (Westminster Abbey), dated before 1278, has arch-
and-gable forms with pinnacles that have been compared to the Westminster Retable, and the charter and seal bag of London (Corporation of
London Records Office), made around 1319, was probably embroidered
105 in London by the makers of the Syon Cope (London, V & A Museum). In
the 1340s the Flemish merchants at Beverley hired the team of masons
working nearby in the Minster to add the north chapel and sacristy, with
43 their beautiful vault supports and flowing tracery, to the parish church
of St Mary.

Although the merchants remained ostentatiously aloof from aristocratic tournaments and jousting, the Londoners not drawn in even to
those held at Cheapside and Stepney, they adopted chivalric references
in their works of art. Sir John Pulteney, mayor of London in 1336 and
financial benefactor to the king, was one of the first citizens of London to
be knighted. The crenellations on the hall at Penshurst and the paintings
of men-at-arms between the windows perhaps reflect both his grati-

105   The Syon cope (London,
Victoria and Albert Museum;
c.1300–20). Other works made by
the embroiderers of this cope
survive. Heraldic orphreys have
been attached at the edge. Both
the spiked quadrilobe frames
and the figure style find parallels
in other media.

106 Stokesay Castle, Salop., built 1294 by the merchant and tax-gatherer Laurence de Ludlow. The polygonal plan of the tower was perhaps a deliberate association of Laurence with the royal works.

fication at this honour and the fact that the king's household records refer to him and his fellow merchant, Sir Richard de la Pole, as 'scutifer regis'. Chivalry and heraldry were reflected in mercantile art and building. If the branches of the de Reymes family are typical, merchants and gentry were often related, and the former certainly modelled themselves on the latter. Heraldry appeared in their wall-hangings and display plate; a chequerwork flint pattern of heraldic derivation has been found in an early fourteenth-century cellar in London. Andrew Horn, a fishmonger in Bridge Street, London, who became City Chamberlain in 1320, assembled a manuscript miscellany of history and statutes (London, Corporation of London Records Office) and had his arms – a fish and St Andrew's cross – painted into the book. Merchant houses were adorned with gatehouses and towers or turrets, which could be octagonal, as at Pulteney's London house. Perhaps the most ostentatious sign of social aspiration is the south tower at Stokesay, the house built in Shropshire by Laurence de Ludlow, who collected an 106 important wool tax for Edward I in 1294 and was much hated; polygonal and crenellated, the tower emulates no less a building than Caernarfon Castle. Laurence was as important to Edward I as Pulteney and de la Pole were to his grandson, and, like Pulteney, he was signalling that he was anyone's equal. The merchants' day as social leaders was, however, yet to come.

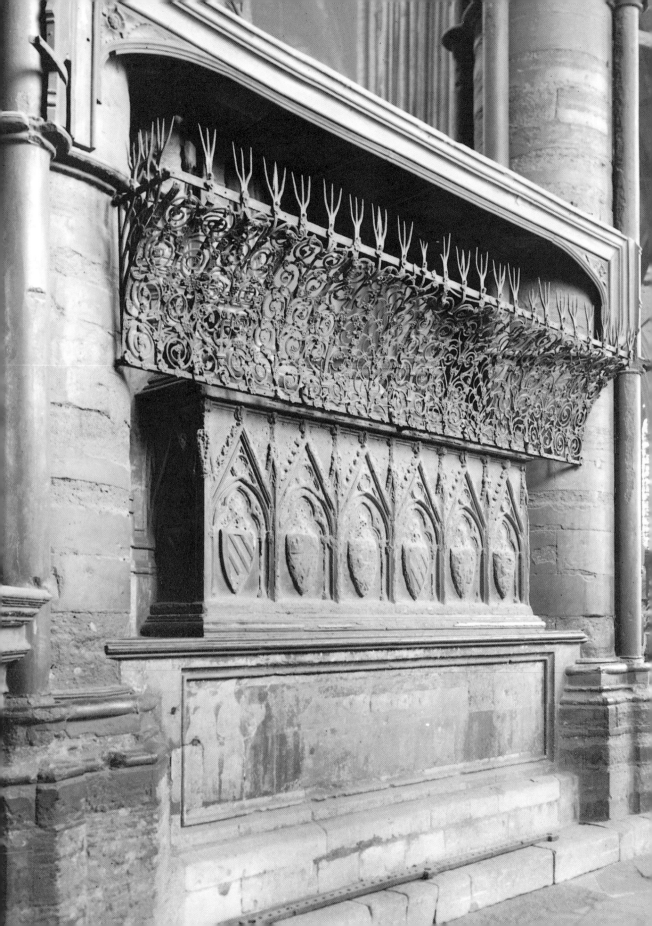

CHAPTER FIVE

Craftsmen and Administrators

So far we have considered the social, religious and cultural conditions within which the Decorated style developed and flourished; but although a style of art may emerge in certain circumstances, it is created not by them but by people. It is now time to look at the people who created Decorated, including not only the architects but the painters, glaziers, carpenters, metalworkers and ancillary smiths and plumbers, who clothed the formal structure in the ornament and colour that endowed it with meaning. The architects were undoubtedly important; they, after all, designed the buildings and ensured their stability. Yet it is important to see their activity in relation to the building as a whole, and to understand the part they played we must try to see them as they saw themselves, disregarding the filter of later scholarly attitudes, which have imposed interpretations of medieval artistic activity that contemporaries would not have recognised.

The architects

At that time an architect, or master mason, would not only build monumental structures such as castles and churches, but he created all forms of stonework, including tombs, church furnishings and wayside crosses. Many masters also ran businesses contracting to quarry and supply stone. Thus Michael of Canterbury, the first architect of St Stephen's chapel, also made the Cheapside Eleanor Cross; John of Battle, undermaster at Vale Royal Abbey, made several of the the Eleanor Crosses and carved statues for Northampton; Thomas of Witney, master 25, 61 mason of Winchester and Exeter Cathedrals, designed the choir fittings IV for the latter; and William Ramsey, architect of St Paul's cloister among many other buildings, also ran the tomb-making business that was continued after his death by his daughter Agnes. The breadth of masonic activity and expertise has deep implications for a style in which monumental and small-scale works constantly enriched and complemented each other.

    Our knowledge of architects and other building workers in this period is drawn from civil and criminal records and building accounts

107 Westminster Abbey, tomb of Eleanor of Castile, 1292–4, seen from the ambulatory (with modern tester). The making of this tomb is unusually well documented, showing how several masters were involved. The work must have been co-ordinated by the administrative clerks. The painting on the base shows Sir Otto de Grandisson praying for the queen's soul.

(fabric rolls); these reveal their existence, and something of their working methods. Other information about how the work was actually done can be deduced from architectural drawings, contracts, masonic writings and craft regulations. There is hardly any of this type of evidence for our period in Britain; except for a few contracts, the famous masons' tracing floors at York and Wells, and the set of regulations made at York in 1352, nearly all our knowledge of these activities has to be extrapolated from sources in other countries or later years. The former type of evidence, however, survives reasonably well, although the fabric rolls exist for only a few places, namely Exeter, which has a continuous run over nearly half a century, York and Ely, which have only a few. Many buildings – for instance, Old St Paul's, Bristol and Tewkesbury – have none at all. Nevertheless, thanks to much careful research, we now know numerous masons from this period by name, and we can even assign certain buildings to specific individuals: Henry of Reyns, for instance, initiated the design of Westminster Abbey, William Joy was architect of the presbytery of Wells Cathedral. These records also help us to follow the careers of some masters as they travelled around the country – Walter of Hereford from Winchcombe Abbey (Glos) to Vale Royal, Carlisle, Scotland, north Wales and London; Thomas of Witney in Winchester and Exeter; William Ramsey in London, Windsor and Lichfield; Michael of Canterbury at Canterbury, Westminster, Winchester and the London area.

Yet these records, abundant and informative though they may seem, need to be treated with care, for they can mislead us into making the wrong assumptions. Not only do they include craftsmen whose works have either disappeared or are insufficiently differentiated to give an idea of a personal style, but scholars still find many styles, or hands, to which they can attach no certain name. Thus, the distinctive styles of Walter of Hereford, Michael of Canterbury and other master masons are still a matter of debate; and often artists have to be identified by such nicknames as the Madley mason, the Madonna Master in the Psalter of Robert de Lisle (London, BL MS Arundel 83 II), or Artist A of the Harnhulle Psalter-Hours. In any event, the whole notion of a personal style may not be wholly appropriate to the Decorated period. Approaches to art that centre on individual attribution are based essentially in ideas first encountered in the Renaissance, which promoted the artist as an original, creative being. When medieval art in general and buildings in particular were thought to be anonymous the problem of attribution scarcely arose; but with the discovery of so many documented names it has become tempting to match buildings to people, both for their own sake and to create a history of medieval architecture that more closely resembles that written for later centuries. That this method can be hazardous is shown by the case of the spire of Salisbury Cathedral, which was for many years dated 1334 and attributed to Richard Farleigh, all on the strength of a contract that he signed with the

108, 116

cathedral authorities in that year. Only recently has it been pointed out that the contract does not mention the cathedral fabric, and that the style of the spire dates it closer to 1300; it was the existence of a documented name that persuaded scholars to link it to an event in the cathedral's building history.

More significantly, perhaps, the pursuit of individual attributions ignores contemporary attitudes and ways of working. The master mason, together with the master carpenter, was undoubtedly the most senior craftsman on the building site, and the responsibilities of both men were reflected not only in their pay but in the confidence placed in them by patrons and administrators alike. Some masters were retained by a particular patron for several years. Ivo de Raghton worked in York for Archbishop Melton, and James of St George and Walter of Hereford worked for Edward I, Walter at one point contracting to work exclusively for the king. Bishop Grandisson wrote in the warmest terms about Thomas of Witney. Yet his words, describing a man who was in our terms an eminent and successful architect as 'a dearly loved member of our household and a valuable and willing servant to us and to our church of Exeter', provide one of the keys to understanding. No amount of professional skill or fame meant that the master mason could act independently of either the administration or the professional requirements of his fellow craftsmen. At whatever scale he was working, on a monumental building or a piscina niche, he was subject to the checks and balances of individual creativity against co-operative enterprise. Attitudes were deeply based in the central tenet of existence that subsumed human individuality into the greater individuality of God, and the notion that the master mason was expected to be original or inventive does not sit with this, or with the surviving evidence, which makes it clear that neither was necessarily a priority. This is not to suggest that no medieval artist was allowed to be creative, or that individual styles cannot be found; but the emphasis that we nowadays place on these things is inappropriate in the context of the Decorated style. The evidence strongly indicates that although individuals were held in great esteem and were often asked to produce original designs, it was not originality as such that earned respect.

The question turns on the matter of design. In any major building, design was the particular responsibility of the master mason. He and his trained colleagues alone possessed the technical knowledge of applied geometry that was required to set out the details of the plan and elevation. The master drew the proposed scheme of the elevation and tracery and vault patterns so that the patron could make a final choice, and he also drew the templates from which the work-force could carve the constituent parts of arches, vaults, piers and windows. Designing the correct curvatures of arches and vaults was the most technically challenging part of the whole process and it is a great irony of architectural history that the master's most important contribution should be effectively invisible in the finished building. Nor is it given much attention in contemporary records. Contracts (for example, that of William Helpeston at Vale Royal in 1359) often specify that the master will draw up designs, but there are few references in the fabric rolls beyond the setting out of the Octagon at Ely, the tracing houses at Exeter and St Stephen's, and a payment at the latter to Thomas of Canterbury for making designs.

34

Even with well-documented works the identity of the designer, as distinct from the makers, can be difficult to establish. The person who set out the Octagon is referred to as 'someone from London', and although the funerary works for Eleanor of Castile are among the best recorded campaigns in the entire medieval period, we can find out only who made them; we are not told who designed them. The tomb base and cross in Lincoln were made by Richard of Stow, with Dymenge de Reyns, Alexander of Abingdon and William of Ireland. John of Battle made his five crosses with the help of several unnamed assistants and William of Ireland; Waltham Cross was made by Roger of Crundale, Dymenge de Reyns and Alexander of Abingdon; Cheapside was by Michael of Canterbury; Alexander helped Roger of Crundale on Charing Cross after Richard of Crundale died, and Alexander and Dymenge also worked on the Blackfriars tomb. The general similarities between the crosses and the tombs show that all the masons were working to master patterns. Logically, the man most likely to have produced these should have been either Richard of Crundale or Michael of Canterbury, although neither is named as master of the project. Cheapside was the second most expensive cross, and Michael took no further part in the enterprise only because in 1292 he became master mason of St Stephen's chapel. The similar motifs in the tombs, crosses and chapel show that Michael was at the very least strongly influenced by the works for Eleanor, and he may even have supplied designs for them all. Yet Richard of Crundale, former chief mason at Westminster Abbey, performed many of the functions of the master mason. He made the Westminster tomb and Charing, the most ostentatious and expensive of the crosses, and he also organised the delivery and despatch of stone from Caen and Purbeck for the entire project. He might reasonably be expected to have produced the designs, but neither monuments nor documents give a certain answer.

One reason for the silence is certainly the nature of the documents, which were to facilitate accounting, and as the master was usually paid a salary details of his work would not be recorded. Others, however, lie in the conditions of the time. All the evidence suggests that the designs belonged not to the master but to the building site; not only was there little, if any, personal identification with a design once it was drawn up, but master masons did not identify themselves with particular designs. Mouldings produced by Thomas of Witney are different in each building with which he was associated. At a time when a building campaign could last indefinitely and be in the charge of several successive master masons, attitudes were dictated by practical realities. If a building were constructed from scratch the first architect at least could realistically expect to have some freedom in the design of the elevation. Yet not even he was necessarily required to be either original or innovatory: new parts of buildings were, as we have seen, often made to resemble adjacent sections that may have been built centuries before. Later masters might have very little scope, as can be seen at Westminster Abbey, where only gentle modifications were made by by Henry of Reyns's successors, John of Gloucester and Robert of Beverley.

The building history of Exeter Cathedral illustrates what could IV happen. Five master masons are recorded for the main building period, but none is likely to be the man who produced the original design of the presbytery, with the two-storey elevation and deeply sloping sill, and the clustered piers. The first master to be mentioned is one Roger; he is probably, but not certainly, the designer of the three-storey choir elevation that established the building's definitive appearance. This design not only survived Roger's two rather short-lived successors, William Luve and William de Schoverville, who seem to have been defeated by the technical difficulties of creating a new crossing while retaining considerable quantities of the constricting Anglo-Norman fabric. It was also left unchanged by Thomas of Witney, who was installed as master 83 mason by 1316 and held the post until 1342. Despite his talent and skill, Master Thomas conformed wholly to the existing plans, confining innovations to the liturgical furnishings, doorways and window tracery. In other buildings changes might be made only to the profiles of capitals and pier bases.

There is some evidence that master masons did not always like losing control of their designs. At least one contract stipulates that the master's designs are not to be modified by anybody, and in later medieval Germany and Italy there were arguments between building administrations and master masons about the ownership of drawings. The drawings, however, were made on the site, and not only could the master be absent, but the labour force was not a fixed entity. Masons were assembled to carry out the job and dispersed at the end of it, and over a long campaign very few journeymen stayed over several seasons. At Exeter only four or five masons (out of a workforce of up to twenty-five) appear in the wages lists year after year; most of the others, the vast majority, were there for a season, often only for a few weeks, and some were called in to perform a specific task. Yet the building reflects none of these changes, for the designs were there to be carried out by whichever masons were present.

Not only was the master often obliged to conform to earlier work, but he also frequently incorporated material brought ready-cut from elsewhere. The bases on the reredos at Beverley, for example, were a standard model that did not change in twenty years, produced by the

108   Madley church, Heref. and
Worcs., built *c.*1320 by masons
who may have worked at
Hereford Cathedral.

Purbeck marblers at Corfe and despatched to order. Yet, despite hints
such as these, and the evidence that Thomas of Witney scarcely ever
used the same design twice, the occurrence of distinctive motifs in
different buildings is often used to attribute the latter to the same
masons. It is on these grounds that the masons who worked at Ely in the
1320s have been identified at Norwich, Bury St Edmunds and Butley
Priory; all the churches in Yorkshire with leafstem patterns of flowing
tracery have been associated with one architect, the micro-architecture
of London and the south-east with another. To some extent this
approach can be justified. The invention of the wave moulding has been
convincingly attributed to Edward I's builders in Wales, tracery patterns
24, 66   with split cusps to the Kentish masons, and in both instances the stylistic
evidence is reinforced by surviving documents. Yet no-one suggests
that every occurrence of these widely distributed motifs indicates the
presence of the inventor; and this exposes the unresolved central difficulty. Although the late medieval controversies referred to above suggest that some notion of copyright was then emerging, at this earlier
date there was no such thing. The constructive geometry needed to set
out architectural mouldings was known to every trained mason, and, as
we have seen, the designs were produced from templates often in the
absence of the designer. Mouldings or whole elevation designs could

V *Right above* Exeter Cathedral, relief of Christ blessing, ?1340s, on the vault of Bishop Grandisson's burial chapel. This figure, flattened and stylised to suit its location, was placed directly above the bishop's tomb, as if to intercede for his soul.

VI *Below* The Peterborough Psalter (Brussels, Bibliotheque Royale, MS 9961-2, fol. 25; *c.*1300–18). The fleur-de-lis backgrounds to the scenes show the influence of heraldry. The *Temptations of Christ* are shown with Old Testament anti-types, here the *Temptation of Adam and Eve.*

VII *Right below* The Barlow Psalter (Oxford, Bodleian Lib., MS Barlow 22, fol. 13; 1321–38). The *Life of Christ* is set against painted and punched diaper grounds, reminiscent of both metalwork and architecture.

VIII Westminster Abbey, the ?high altar retable, ?c.1270. This once-magnificent panel is thought to have been the retable of the high altar. Its architectural framework, imitation enamel, cameos, gilding, gemstones and decorative glass share the ornamental qualities of other work in the building and of the building itself. The paintings, now damaged, but once of exceptional quality, show Christ blessing and holding a small globe, between the Virgin and St John. Scenes of His Ministry in spiked quadrilobes are flanked by St Peter and (probably) St Paul.

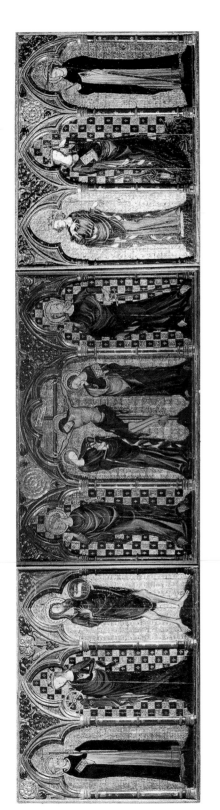

IX Retable (Thornham Parva church, Suffolk).

X Altar frontal (Paris, Musée de Cluny). The two panels are from the same set of altar furniture, c.1325–50. The presence of St Thomas Aquinas among the saints in the retable indicates that they come from a Dominican house. The scenes of the Virgin on the frontal include (right) the recently invented scene of *St Anne teaching the Virgin to read*. The draperies in the narratives are powdered with devices in current fashion, and the alternating colours and devices in the diaper backgrounds show the influence of heraldry.

in consilio impiorum: & in uia pec
catorum non stetit: & in cathedra pe
stilentie non sedit.
Sed in lege domini uoluntas eius:
& in lege eius meditabit die ac nocte.
Et erit tanquam lignum qd plan
tatum est secus decursus aquarū:

XI The Windmill Psalter (New York, Pierpont Morgan Lib., MS M.102, fol. 2; *c*.1290). The second letter, E, of the opening to Psalm I has an illustration of the *Judgement of Solomon*, and the windmill from which the book takes its name. A naturalistic pheasant is painted in the lower margin. The book is associated with Edward I.

easily be copied or adapted. Henry III's request for a copy of the vault at Lichfield is recorded, but something similar must have happened with the chancel fittings at Hawton, which are an adaptation of the design at Heckington, and the choir elevation of Selby Abbey, which is a close adaptation, but not a replica, of the choir of Howden. Indeed, the nave of Lichfield has many of the characteristics of Westminster Abbey, but is not thought to be by the same masons. Later works certainly could have been made by masons who had been present at the other site, although, as we shall see, there are reasons to suppose that the Hawton fittings were made by a different workshop. The occurrence in churches built in the Hereford area from about 1320 of tracery and mouldings clearly dependent on the cathedral has suggested that they were built by a mason from the cathedral workshop. Yet once a design became known it passed into general use, and any argument that seeks to identify a particular mason or workshop with a particular motif or set of motifs requires very great care. 108

This, then, is the background against which the achievements of any one master mason of the time should be seen. To fit him into the overall scheme of artistic production requires a small shift in thinking, away from the architect as an individual genius and towards the architect as a great artist who was part of a larger whole. It may help to look at the people, both artists and administrators, with whom he collaborated.

The building administrator

The building authorities were essential to realising the construction, and the administrative clerk could be a prominent and powerful figure. In this period a Clerk of the Works was sometimes appointed to look after a royal building campaign, and if there was no officially titled appointment, a clerk still took over most of the administration. A Cathedral Works was run by a member of the chapter, and in monasteries it was the job of the Sacrist. Although we have no evidence about a non-royal secular building programme, it is likely that it would have been run by a member of the household. The clerk was often interested and knowledgeable in matters of art: Henry III certainly respected the expertise and taste of his clerk, Edward of Westminster, whose advice he followed on at least one occasion; and Thomas Ludham, clerk to the fabric at York Minster in the 1340s, took the kind of active interest in the building plan that gives weight to the traditions surrounding the parts played by the monks Alan of Walsingham and John of Wisbech in the Decorated work at Ely.

Some idea of the clerk's co-ordinating function can be gained from the records of the funerary works for Eleanor of Castile. Richard of Crundale, the maker of Charing Cross and the tomb at Westminster, seems to have organised the delivery and distribution of all the stone, and as different items were finished, masons were smoothly reallocated to new tasks; but that Richard was not in sole charge is suggested by the absence

of fuss at his premature death in 1293, when Roger of Crundale collected his outstanding pay and took over work on Charing Cross. The West-
107 minster tomb was not solely a work of masonry but involved several craftsmen with different skills; each was hired separately and his materials were supplied either by him or by the clerks, but not by Richard of Crundale, whose responsibility did not extend beyond the stonework. Walter of Durham painted the tomb base; Thomas Hocton
73 made the destroyed wooden tester; the gilt-bronze effigy, by William Torel, was cast at the abbey, but Thomas of Leighton brought the iron grille ready-made from his own workshop outside London. Torel also cast the effigy for Lincoln, as well as that of Henry III at the Abbey. The images at Blackfriars, however, were made by William of Suffolk and Alexander of Abingdon, and Alexander in particular was one of those who seem to have travelled widely in the service of the project. Yet what emerges from the record is the careful co-ordination of the whole group of masons, carpenters, painters and metalworkers and the pressure towards the end of 1293 to finish the complete programme of tombs and crosses; but it could not have been managed without the clerks of the works, and it helps also to emphasise the point that a master mason's responsibility stopped with the stonework. There is no evidence that Richard of Crundale, for all his importance as co-ordinator of stone and masons, was involved in any way with other aspects of the project.

Collaboration

The only craftsman with skills equal to those of the master mason was the master carpenter, whose expertise was complementary. In any building campaign the collaboration between these two was the most important. Every stone building contained substantial quantities of woodwork. In churches, where it included the choir stalls, screens and other wooden furnishings, the most technically demanding carpentry was in the trusses supporting the pitched outer roof. In barns, where there was no point in incurring the extra cost of concealing them, and in halls, where their structural details could be both an object of beauty and a status symbol, the roof timbers were exposed; but in churches they were often hidden by stone vaults. The masonry walls, however, had to accommodate the immense pressure exerted by the angle and weight of the timber trusses. Working so closely together, masons and carpenters could not but be aware of one another's work. The heavy, emollient mouldings of late Decorated may well be influenced by the soaplike effects obtainable in wood, and references to arch-brace and crown-post
4 construction have been detected in the aisle vaults of St Augustine's, Bristol, and the superstructure of the door to the chapter house vestibule in York Minster. Wooden vaults imitating masonry, with ribs and carved bosses, occur from the thirteenth century, usually over square or rectangular bays; but in York chapter house c.1280 and over the crossing
34 at Ely from 1328, they are octagonal, and both show signs of close

co-operation between the masons and the carpenters.

In York chapter house, where a stone vault was planned but later abandoned, perhaps because they decided not to have a central column, the masons altered the buttresses in anticipation of the different thrusts that would be exerted by the timber roof. At Ely the stonework in the upper Octagon is designed exactly to accommodate the timber frame that supports the lantern and from which the vault panels are suspended. Some masons were familiar with both materials. Thomas of Witney advised the chapter of Exeter on timber for the bishop's throne, IV and the architectural character of the finished piece suggests that he designed it; and the great wooden vault in the south transept tower was made from 1316 while he was master mason. Yet there is scant evidence that he or any other mason worked the timber himself, nor is there evidence that carpenters worked in stone. The Octagon, moreover, cannot be treated in isolation from its contemporary buildings at Ely, with which it closely shares designs of both mouldings and decorative details.

The Octagon, Lady chapel and Prior Crauden's chapel were fully 32, 33, sculpted, painted and gilded, and like all Decorated structures they pose 34 acute questions about responsibility for design. We do not know, for instance, how far a tracery pattern was dictated by the requirements of the stained glass programme; or whether, in a building encrusted with sculpture, the ornament was designed by the master mason or adapted from patterns supplied by another type of craftsman altogether, such as a painter or a goldsmith. The designs of diaper and draperies so exactly x conform to those in other media that it is quite legitimate to wonder whether they were not adapted directly from them. Nowadays we regard this kind of relief decoration – diaper, ballflower, foliage and figures – as sculpture, and distinguish it from architecture. We might be tempted to conclude that, for example, the leaf sculptures in the chapter houses of Southwell and York, or long sequences of figured bosses like those in the cloister of Norwich Cathedral, were carved by specialist sculptors. The temptation is even greater when considering architectural sculpture that includes figures carved more fully in the round – those on the prior's door at Norwich, the minstrels' gallery at Exeter, the 114 reredos of Christchurch priory, the Grandisson tomb at Hereford or the 40 Tomb of Christ at Hawton. At Hawton the weighty, graceful style of 95 Christ and the Marys is distinct enough from that of the smaller figures 109 to suggest that they were by another hand. Although even there the figures are extensions of and subordinate to the architectural setting, physically attached to the mouldings and carved from the same blocks, the building masons could have left uncut, rough stone for specialist sculptors to shape. Yet there is no evidence that in the thirteenth and fourteenth centuries this essentially architectural sculpture was distinguished from the structural blocks upon which it was carved. Building accounts describe masons either by the type of stone they worked –

marblers – or by what they did – paviours. Stone cutters are known as *cissores* or *taylatores*. By the fifteenth century the latter, now *enteilers*, were specifically carvers; but in the fourteenth they were not distinguished from cutters. At Exeter, and to a lesser extent Ely, where the vast programme of decorative sculpture can be related to a long series of wages lists, there is no reference to any category of mason that seems to have specialised in decorative sculpture. The only type of carving that is occasionally singled out is the making of images.

This was still very tentative, and few image makers yet specialised exclusively: John of Battle, for instance, was also an architect. Only Alexander of Abingdon, who is cited in various documents until *c*.1317, is invariably referred to as a maker of images; but other craftsmen were paid specifically for carving images, notably the 'carver from London' who made images at Exeter in 1324, and the carpenter John de Burwell, who in 1339–40 carved 'one image' (the blessing Christ) for the great central boss of the lantern at Ely. The criterion for qualifying as an 'imagier' is not clear, but the slender evidence suggests that those who were seen as specialists were not the makers of images that were included in the general architectural ornament, but the makers of such figures as statues and effigies that were carved more or less in the round. Alexander of Abingdon's known work consisted of statues, and a further hint comes from the topmost figures, Christ and the attendant angels, on the Percy tomb at Beverley; these are the only discrete pieces of the entire structure, and they were apparently carved by a sculptor who did no other work on the tomb, but whose hand has been detected on effigies at Alnwick and Staindrop. The effigy at Bainton church (Humberside) is in a different stone from the tomb niche, and although it was clearly made for the niche, it was carved by another workshop. [frontis]

The different styles of the statues of Queen Eleanor suggest that John of Battle, Alexander of Abingdon and William of Ireland were allowed some freedom in presentation; and decorative carving is of equal interest because, unlike purely moulded work, it is sufficiently varied to allow the identification of different hands. At Heckington, for example, the architectural mouldings on the Tomb of Christ and the sedilia are identical; but the foliage and figure sculpture are so dissimilar that it has been suggested that they were executed by two different people, one of whom also carved the smaller Tomb of Christ at Navenby. [61] [110]

The execution of all the stonework, however, seems to have been under the control of the master mason, even that of the 'imagiers', whose figures had to fit the dimensions of their settings, which were fixed by the master. At least one of the other sculptors of the Percy tomb did other carving around the Minster, notably in the north aisle of the nave, carving that, like the tomb, involved architectural mouldings as well as figures, and was part of a programme including elaborate window tracery. Such features as tracery are crucial to the question, for tracery was integral to elaborate decorative schemes, but it also had an

109   Hawton church, Notts., Tomb of Christ (centre) and tomb of the benefactor, *c*.1340, on the north side of the chancel. The Tomb of Christ, used for Corpus Christi ceremonies, has an *Ascension* scene at the top and the sleeping soldiers below. The middle register contains carvings in high relief of Christ and the Maries. This outstanding work is a later version of the Tomb of Christ at Heckington.

independent existence. Tracery patterns that can be associated with sculpture at one place can appear without it at another: the pattern adorning the south transept of Heckington and the chancel of Hawton, where it is related to the distinctive sculpture programme, was also used without the sculpture at Sleaford, Algarkirk and Selby Abbey. Selby has in common with Heckington a type of gargoyle in the form of a boat, but its other sculpture, though once extensive, is unrelated. If a chancel or chapel was built or refurbished in association with a burial, tracery was put in as a matter of course. In the Despenser chapel at Winterbourne Basset and the chancels of Elsing, Bainton and Halsham, the tomb is accompanied by flowing tracery and, at Halsham, additional grotesque sculptures. At Dorchester, in the *Tree of Jesse*, the sculpture and tracery are one, just as they are on the Luttrell tomb at Irnham. Tracery was among the elements from which a patron could choose according to his taste or pocket; but this alone indicates that the masons made no clear distinctions between one type of carving and another. It is always possible that the works team would include masons with an aptitude for decorative work; but in our period they had not yet established a specific identity.

In a large programme of ornament, direction and collaboration were vital. The latter could be of two kinds: either several people working together on different phases of one operation, or several people each responsible for an area within it. This happened frequently in manuscript illumination, where, for example, the constant collaboration of

110 Heckington church, Lincs., upper part of the sedilia, *c.*1330. Adorned with figures, foliage, gables, ogees, birds and grotesques, it was carved by several craftsmen.

111 Hawton church, Notts., east window of the chancel, *c.*1340. This distinctive design was used at Heckington and other Lincolnshire churches, and also at Selby Abbey (see p. 34).

certain hands has been isolated within the group of manuscripts dependent on Queen Mary's Psalter. A famous instance of the former type of shared work is the great early fourteenth-century programme of sculptures at Orvieto Cathedral in Italy, which was almost certainly devised and partly carved by the master mason, Lorenzo Maitani. Its unfinished condition has revealed all stages of the carving from initial roughing out to the final burnishing, each stage apparently carried out by craftsmen of appropriate skills, the masters putting the finishing touches. Unfortunately we have no comparable evidence in Britain, but we must remain aware that such a division of labour was a possibility here. On the other hand, evidence for the latter form of collaboration, several workers each concentrating on a particular zone of relief carving, survives not only at Heckington, as we have seen, but in several other places, notably Beverley and Ely.

Detailed study of the Percy tomb at Beverley has indicated that there the work was divided between five people, each wholly responsible for a particular zone, with the odd irrational intrusion of one sculptor into another's area. This is not unlike the vastly more complex operation in the Lady chapel at Ely. The extent of the destruction at Ely makes study of the surviving sculpture both rewarding and frustrating: it is useless to dado were made by 'imagiers', for the records do not exist. The local speculate whether the large, virtually free-standing figures that once 113 lined the upper walls and the smaller ones atop the nodding ogees of the dado were made by 'imagiers', for the records do not exist. The local clunch, or chalky limestone, is soft and easily carved and the high finish of the undamaged parts of the dado sculptures prevents any study of working methods. Conclusions must be drawn on the basis of style; but the evidence of different styles and the relation of the sculptural ornament to its backing stones do invite comment. The entire dado level, from the narrative reliefs on its rear plane to the gables and nodding ogees of the forward plane, is made up of structural blocks that were put in as the walls rose. The sculpture was already carved at least to some degree, for the figures are carefully disposed to avoid the masonry joints, which are themselves often ineptly handled. Each block includes both figure work and architectural ornament and foliage. In the ninety-three surviving scenes of the *Life and Miracles of the Virgin* there are several styles of drapery carving, although some of the distinctions are so fine that they may not always reflect a different hand. The figure types appear mainly in sequential groups of scenes, with the occasional intrusion of a different manner for one or two scenes. While the same style normally appears on both sides of the gable over any one niche, sometimes the styles are different. Two 'hands', both carving graceful, unfussy tubular folds, but one with deep, fine curves across the body, seem to have been responsible for most of the work, with the assistance of another hand at the east end and a possibly different hand at the west. The foliage cresting on the gables and nodding ogees, however, is arranged quite differently. There are seven distinct varieties of foliage,

112   Elsing church, Norfolk. The chancel, with curvilinear tracery, was built in association with the burial of Sir Hugh Hastings, d. 1347 (see p. 152).

113 Ely Cathedral, Lady chapel, narrative relief of a *Miracle of the Virgin*, ?late 1320s. A vision of the Virgin appeared to a usurer who gave away a loaf of bread. The Virgin is accompanied by an angel, and at the bottom demons are being vanquished. Miracles of the Virgin occur to all classes of society. The figures, which were fully painted against a gilded diaper background, are in one of the two main styles of sculpture in the chapel.

from bulbous, ribbed, cabbage-like leaves to undulating, attenuated seaweed. Not only is their distribution apparently random, but none is associated with any particular drapery form. The predominating figure styles appear with every kind of foliage. Occasionally the same foliage type appears on adjacent gables, and patterns even sometimes alternate for a few bays. This distribution of styles can be interpreted in a number of ways: that the foliage and figures were carved by different people; that they were carved in different phases by the same people; or that many blocks were being carved at the same time and carvers were directed from one block to another as they finished a task. The drapery of the Ancestors of Christ in the double niches on the wall-piers strongly suggests that they were also by the makers of the narrative reliefs; additionally, although they are carved nearly in the round, they are made from the same blocks as the architectural mouldings around them, and are wholly integrated with them.

If the decorative sculpture was carved by the cutting masons, who designed it? The variations in pattern of the diaper and seaweed foliage at Ely are reminiscent of the minor decorative changes made to relieve monotony in a street of 1930s semi-detached houses; but in the Decorated period this kind of variety was an established ornamental approach. Master masons may have possessed collections of stock foliage- and figure-types, although, if they did, there are no hints in the documents and, despite efforts to attribute manuscripts containing random sketches, no contemporary example has certainly survived. What a master mason could use, however, was the resident expertise of the painters, glaziers and metalworkers. It has to be admitted that the evidence of their participation in the design is as circumstantial as that of pattern-books; but it is thought that painters drew designs of figures for 105 *opus anglicanum*, and it is reasonable to suppose that a painter sketched out the scheme for the narrative scenes in the Lady chapel and Octagon at Ely; he might also have supplied models for the figures. When, as in the Lady chapel, figures are of high quality and their styles resemble those in manuscript illuminations, the conclusion seems plausible. Unfortunately, however, it is much less convincing when the carved figures are of lesser quality, as in the scenes of St Etheldreda in the Octagon or, 114 for example, in the cloister at Norwich. Confronted by such stiff, ungainly forms as these, it is possible to conclude only that if a painter did supply models either he or the sculptor was not very competent.

114   Norwich Cathedral, prior's door, *c*.1310. The figures are set against the arch mouldings, under alternating gables and ogee arches. They include Christ, St John the Baptist and an angel. It is uncertain whether they were carved by the cutting masons or by specialist figure sculptors.

115 Westminster Abbey, St Faith's chapel, wall painting of St Faith, *c*.1300. A painted retable, in an architectural setting and with some attempt at illusionistic recession in the pedestal. The drapery style is similar to that associated with William Torel (see p. 119).

Nevertheless, figure styles in particular show a striking convergence in this period. Both before and after this time figure styles in different media bear only a general resemblance to one another, but in these years artists seem deliberately to have drawn closer together. The style associated with William Torel in the effigy of Eleanor of Castile, which 73 employs straight, vertical drapery folds that are disturbed only by a break sideways across the foot, has no surviving precedents. It appears on her seal, which on these grounds has been attributed to Torel, and on the engraved figures sketched on the reverse of the cushion behind the effigy of Henry III, which are presumably also by Torel. As a goldsmith, Torel would have made his figures by modelling rather than chiselling; but his style was immediately imitated by Alexander of Abingdon in the statues for Waltham Cross, and after an interval it was adopted for monumental painting by the painter of St Faith in Westminster Abbey, 115 and for miniatures, by the Madonna Master of the De Lisle Psalter. It 116 was also adopted by the brass makers of the Camoys group.

Whatever part the painters may have played in designing ornamental sculpture, they were essential to the creation of Decorated. Some details of the craftsmanship of St Edward's chair at Westminster suggest that it was the painter-decorators who acted as the catalyst in making the works in combined media that are the essence of the style. The chair was made by Walter of Durham, the King's painter; and the decorative carving of foliage and pinnacles was done not directly into the wood but into the chalk ground that acted as underlayer to the paint. Walter was evidently familiar with many different materials. Yet not only did the painter-decorators add to the architectural mouldings the stamped and stencilled patterns familiar in panels, textiles and metalwork; they also ix supplied much of the complex play on illusion that lies at its heart. Paint x covered all surfaces, whether two- or three-dimensional; and flat surfaces were often deliberately juxtaposed to sculptures and mouldings, as can still be seen in Westminster Abbey and Prior Crauden's chapel at Ely, where polychrome sculpture was placed alongside figures painted on the flat wall. The *Annunciation* and *Crucifixion* painted at the west end of Prior Crauden's chapel were opposed to sculpted and painted figures at the east; and in the south transept at Westminster the sculpted figures in the upper registers stood above the painted saints Christopher and Thomas in the dado. Sometimes the illusionistic trick was played back on itself, as in the grisaille figures at St Stephens chapel, in which the 'stone' was left plain to underscore the joke. The painted retable of St Faith in the Abbey, however, contains hints of three-dimensionality in both the modelling of the figure and the pedestal on which it stands. Painters not only used micro-architectural frames on panels, but increasingly added fictive architectural settings to manuscript illumin- 53 ations, wall-paintings and stained glass (as, for example at Merton 89 College), which in the two latter instances reflected the architecture around them.

Stylistic exchange

The opportunities for craftsmen to absorb one another's styles and ideas were almost limitless, for medieval art reflects the mobility of medieval life. A patron could employ any number of craftsmen in different places; and a craftsman, or group of craftsmen, could make any number of works for any number of patrons, as can be seen from the manuscripts made by artists of the Queen Mary's Psalter, which are varied and seem to have been destined for many different kinds of patron. A design could be used by different groups of craftsmen. Each occasion provided an opportunity for ideas to intermingle. Not only did patrons and craftsmen constantly move about, but so did the works themselves. Portable objects travelled with other household goods; in any case, they had not necessarily been made where they were bought, and bespoke works could also be despatched long distances from their centres of production. The 'East Anglian' Madresfield Hours went to Cumberland; and the great alabaster reredos of St George's chapel, Windsor, was transported thither from Nottingham. Not even a monumental building can be said to be wholly fixed in its location until it was actually assembled on its foundations, on account of the many building components that were precut in one place and sent for use in another, for example the products of the Purbeck 'marble' quarries. The identical details on the screens at Exeter and Beverley demonstrate the extent of the trade in prefabricated parts; and the accounts for the Eleanor Crosses show how templates could be sent to Corfe from elsewhere for execution by local marblers. It also worked in reverse, however, for as Purbeck stone required specialist cutters, the marblers often also travelled with it to a distant building site. They also set up permanent workshops in London, the most prominent in the early fourteenth century being Adam of Corfe, who had a workshop and business in St Paul's churchyard, and supplied marble to St Paul's, St Stephen's and to the shrine of St Thomas Cantilupe. When Walter of Hereford needed pieces cut to his designs for Vale Royal, he sent to the marblers of London rather than Corfe. Yet Corfe remained effectively a centre for both the reception and the dissemination of designs.

Together with the larger towns and the building sites themselves, such quarries formed an essential antithesis to the mobility of the work-force, for they were fixed locations, and it was the interaction of mobility and fixity that provided the dynamic of artistic creativity. Quarries were more than mere sources of stone. They were training grounds for masons, some of whom, for instance Peter de Barnack, who worked at Leicester in 1325–6, are identified with quarry names in the wages lists. The long-established building sites – St Albans, Exeter, York, Bristol, Hereford, Tewkesbury, Lichfield – provided continuous work, in some instances for more than a generation, while between them Westminster Abbey and Old St Paul's were in building for the entire

116 The Psalter of Robert de Lisle (London, BL, MS Arundel 83 II, fol. 131v; 1300–10). The painter, known as the Madonna Master, worked in a style related to that associated with William Torel. The setting of a large, cusped arch-and-gable, with figures in niches, diaper and censing angels, should be compared with all types of work in this period, from monumental tombs to stained glass, brasses, ivories, metalwork etc.

Decorated period. As we have seen, the permanent work-force at these sites was enriched by the presence of transient workers. Alongside these protracted operations were brief but intensive campaigns that occupied an enormous number of masons and other workers for a relatively short time. For the castles in Wales masons were drawn by decree from all over the country except the granite-working south-west, and when the campaigns ceased they were released to go to other sites.

It was in towns, however, that craftsmen found the widest opportunities to discover new ideas and influences, particularly if there was a settled market for a variety of luxury goods, such as goldsmiths' work, books and embroidery. Oxford, where the university created a local demand for books, supported booksellers and illuminators as well as masons and glaziers. This should be true of Cambridge, although it cannot certainly be demonstrated; it was certainly true of the flourishing port of Norwich, which may have supplied the Cambridge demand. By the 1330s York, already a source of work for painters and glaziers at the Minster and elsewhere, had at least one goldsmith, Hugh le Seler, who made the great seal of the diocese of Durham. Merchants, gentry and the local nobility, particularly those who were not drawn to London – the Percies at York, the Lancasters at Leicester – provided local patronage. Sometimes, especially in such east coast ports as Hull and Beverley, there was a sufficient community of foreign merchants. The corbel of a sheep's head in the north chapel of St Mary's, Beverley, indicates why the Flemish merchants were there. The city that above all could support the ideal conditions for the intricate web of artistic connections that underlies Decorated was, of course, London.

London was a natural centre of art production. Supplying both local and national markets, an entrepôt for finished goods and raw materials for home-produced craft, it attracted large numbers of people and exported both them and their wares. The clergy of Beverley Minster ordered the new shrine of St John from Roger de Faringdon in London, and many 'East Anglian' manuscripts were also probably ordered from there; hence the difficulty in deciding their provenance. Many funerary brasses were despatched from London workshops; those of Sir Hugh Hastings at Elsing in Norfolk and Lawrence de St Maur at Higham Ferrers in Northamptonshire were sent out from the same London shop. Some of the statues for the Northampton Eleanor Cross were carved in London and London craftsmen also supplied effigies and other components of tombs: the alabaster effigy of Edward II at Gloucester was almost certainly made in London, whither at that time alabaster was sent uncarved from the quarries, as the carvers who were to produce such works as the Windsor retable were not yet established.

The diverse geographical origins of London craftsmen can be deduced from their topographical surnames. Some, the goldsmiths Walter of Colchester and Roger de Faringdon, the masons Michael of Canterbury and Richard of Crundale, the painter Hugh of St Albans, were from London's natural catchment area of the Home Counties. Others, however, were from much further off: the masons Robert of Beverley and John of Gloucester; the goldsmith William of Gloucester; the glazier John of Lincoln; the painter John of Bristol; and the carpenter Edmund of St Andrew from Worksop in Nottinghamshire. Not all these men came of their own free will. Painters, for example, were impressed for work at St Stephen's from all over the south-east, East Anglia and the Midlands. Yet many who came voluntarily stayed and established businesses. Among these, if the documents have been interpreted correctly, were members of the East Anglian Ramsey family of masons, one of whom, William Ramsey, set up alongside his peripatetic architectural work the stone contracting and tomb-making business that was continued by his daughter Agnes. An enormous variety of craftsmen was settled in London, from alabasterers and marblers through jewellers, seal-engravers and metalworkers, to members of the textile trades, who made tents and banners, bedding, domestic hangings, clothes and ecclesiastical vestments. Painter-decorators lived alongside parchment makers, scribes, illuminators and bookbinders. The London craftsmen were among the first to form guilds and fraternities, in particular the goldsmiths, painters and tailors; and they tended to congregate: the painters around Cripplegate, the goldsmiths in Cheapside, bronze- and iron-founders at Aldgate, the tailors at Cornhill, where the house of Edward III's tentmaker, John de Yakeslee, eventually became the hall of the Merchant Tailors' livery company.

What gave London another clear advantage over other cities was Westminster, the administrative centre of the kingdom, which, although distinct, existed in close proximity, to their mutual benefit. While other towns – York, Chester, Carlisle – became seats of government for a time, the Westminster institutions were permanent, and they attracted a settled population of civil servants, bankers, lawyers and merchants. The two great households of Westminster, the abbey and the palace, were significant employers of craftsmen, both from as far afield as Italy and from London. The royal accounts show clearly the benefit that accrued to both towns from the demand for jewellery, plate, hangings, clothes and vestments, as well as building and decorating work. The London-based workshops were not employed exclusively by the king, even the master masons having independent practices. Perhaps as important as the craftsmen were the suppliers of materials and finished goods. These people emerge clearly from the royal records, but it is safe to presume that other great households were similarly organised. The clerks of the works acted as liaison between the craftsmen and the suppliers, buying, for example, the metal for the royal effigies at Westminster from John de Ware and William Sprot of London, even though William Torel himself supplied the wax for the models. Adam de Basing, a prominent London draper whose name lives on in Basing Hall Street, the site of his mansion, supplied textiles, jewels and metalwork to Henry III. Working directly to the clerk Edward of Westminster, he not only produced worked cloths, for instance orphreys for the chasuble embroidered by Mabel of Bury St Edmunds, but he had garments and vestments made up from materials given to the king, including a tunicle and dalmatic made of damask given to Henry by his wife's uncle, Peter of Savoy. Adam supplied the trousseau of Henry's half-sister, Alice de Lusignan, and banners and hangings for Westminster Abbey were made through him. With the clerk, such suppliers may well have been able to influence the taste of the patrons and therefore the appearance of what was made.

Once the clerks of the works had found reliable suppliers and craftsmen they tended to go on using them. Adam de Basing worked for the king for more than twenty years, even at times supplying such materials as wool and corn, which were outside his normal business. Walter of Durham was continuously employed either in the abbey or the palace for several years. More significant, perhaps, was the use made of London workshops by the royal works wherever they may be. We have seen that Walter of Hereford sent templates of capitals and bases from Vale Royal in Cheshire to be made by the London marblers; and the Wardrobe accounts for the 1340s show that wherever the king was in residence for the great feasts, the stamped, painted, stencilled and appliquéd festive cloths were made up in London. Required in a hurry, these textiles were decorated using techniques that could produce a showy result at speed; the similar techniques employed on tombs and buildings, where such considerations hardly applied, shows the transposition of techniques for one medium and purpose to those of another that is typical of the period.

Such commissions often required the combined skills of tailors, painters and embroiderers, just as funerary monuments needed masons, metalworkers and sometimes painter-decorators. Surviving metalwork 99 – for instance, the Swynburne pyx – shows the close relation between painters and metalworkers, and the influence of metalworkers shows 93 again in the flying equestrian figures on the Crouchback and Valence tombs, which closely resemble seal impressions. London above all provided the conditions in which craftsmen could automatically draw together for mutual inspiration. It can be no accident that the goldsmith, sculptor, brass-maker and illuminator who worked in the style associated with William Torel were all based in London.

At one level, then, the cohesion of Decorated depended on the settled presence of a wide variety of craftsmen; but what continually renewed it were the ideas brought in by their more mobile colleagues. The new patterns of window tracery that adorned Westminster and St Paul's were not local inventions, but were imported from France and imposed on local designs. Thence they were adapted into a typically Cistercian 17 elevation at Tintern, and into interiors rich in architectural mouldings at 27 Exeter and Wells. Ogival traceries that began life in reticulated form were transposed into the foliate and leaf patterns of the east and north. The leading master masons travelled extensively both on the king's business and in private practice. King's Master Masons covered enormous distances, being required to care for all castles north or south of the River Trent. James of St George, having been brought all the way from Savoy to north Wales, went from there to Linlithgow in Scotland. Walter of Hereford, as we have seen, worked at Winchcombe in Gloucestershire, Vale Royal, north Wales, Scotland and London; John of Battle worked at Vale Royal and on the Eleanor Crosses in Bedfordshire, Northamptonshire and Hertfordshire. Alexander of Abingdon was sent 25 to Waltham, London and Lincoln. Masters with independent practices might stay within a particular region – William Joy worked at Wells and Exeter – or go further afield. Nicholas de Derneford worked at Bristol, Burton-on-Trent, Repton and the castles in Wales; William Ramsey combined working for the king with a practice that was based in London but took him to Norwich and Lichfield.

Whether or not the presence of such a craftsman can be associated with the specific appearance of a motif is, as we have seen, debatable. The appearance of flowing tracery at Astley church has been related to 98 Ramsey's presence at Lichfield; but the patron or his master mason could have discovered the motif by many different ways, and the Kentish tracery at Kirkham Priory and Whitby Abbey in Yorkshire 66 should remind us that motifs become independent of their source. The point is the network of connections that such men created. Robert of Beverley, Richard of Crundale, Walter of Hereford and William Ramsey worked on both castles and churches, and were therefore familiar with the motifs and iconography of very different kinds of building. Walter of Hereford, assistant to James of St George, had as his own assistant John of Battle, who himself worked with Alexander of Abingdon and the group around Richard of Crundale.

What these men represent is the largest of a series of decreasing circles of mobility, moving around and towards those craftsmen who scarcely moved at all. It is their perpetual, kaleidoscopic mingling that explains how the Decorated style can be at once national and regional, architecture and anti-architecture. Yet they also represent only one of the main contributory threads. In the final chapter, we shall attempt to weave the threads together.

Epilogue

The Decorated style was devised in a society in which only a few people were wealthy; but it was appropriate both to grand ceremonial spaces and to tiny, reduced niches; to huge expanses of stained glass, tapestry and wall painting, and to little ivory diptychs, manuscript miniatures, pilgrim badges and rings. A pilgrim scarcely above villein status could wear a badge adorned with the same devices of the ogee arch, foliage cresting and filigree quatrefoils that appeared in the buildings, furnishings and tombs of the king and bishops. If Decorated flourished amid court ceremonial it was equally suited to more modest surroundings, and its success is reflected in the survival for two centuries, until the Reformation, of the type of setting for devotion that developed in the later thirteenth century.

In the second half of the twentieth century there has been increased scholarly emphasis on the part played by the court in the creation of Decorated, with the isolation of a court style centred on Westminster. Works outside Westminster that display similar motifs, especially those that can be associated with patrons close to the king, are identified as in the court style. The presumption is that Decorated is a style that will be created for the higher ranks of society, and filter down as the lesser ranks adopt it to claim status by association. Manifestations of the court style include the obvious influence of Westminster Abbey at Lichfield and Hereford; the intrusion of London-derived proto-Perpendicular forms at Edward II's burial church in Gloucester; and the spread of such motifs as the ogee and arch-and-gable from their early appearance on the Eleanor Crosses, the Westminster tombs and St Stephen's chapel.

That the king's works included foremost exponents of Decorated is undeniable, and reflections of them are found in buildings associated with men close to the king. In addition to the nave of Lichfield and the transept at Hereford, both built by allies of Henry III, a declaration of allegiance, or at least a claim to association, can be seen in the towered gatehouses built by Edward I's captains and followers. Whether there was a definable court style, however, is doubtful: once pursued, both the style and the court become elusive, and concentration on the courtly element in Decorated diminishes the significance of other aspects, to the detriment of understanding the style as a whole.

For the idea of a court style to have any substance it has to be shown that there was a court with a consistent artistic policy, and a group of artists to put the policy into effect. The comparative wealth of evidence surrounding the king's works can give that impression; but it can also mislead. At this period the English court is not easy to define. Strictly speaking, it consisted of the people in the immediate vicinity of the king at any one time. The court was certainly not synonymous with Westminster, which was becoming the centre of administration, not the main residence of the king. The court had no fixed geographical location, nor any permanent members apart from the king himself. Nor can it be equated with the household, for it was smaller than the *familia* and only overlapped the *domus*: personal friends and relatives could be summoned to court for brief periods, particularly at Christmas or Eastertide. On these and like occasions, in the king's as in other noble households, a distinct culture can be identified. Court culture has been characterised as patterns of behaviour that originated with the king and his circle, and devolved to the fringes. It was expressed in music, poetry, romances and chivalry, and certainly by the later thirteenth century an essential form of expression was the setting of joust and festival, in the chosen colour schemes of liveries, banners and hangings, which denoted belonging and encouraged the sense of a group. The epitome of this aspect of court culture was the ceremonial of the Order of the Garter. We have seen how such things influenced the Decorated style; but they scarcely amounted to a policy on the monumental arts.

A court style – or styles, for the period was long, and Decorated changed over time – depends for its existence on a settled team of craftsmen. The evidence for such a team in royal circles is equivocal: a group of carpenters did work for Edward II for a few years, but most craftsmen were employed as individuals for specific tasks. Some master masons, notably Walter of Hereford and John of Battle, do seem to have worked fairly consistently on buildings for the king and queen; but they may well have had substantial non-royal clientèles for whom the records do not survive. Other artists, Alexander of Abingdon for instance, or Michael of Canterbury, did work for other patrons. The superb quality of William Torel's gilt bronze royal effigies shows that by the 1290s he was a mature craftsman, but his previous career is entirely unknown to us. Such continuity as did exist would have been maintained by the clerks of the works; but whether they consciously pursued a style in royal architecture is debatable. Modern scholars broadly define the court style as the strand that most consistently and closely reflected the influence of French Rayonnant, particularly in the debt of Westminster Abbey to the Sainte-chapelle, in Edward I's works of the 1290s, and through St Stephen's chapel, the proto-Perpendicular choir of Gloucester. In France, Rayonnant has been closely associated with the

67, 73

117 Lead pilgrim badge (H. 86 mm; London, Museum of London; fourteenth century) showing the *Annunciation*. It was made for pilgrims to Walsingham, and sets the scene beneath a cusped and crested ogee arch with flanking pinnacles and a base of quadrilobes. A lily, symbol of the Virgin, occupies a prominent central position.

personal patronage of Louis IX, and as such regarded as the French court style. This naturally enhances the courtly claims of Rayonnant-inspired works in England.

Given contemporary developments in mainland Europe, the scholarly need to find a court style of exactly this sort in England was inevitable. This was a time when sophisticated court cultures were flourishing not only in France but in the Spanish kingdoms, Naples, north Italy and the Empire, especially in such areas bordering on France as Hainault and Artois. The court cultures of Savoy, Hainault and Castile were all influential in England. In architecture, court styles have been isolated in the thirteenth century in the patronage of Charles II of Anjou in Naples, and in the fourteenth under Kasimir the Great (*reg* 1323–70) in Lesser Poland and Charles IV (Emperor 1355–78) in Prague. All three were inspired by the example of French Rayonnant. It was necessary only to fit the English evidence into the existing pattern. The English case was further strengthened by the close relation of the French and English royal families (Louis IX and Henry III were married to sisters, daughters of the count of Provence), and by the moral authority that Louis exerted on Henry III and, even in death, on Edward I.

Louis IX was undoubtedly a strong influence on Henry III; but not at the institutional level; nor did Henry or Edward merely ape the visual propaganda of the French royal house. What impressed Henry was Louis' acquisition of relics and the ceremonial surrounding their display, which was clearly reflected in Henry's arrangements for the procession and reception of the Holy Blood. Yet although a contemporary popular song maintained that when Henry finally saw the Sainte-chapelle in 1254 he declared a wish to bring it home in a cart, at no time did he contemplate building a separate chapel for his own relic of the Passion, but he simply had the decorative ideas of the Sainte-chapelle incorporated into a monumental basilica that was based on a different building altogether, the French coronation church of Reims Cathedral.

The ceremonial function of Westminster is not directly comparable to any one building in France, and this reflects the differences in the ways that the two monarchies promoted themselves. This can partly be explained by their different relations with the Church. The kings of France did not suffer the conflicts with the Church that beset other rulers in Europe, and they owed their position of power in the thirteenth century as much to the support of the Church as to their own military skill. Ever since the early twelfth century, when Abbot Suger of Saint-Denis took under his guidance and protection the future Louis VII, and identified the interests of his abbey with those of the monarchy, the French monarchy had become closely linked to Saint-Denis, the shrine of the patron saint and the established French royal necropolis since Carolingian times. The latter was to be further emphasised in the 1260s when the series of new tombs for the early kings was initiated, probably by the monks, if with Louis' support. Reims Cathedral, in the meantime, jealously guarded its equally traditional rights to the crowning. In England the rights to the coronation had hitherto been shared by Winchester and Westminster, and other traditions were also different. No king since the Norman Conquest had had what amounted to a pupil-tutor relationship with the Church hierarchy, and the royal abbey of Westminster was not equivalent to that of Saint-Denis. It was not the shrine of the patron saint: in the thirteenth century England had three guardian saints, the Confessor, St Edmund and St George, and there is no evidence that Henry was trying to create a national saint from the figure that he saw as his own patron. Nor was the abbey the royal necropolis. The kings of England had either founded their own burial churches or been buried near their place of death, often on French soil; Henry appears not to have intended Westminster for the interment of anyone other than himself and the Confessor. The sequence of kingly burials after him was broken (not always voluntarily), and Edward I and his successors allowed many of their relatives to be entombed at the abbey too, so that it became a family, rather than a kingly, burial church. In any case the abbey church contains elements that are not French. The Italian associations of the pavements, if diluted, like the architecture, by English characteristics, are too insistent to ignore. Henry drew on specific French and Italian sources, using the recognition of their original purpose to indicate a related but distinct usage at Westminster.

Edward I's attitude to his counterparts in France also requires scrutiny. His use of French royal prototypes for the Eleanor Crosses and possibly for the metal effigies of his father and his wife, suggest that he was particularly impressed by the death rituals and ceremonial of the French kings. He may, however, have had particular kings in mind, for both Philip Augustus and Louis IX were distinguished military and chivalric heroes, the latter also a saviour of Christianity. The openings in the sides of Henry III's tomb sarcophagus, which hint strongly at a shrine, perhaps indicate a desire to associate Henry's body with miracles in the manner of Louis IX, although there ends any resemblance between Henry's tomb and those of France. The making of the former is a mystery. Its type is based on papal tombs in Italy, and why it was chosen for Henry, and by whom, is unknown. The tomb was probably made during Edward's reign – he supplied 'jasper' stones (presumably the porphyry slabs in the sides) – but the design could have been chosen by the dying Henry, or by Abbot Richard Ware, who perhaps wished to flatter the king. For Edward, however, it was a highly significant monument, and that he did not follow a French form for it seems to belie the notion that he was a slave to French court fashion. In addition, the most unequivocally French types of tomb in the abbey are those of the Earl and Countess of Lancaster in the sanctuary, which were almost certainly 28, 93 not paid for by Edward. St Stephen's chapel is often compared to the Sainte-chapelle, its differences in form, with a rectangular ground-plan and wooden vault, being explained away as English characteristics.

Insofar as it was the palace chapel, no doubt greatly in need of rebuilding, it shared the function of the Sainte-chapelle; but it was never associated with a great relic, and there is no evidence that the cult of kingship apparently practised there by Edward III was intended in 1292.

The artistic links between the kings of France and England were not, then, as straightforward as they seem; nor is the association of Rayonnant with royalty. Recent scholarship in France has revised the close identification of Rayonnant with Louis IX; and in England Rayonnant ideas were adopted ostentatiously in buildings that had no links to the king. Old St Paul's, indeed, with its Rayonnant tracery, rose window and buttresses, is usually interpreted as a rival to the king's interests. The Rayonnant style of York Minster, which is presented as a reflection of the presence of the court in the city between 1298 and 1305, is based on a misunderstanding, and it reflects nothing of the kind. The late thirteenth-century rebuilding at the Minster began with the chapter house; and by the time the Exchequer arrived in 1298 the nave itself had already been in building for seven years. There is no sign of a change in style after 1298, nor, beyond the status of the archbishops, is there any reason to connect York with the court before then. Nor was the court, as such, present in York for any significant period, for it was the Exchequer, not the king, that had settled there. Between 1298 and 1305 Edward I spent only a few isolated days in the city. In any case, York itself quite transcended the presence of the royal finance office. Notwithstanding the troubles of the Scottish wars, the city was the centre of a wealthy region, with powerful magnates and rich churches. It was, and is, the metropolitan seat of the northern archdiocese of England, a rival to Canterbury. The grandeur of the Minster both reflected and proclaimed not a royal association but the status of the see and of the archbishop.

The complex structure of ideas that supports the notion of a French-based English court style is thus beginning to disintegrate. We are now in a position to ask whether, apart from the associative instances outlined above, there was an English court style of any kind, and if the widespread response to the royal works actually reflected their royal connotations. The dramatic interior, with large-scale figure sculpture, was revolutionary in England; but the dramatic interior itself was introduced into a receptive culture whose love of ornament and bright surfaces went back to Anglo-Saxon times, and which had already devised for itself the decorated settings of the cathedrals of Canterbury, Lincoln and Ely. The association of architecture and reliquary had been made in the façades of Wells Cathedral and Binham Priory; the latter may well have had geometrical bar tracery before Westminster, and a simpler kind certainly existed at Lincoln. Although the wave moulding appeared first in royal buildings, that other delineator of late Decorated, the ogee curve, was used simultaneously on the Hardingstone Cross and Archbishop Pecham's tomb at Canterbury, and it is a moot point whether any such motifs passed into common use because of their known royal associations or because their inventors took them on into their work for other patrons. There is no obvious sign that the king's craftsmen made a point of producing innovatory or unusual work exclusively for the king. The evidence broadly indicates that the king employed individual artists of established reputation. Michael of Canterbury and William Hurley, for instance, were experienced in their crafts before they came to work for the king, as were the embroiderers Johanna Heyroun and Matilda la Settere. The king wanted the best, and his clerks ensured that he got it; but this is not necessarily to be equated with defining taste or introducing novelty, even though in some instances the royal works undoubtedly did.

The truly 'courtly' aspects of royal patronage were expressed not so much through architectural style and decorative motifs as through imagery. Where the kings differed from their peers was in their need to distinguish themselves as monarchs, and this, as we have seen, was done through illustrative subject matter, which was largely exclusive to their position and inappropriate to others. The iconography of the north transept portal at Westminster was taken up at Higham Ferrers and Lincoln Cathedral; but the former was held by Henry III's son, and the use at Lincoln of the Holy Blood imagery more likely represents Grosseteste's interest in the subject rather than particular allegiance to Henry III.

The controversy over proto-Perpendicular and the sources of Gloucester has done much to encourage the idea of Westminster as a centre opposed to the rest of the country, and this has led to the wholly anachronistic view of a courtly centre surrounded by the provinces, provincial being used in its most pejorative sense. Westminster was indeed a centre, but it was one among many. In this period, in architecture as in other things, England was strongly regional, with firmly established cathedral and monastic centres, and others maintained by the patterns imposed by a peripatetic society with scattered estates. Architectural regionalism is manifest in the different emphases in different areas: vaulting in the south-west, and tracery in the north and east. Yet a stylistic lead might be established anywhere, as at Old St Paul's, the tracery designs of which were so influential across the country, at Wells, Exeter, Tintern and York, as well as in countless lesser buildings. It is the interaction between the local and the distant that is significant. Decorated came about through the random concatenations of patrons, designers and places. This can be seen in the series of so-called Court tombs, where initiative seems to have passed between the bishops and the higher nobility; or in the Kentish work at St Stephen's and Canterbury, where stylistic refinements were made at a particular centre because that was where the artists were working at the time. *84, 28, frontis, 29*

This may seem entirely obvious, but if it were, it would not need to be stated. No aspect of Decorated, or any other style, can be identified with a particular patron or craftsman. French styles, for example, interested large numbers of people besides the kings: artists of all kinds and other patrons. The forms of Rayonnant that appeared at St Paul's and York were introduced not by the king but by bishops. The significance of the bishops and higher clergy generally in the development and dissemination of the Decorated style cannot be too strongly emphasised: many of the motifs that are said to reflect the court were devised not for the king but for clerical patrons, and many influences that seem to emanate from the king's works had originally come from a clerical milieu. The decorative interiors of Ely and Lincoln, the vaults and tracery of Exeter, the elevation and tracery at York, ground-plans at Ely and Wells, were all devised under the auspices of the higher clergy. Decorated buildings owed their existence to such men as Bishops Kirkby and Hotham and Prior Walsingham of Ely; Bishops Bronescombe, Quinil, Bitton, Stapeldon and Grandisson of Exeter; Archbishop le Romeyn at York. The chapter house and new east end of Wells Cathedral were built by the canons. At Canterbury Prior Eastry and those responsible for Pecham's tomb introduced the latest motifs. Innovations in tomb design almost all occurred in episcopal circles: the canopied tombs of Grosseteste at Lincoln, Aigueblanche at Hereford, Grey at York and Bridport at Salisbury; the bronze effigies of Grosseteste and of Bitton I and Jocelin at Wells. The appearance of such motifs as Kentish tracery and the ogee are associated with bishops' tombs, the former on that of Bradfield at Rochester, the latter on the tomb of Pecham.

Works such as these were as essential to the development of Decorated as those commanded by the kings. One reason is that the bishops, while not individually as wealthy as the king, were far more numerous. Another, linked, reason, is that the artists who created the style worked at it regardless of whom they were working for, so that innovation oscillated between buildings and objects made for the clergy and those made for lay patrons. It simply depended on where and for whom the craftsmen were working. The third, main, reason is the purpose of Decorated itself. The ostentation and display were primarily directed towards Christian cult and Christian devotion. Lay benefactions, however exalted, were exercised on the Church's terms. The first dramatic interior, the royal abbey at Westminster, was created in the interests of spiritual salvation. Encroaching motifs and techniques of the secular world were immediately encompassed and transformed into Christian metaphor and symbol. The vaults of Bristol and the self-serving imagery in the choir of Tewkesbury were both created under the wing of the Church. The importance of the clergy in all this was inevitable: while their aims may on occasion have run parallel with those of the laity, it was their professional concern to reconcile the material and the spiritual on behalf of the lay world, a lay world that included not only the king and magnates but all classes of society. The Decorated style may have found favour with kings and princes, but it was created by and on behalf of all who could afford a share in it. The style was not the expression of kingly magnificence. It was the expression of religious devotion.

Genealogical Tables

The following genealogical tables are intended to show some of the family relationships and connections mentioned in this text. In this period family ramifications were extensive and complicated, and in the interests of clarity these tables have been reduced and simplified. People cited in bold type are of particular interest in the context of this book.

England 1

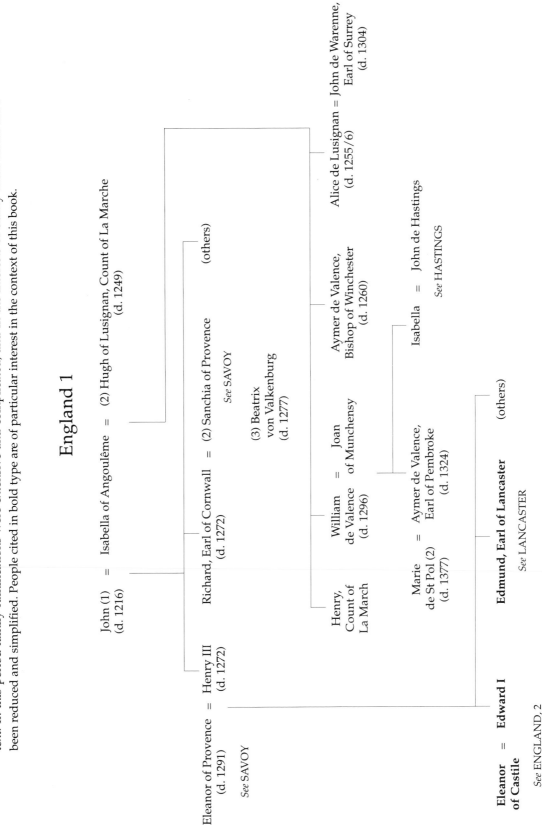

England 2

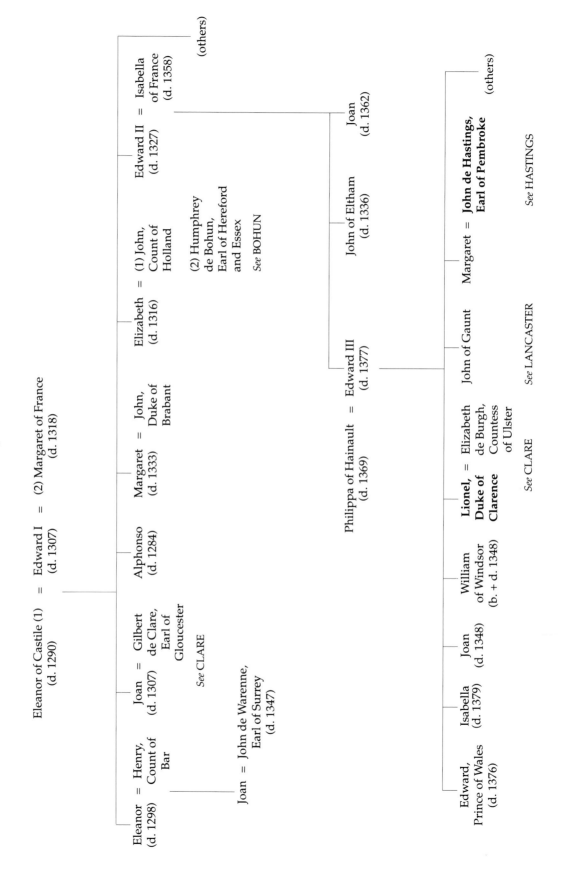

Lancaster

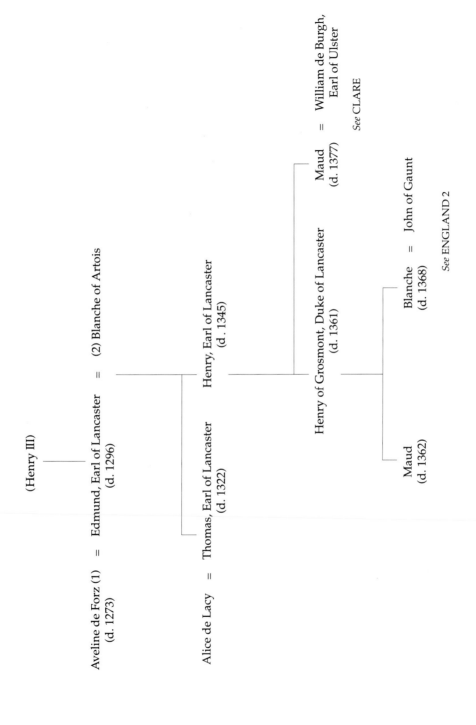

(Henry III)
|
Aveline de Forz (1) = Edmund, Earl of Lancaster = (2) Blanche of Artois
(d. 1273)   (d. 1296)

Alice de Lacy = Thomas, Earl of Lancaster   Henry, Earl of Lancaster
(d. 1322)   (d. 1345)

Maud   Henry of Grosmont, Duke of Lancaster   Maud
(d. 1362)   (d. 1361)   (d. 1377)

Blanche = John of Gaunt
(d. 1368)

Maud = William de Burgh,
Earl of Ulster

See CLARE

See ENGLAND 2

Clare

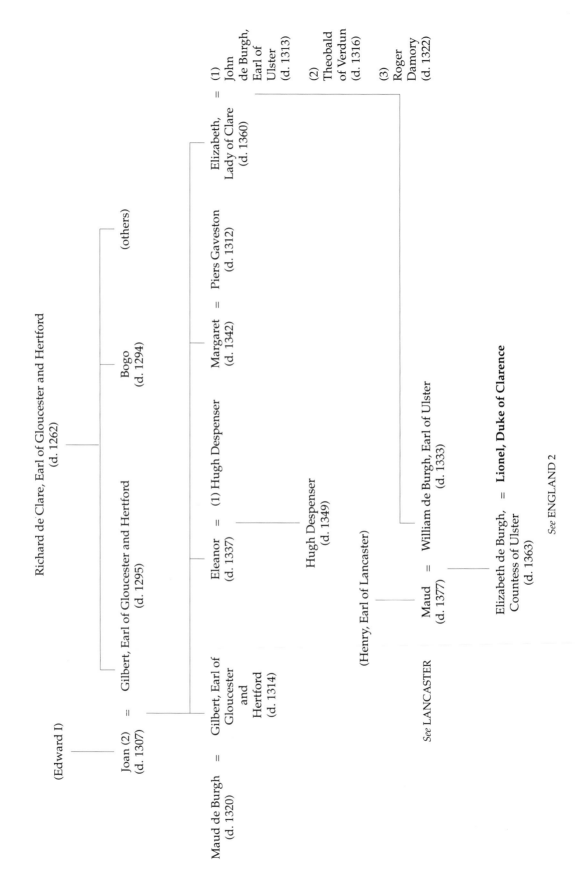

Richard de Clare, Earl of Gloucester and Hertford
(d. 1262)

(Edward I)

Joan (2) = Gilbert, Earl of Gloucester and Hertford
(d. 1307)   (d. 1295)

Gilbert, Earl of Gloucester and Hertford   Bogo   Margaret = Piers Gaveston   Elizabeth, = (1) John
(d. 1314)   (d. 1294)   (d. 1342)   (d. 1312)   Lady of Clare   de Burgh,
                                                                                             (d. 1360)   Earl of
                                                                                                                Ulster
                                                                                                                (d. 1313)

Maud de Burgh = Gilbert, Earl of   Eleanor = (1) Hugh Despenser   (others)   (2)
(d. 1320)   Gloucester   (d. 1337)   Theobald
                and   of Verdun
                Hertford   (d. 1316)
                (d. 1314)   Hugh Despenser
                                        (d. 1349)   (3)
                                                                                                             Roger
                                                                                                             Damory
                                                                                                             (d. 1322)

(Henry, Earl of Lancaster)

Maud = William de Burgh, Earl of Ulster
(d. 1377)   (d. 1333)

See LANCASTER

Elizabeth de Burgh, = **Lionel, Duke of Clarence**
Countess of Ulster
(d. 1363)

See ENGLAND 2

196

Savoy

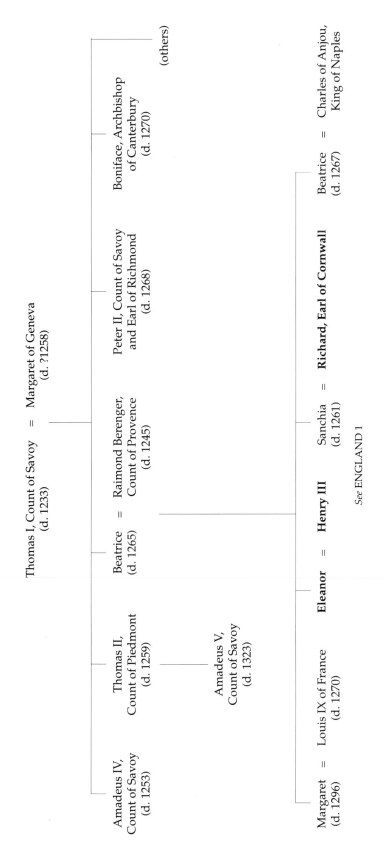

Thomas I, Count of Savoy = Margaret of Geneva
(d. 1233)   (d. ?1258)

Amadeus IV,
Count of Savoy
(d. 1253)

Thomas II,
Count of Piedmont
(d. 1259)

Amadeus V,
Count of Savoy
(d. 1323)

Beatrice
(d. 1265)
=
Raimond Berenger,
Count of Provence
(d. 1245)

Peter II, Count of Savoy
and Earl of Richmond
(d. 1268)

Boniface, Archbishop
of Canterbury
(d. 1270)

(others)

Margaret
(d. 1296)
=
Louis IX of France
(d. 1270)

Eleanor = **Henry III**

Sanchia
(d. 1261)
=
Richard, Earl of Cornwall

Beatrice
(d. 1267)
=
Charles of Anjou,
King of Naples

See ENGLAND 1

Bohun

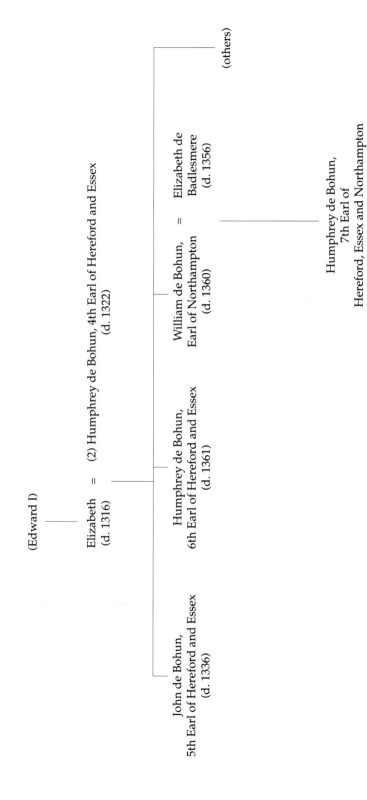

(Edward I)

Elizabeth = (2) Humphrey de Bohun, 4th Earl of Hereford and Essex
(d. 1316)   (d. 1322)

John de Bohun,
5th Earl of Hereford and Essex
(d. 1336)

Humphrey de Bohun,
6th Earl of Hereford and Essex
(d. 1361)

William de Bohun, = Elizabeth de
Earl of Northampton   Badlesmere
(d. 1360)   (d. 1356)

(others)

Humphrey de Bohun,
7th Earl of
Hereford, Essex and Northampton
(d. 1372/3)

Hastings

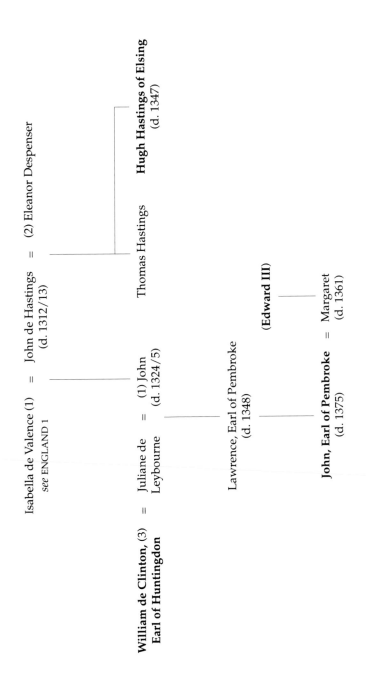

Isabella de Valence (1)   =   John de Hastings   =   (2) Eleanor Despenser
see ENGLAND 1   (d. 1312/13)

Thomas Hastings

Hugh Hastings of Elsing
(d. 1347)

William de Clinton, (3)   =   Juliane de   =   (1) John
Earl of Huntingdon   Leybourne   (d. 1324/5)

Lawrence, Earl of Pembroke
(d. 1348)

(Edward III)

John, Earl of Pembroke   =   Margaret
(d. 1375)   (d. 1361)

Grandisson

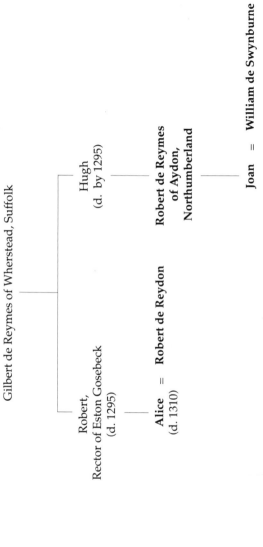

Louis de Brienne, Vicomte de Beaumont

Otto de Grandisson
(d. 1328)

William de Grandisson
(d. 1335)

Blanche = Peter
de (d. 1352)
Mortimer
(d. 1347)

John, Bishop of Exeter
(d. 1369)

Otto
(d. 1359)

Beaumont

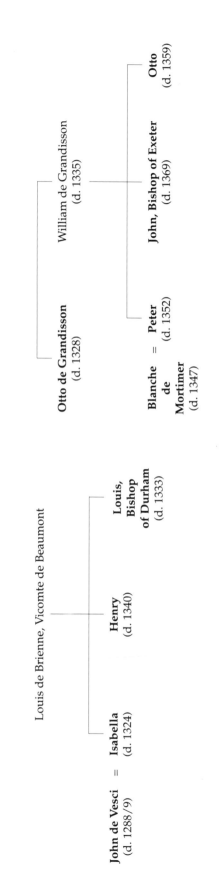

John de Vesci = Isabella
(d. 1288/9) (d. 1324)

Henry
(d. 1340)

Louis,
Bishop
of Durham
(d. 1333)

Reymes and Reydon

Gilbert de Reymes of Wherstead, Suffolk

Robert,
Rector of Eston Gosebeck
(d. 1295)

Hugh
(d. by 1295)

Alice = Robert de Reydon
(d. 1310)

Robert de Reymes
of Aydon,
Northumberland

Joan = William de Swynburne

Glossary of architectural and decorative terms

Arch-and-gable Decorative architectural motif of an arch contained within a triangular gable.

Ballflower Decorative motif of a small globular ball encased in a three-petal flower.

Boss Keystone of a vault, usually ornamented with decorative carving.

Buttress Projecting mass of masonry built up against a wall to give extra support. *Flying buttress* Arch transmitting the thrust of a vault over an aisle to the main buttress.

Canted Of a ground-plan, walls that incline towards one another at an angle.

Capital The head, usually carved, of a column or pier.

Chamfer A cut along the sharp edge of a squared block or moulding, usually at 45° to the other surfaces.

Chevet (French) The east end, comprising the apse and ambulatory, of a church.

Choir The part of the church in which the choir is seated. It can also refer to the presbytery east of the choir proper.

Clerestory The topmost level of windows in the main wall of a church.

Colonnette Small, decorative column.

Corbel A projecting block, often carved, used as a support.

Cornice In Gothic architecture, a projecting moulding along the top of a wall.

Crocket A projecting feature, often foliate or figured, that adorns gables, pinnacles, capitals etc.

Cusp The small points that project where tracery foils meet.

Diaper All over decoration of repeated squares, filled with rosettes or other ornamental devices.

Diaphragm arch Transverse arch across a building carrying a section of wall or gable.

Elevation The wall of a building, or the design thereof.

Finial The ornament, usually foliate, that caps off a gable or canopy.

Gable Triangular feature, in monumental architecture a wall end that carries a pitched roof; used decoratively on smaller structures.

Gothic Style of church architecture prevalent in Europe between the mid-twelfth century and the mid-sixteenth.

Lancet Single-light, pointed-arched window without tracery.

Lierne A short vault rib that connects two bosses but does not spring from the main vault springers.

Moulding Carved, decorated outline given to an arch or stringcourse.

Mullion Vertical division of a window.

Oculus Circular window; also a circular shape in tracery.

Ogee Reversed, s-shaped curve.

Pier Masonry support to an arch.

Pinnacle Decorated pyramidal top to a buttress, gable etc.

Quadrilobe Tracery design of four lobes or leaves partitioned by cusps.

Quatrefoil Circle of tracery partitioned by cusps into four lobes or leaves.

Rayonnant Style of French Gothic architecture fashionable in the thirteenth century.

Reredos Permanent screen behind an altar, usually of wood or stone.

Retable Painted or carved wooden altarpiece, sometimes portable.

Retrochoir Strictly, the passage at the west of the choir dividing the choir entrance from the nave altar and rood screen; nowadays more often denotes the area in a church east of the high altar.

Rib Projecting moulding on a vault surface.

Romanesque Architectural style prevalent in Europe from the eleventh century to the mid-twelfth; English Romanesque is often termed *Anglo-Norman* or simply *Norman*.

Roodscreen Screen at the east end of the nave that carried the rood, the sculptured figures of the crucified Christ between the Virgin and St John.

Sedilia Seats for the clergy beside the main altar.

Sexfoil Circle of tracery partitioned by cusps into six lobes or leaves.

Shaft Trunk of a column; also used of unstructural, decorative columns.

Spandrel Triangular space next to the haunch of an arch.

Springer Masonry of a vault at the point at which it arches away from the wall.

Stringcourse Horizontal moulding that defines the division of two storeys.

Tierceron Secondary vault rib that rises from the springer.

Tracery Bars of stone that make up the pattern in a window. *Curvilinear* or *flowing* tracery is composed of ogee curves. *Kentish* tracery is a quadrilobe or trilobe with spurs between the lobes.

Transept Cross-arms of a cruciform church plan.

Transom Horizontal bar dividing a window.

Trefoil Circle of tracery partitioned by cusps into three lobes or leaves.

Triforium Low arcaded passage or space above the main arcade of a church wall.

Trilobe Tracery design of three lobes or leaves partitioned by cusps.

Vault Arched masonry ceiling. A *barrel vault* is a continuous tunnel roof of pointed or semi-circular section. A *rib vault* is based on diagonal arched ribs (q.v.).

Weeper Small sculptured figure, often a mourner, attached to the side of a tomb sarcophagus.

Bibliography

General historical and cultural overviews of the period include:

Alexander, J. and Binski, P. ed., *Age of Chivalry. Art in Plantagenet England 1200–1400* (exhibn. cat. London, Royal Academy, 1987)

Ford, B. ed., *Medieval Britain*, vol. 2 of *The Cambridge Cultural History* (Cambridge, 1992)

Medcalf, S. ed., *The Later Middle Ages* (London, 1981)

British Archaeological Association Conference Transactions, I. Worcester Cathedral (1975); II. Ely Cathedral (1976); III. Durham Cathedral (1977); IV. Wells and Glastonbury (1978); VI. Winchester Cathedral (1980); VII. Gloucester and Tewkesbury (1981); VIII. Lincoln Cathedral (1982); IX. East Riding of Yorkshire (1983); X. London (1984); XI. Exeter Cathedral (1985); XIII Lichfield (1993), are very useful collections of papers on the architecture, furnishings and liturgical arrangements of the cathedrals and other buildings in their localities.

For further useful collections of conference papers and articles on widely varied, but related themes, see:

The Burlington Magazine, cxxx (1988), published to complement the *Age of Chivalry* exhibition (see above) [articles by M. Camille, M. Michael, M. Roberts, N. Morgan]

Fernie, E. and Crossley, P., ed., *Medieval Architecture and its Intellectual Context. Studies in Honour of Peter Kidson* (London, 1990) [articles by P. Draper, N. Coldstream, T. A. Heslop, R. Morris]

Ormrod, W. M. ed., *England in the Thirteenth Century*, Proceedings of the 1984 Harlaxton Symposium (Harlaxton, 1985) [papers by M. Clanchy; E. Fernie; B. Golding; F. Lewis; M. Prestwich; M. Roberts; D. Stocker]

Ormrod, W. M. ed., *England in the Fourteenth Century*, Proceedings of the 1985 Harlaxton Symposium (Woodbridge, 1986) [papers by P. Binski and D. Park; P. Lindley; R. Morris; M. Roberts; L. F. Sandler; K. Staniland]

Ormrod, W. M. ed., *England in the Thirteenth Century*, Harlaxton Medieval Studies, I (Stamford, 1991) [papers by J. Cherry, T. Tolley]

Chapter One
ILLUMINATED ARCHITECTURE

General

Art and the Courts: France and England from 1259 to 1328 (exhibn. cat., Ottawa, National Gallery of Canada, 1972)

Bock, H., *Der Decorated Style. Untersuchungen zur Englischen Kathedralarchitektur der ersten Hälfte des 14. Jahrhunderts* (Heidelberg, 1962)

Bony, J., *The English Decorated Style. Gothic Architecture Transformed 1250–1350* (Oxford, 1979)

Brieger, P., *English Art 1216–1307* (Oxford, 1957; repr. 1968)

Cherry, J., *Medieval Decorative Art* (London, 1991)

Colvin, H. M., ed. *The History of the King's Works*, i and ii, The Middle Ages (London, 1963)

Evans, J., *English Art 1307–1461* (Oxford, 1949)

Kidson, P., Murray, P., and Thompson, P., *A History of English Architecture* (2nd edn., Harmondsworth, 1979)

Platt, C., *The Architecture of Medieval Britain* (Yale, 1990)

Stone, L., *Sculpture in Britain: The Middle Ages*, Pelican History of Art (2nd edn., Harmondsworth, 1972)

Webb, G., *Architecture in Britain: The Middle Ages*, Pelican History of Art (2nd edn., Harmondsworth, 1965)

Wilson, C., *The Gothic Cathedral* (London, 1990)

Individual Church Buildings

There are very few monographs on English buildings. Some are given below. More discussion and full references can be found in the surveys cited above. For castles and houses, see under Chapter Four below.

Aylmer, G., and Cant, R., ed., *A History of York Minster* (Oxford, 1977)

Colchester, L. S., ed., *Wells Cathedral: a History* (Shepton Mallet, 1982)

Crook, J., ed., *Winchester Cathedral. Nine Hundred Years 1093–1993* (Chichester, 1993)

Hastings, M., *St Stephen's Chapel and Its Place in the Development of Perpendicular Style in England* (Cambridge, 1955)

Swanton, M., ed., *Exeter Cathedral. A Celebration* (Exeter, 1991) [chapters by J. Givens, V. Sekules, M. Glasscoe, P. Tudor-Craig, N. Stratford, N. Coldstream]

Wilson, C., et al., *Westminster Abbey*, New Bell's Cathedral Guides (London, 1986)

Woodman, F., *The Architectural History of Canterbury Cathedral* (London, 1981)

Chapter Two
KINGDOM, LAND AND PEOPLE

The historical, political and social background to the period is discussed in the following works, all with useful bibliographies:

Altschul, M., *A Baronial Family in Medieval England: The Clares 1217–1314* (Baltimore, 1965)

Edwards, K., *English Secular Cathedrals in the Middle Ages* (Manchester, 1967)

Fowler, K., *The King's Lieutenant: Henry of Grosmont, first Duke of Lancaster 1310–1361* (London, 1969)

Fryde, N., *The Tyranny and Fall of Edward II* (Cambridge, 1979)

Given–Wilson, C., *The Royal Household and the King's Affinity* (New Haven and London, 1986)

Highfield, J. R. L., 'The English Hierarchy in the reign of Edward III', *Transactions of the Royal Historical Society*, 5th ser., vi (1956), pp. 115–38

Highfield, J. R. L., *The Early Rolls of Merton College, Oxford*, Oxford Historical Society, NS xviii (Oxford, 1964)

Hilton, R. H., *A Medieval Society: the West Midlands at the end of the 13th Century* (London, 1966)

Holmes, G. S., *The Estates of the Higher Nobility in Fourteenth Century England* (Cambridge, 1957)

Holt, R., and Rosser, G., ed., *The Medieval Town: A Reader in English Urban History 1200–1540* (London and New York, 1990)

McFarlane, K. B., *The Nobility of Later Medieval England* (Oxford, 1973)

Maddicott, J. R., *Thomas of Lancaster 1307–22* (Oxford, 1970)

Ormrod, W. M., *The Reign of Edward III* (New Haven and London, 1990)

Pantin, W. A., *The English Church in the Fourteenth Century* (Cambridge, 1955)

Phillips, J. R. S., *Aymer de Valence, earl of Pembroke 1307–24* (Oxford, 1972)

Prestwich, M., 'Exchequer and Wardrobe in the later years of Edward I', *Bulletin of the Institute of Historical Research*, xlvi (1973), pp. 1–10

Prestwich, M., *Edward I* (London, 1988)

Rosenthal, J. T., *The Purchase of Paradise: Gift Giving and the Aristocracy 1307–1485* (London and Toronto, 1972)

Rosser, G., *Medieval Westminster 1200–1540* (Oxford, 1989)

Salzman, L. F., *Edward I* (Oxford, 1968)

Saul, N., *Knights and Esquires: The Gloucestershire Gentry in the 14th Century* (Oxford, 1981)

Stones, E. L. G., 'Sir Geoffrey le Scrope (c.1285–1340), Chief Justice of the King's Bench', *English Historical Review*, clxx (1954), pp. 1–17

Taylor, A. J., 'Castle building in thirteenth–century Wales and Savoy', *Proceedings of the British Academy*, lxiii (1977), pp. 265–92

Thrupp, S. L., *The Merchant Class of Medieval London* (Ann Arbor, 1948, repr. 1962)

Vale, J., *Edward III and Chivalry* (Woodbridge, 1982)

Waugh, S. L., *England in the Reign of Edward III* (Cambridge, 1991)

Chapter Three
M I N D A N D S P I R I T
Much of the material in this chapter is covered in works already cited. See also:

Boitani, P., and Torti, A., ed., *Religion in the Poetry and Drama of the Late Middle Ages in England* (Cambridge, 1990)

Clanchy, M., *From Memory to Written Record* (London, 1979)

Coales, J., ed., *The Earliest English Brasses* (London, 1987) [full bibliography]

Coldstream, N., 'English Decorated Shrine Bases', *Journal of the British Archaeological Association*, cxxix (1976), pp. 15–34

Coldstream, N., 'Fourteenth-Century Corbel Heads in the Bishop's House, Ely', in *Studies in Medieval Sculpture*, ed. F. H. Thompson, Society of Antiquaries, Occasional Paper (NS) III (1983), pp. 165–76

Erbe, T. ed., *Mirk's Festial: a Collection of Homilies by Johannes Mirkus*, pt. 1, Early English Text Society (London, 1905)

Evans, M., 'An Illustrated Fragment of Peraldus's *Summa* of Vice: Harleian MS 3244', *Journal of the Warburg and Courtauld Institutes*, xlv (1982), pp. 14–68

Fairweather, F. H., 'Colne Priory, Essex, and the Burials of the Earls of Oxford', *Archaeologia*, lxxxvii (1938), pp. 275–95

Hepburn, F., *Portraits of the Later Plantagenets* (Woodbridge, 1986)

James, M., 'Ritual, Drama and the Social Body in the Late Medieval English Town', *Past and Present*, xcviii (1983), pp. 3–29

Ladner, G. B., 'Medieval and Modern Understanding of Symbolism: a Comparison', *Speculum*, liv (1979), pp. 223–56

Lankester, P., 'A military effigy in Dorchester Abbey, Oxon', *Oxoniensia*, 52 (1987), pp. 145–72

Lewis, S., *The Art of Matthew Paris in the Chronica Majora* (Berkeley, 1987)

Lindley, P., 'The Imagery of the Octagon at Ely', *Journal of the British Archaeological Association*, cxxxix (1986), pp. 75–99

Marks, R., *Stained Glass in England during the Middle Ages* (London, 1993)

Moore, S. A., 'Documents relating to the Death and Burial of King Edward II', *Archaeologia*, l (1887), pp. 215–26

Morgan, N. J., *Early Gothic Manuscripts (ii) 1250–85*, A Survey of Manuscripts Illuminated in the British Isles, IV (London, 1988)

Morris, R., 'Tewkesbury Abbey: the Despenser Mausoleum', *Transactions of the Bristol and Gloucester Archaeological Society*, xciii (1974), pp. 142–55

Morse, R., *Truth and Convention in the Middle Ages* (Cambridge, 1991)

Norton, C., Park, D., and Binski, P., *Dominican Painting in East Anglia. The Thornham Parva Retable and Musée de Cluny Frontal* (Woodbridge, 1987)

O'Neilly, J. G., and Tanner, L. E., 'The Shrine of St Edward the Confessor', *Archaeologia*, c (1966), pp. 129–54

Ormrod, W. M., 'The Personal Religion of Edward III', *Speculum*, lxiv (1989), pp. 849–77

Owst, G. R., *Literature and Pulpit in Medieval England* (Cambridge, 1933; 2nd edn., 1961)

Pevsner, N., *The Leaves of Southwell* (London, 1945)

Salter, E., and Pearsall, D., *Landscapes and Seasons of the Medieval World* (Toronto, 1973)

Sandler, L. F., *Gothic Manuscripts 1285–1385*, A Survey of Gothic Manuscripts Illuminated in the British Isles, V, 2 vols (London, 1986)

Sekules, V., 'The Tomb of Christ at Lincoln and the Development of the Sacrament Shrine: Easter Sepulchres Reconsidered', *Medieval Art and Architecture at Lincoln Cathedral*, British Archaeological Association Conference Transactions: Lincoln, 1982, pp. 118–31

Staniland, K., 'Clothing and Textiles at the Court of Edward III 1342–52', in *Collecteana Londoniensia. Studies in London Archaeology and History presented to Ralph Merrifield*, London and Middlesex Archaeological Society, Special Paper, no. 2 (1978), pp. 223–34

Staniland, K., 'Medieval Courtly Splendour', *Costume*, xiv (1980), pp. 7–23

Stapleton, T., 'A Brief Summary of the Wardrobe Accounts … of Edward the Second', *Archaeologia*, xxvi (1836), pp. 318–45

Thompson, A. H., *The History of the Hospital and New College of the Annunciation of St Mary in the Newarke, Leicester* (Leicester, 1937)

Tristram, E. W., *English Wall Painting of the Fourteenth Century* (London, 1955)

Ward, B., *Miracles and the Medieval Mind* (Aldershot, 1982)

Chapter Four
T H E P A T R O N S
Little has been published on medieval art patronage as such, but it is dealt with in many of the works already cited. See also:

Alcock, N. et al., 'Maxstoke Castle, Warwickshire', *Archaeological Journal*, cxxxv (1978), pp. 195–233

Austin, R., 'Some Notes on

the Family of Bradeston',*Transactions of the Bristol and Gloucester Archaeological Society*, xlvii (1925), pp. 279–86

Badham, S., 'A lost bronze effigy of 1279 from York Minster', *Antiquaries Journal*, lx/i (1980), pp. 59–65

Binski, P., *The Painted Chamber at Westminster*, Society of Antiquaries Occasional Paper (N.S.), ix (London, 1986) [cites the earlier literature in full]

Crooks, F., 'John de Winwick and his Chantry in Huyton Church', *Transactions of the Historical Society of Lancashire and Cheshire*, lxxvii (1925), pp. 26–38

Dixon, P., *Aydon Castle* (London, 1988)

Douch, R., 'The Career, Lands and Family of William Montague, Earl of Salisbury 1301–44', *Bulletin of the Institute of Historical Research*, xxiv (1951), pp. 85–8

Giuseppe, M., 'The Wardrobe and Household Accounts of Bogo de Clare, AD 1284–6', *Archaeologia*, lxx (1920), pp. 275–95

James, T. B., *The Palaces of Medieval England* (London, 1990)

Jenkinson, H., 'Marie de Sancto Paulo, Foundress of Pembroke College, Cambridge', *Archaeologia*, lxvi (1915), pp. 401–46

Johnstone, H., *Edward of Caernarvon* (Manchester, 1946)

Michael, M. A., 'The Harnhulle Psalter-Hours: An Early Fourteenth-Century Manuscript at Downside Abbey', *Journal of the British Archaeological Association*, cxxiv (1981), pp. 81–99

Nicolas, N. H. ed., *Testamenta Vetusta*, 2 vols (London, 1826) [early wills]

Parsons, D. ed., *Eleanor of Castile 1290–1990. Essays to Commemorate the 700th Anniversary of her Death: 28 November 1290* (Stamford, 1991)

Parsons, J. C., *The Court and Household of Eleanor of Castile in 1290* (Toronto, 1977)

Schofield, J., *The Building of London from the Conquest to the Great Fire* (London, 1984)

Schramm, P. E., *History of the English Coronation* (Oxford, 1937)

Tummers, H., *Early Secular Effigies in England* (Leiden, 1980)

West, J., 'Acton Burnell Castle, Shropshire', in *Collectanea Historica. Essays in Memory of Stuart Rigold*, ed. A. Detsicas (1981), pp. 85–92

Williams, G., 'Henry de Gower (?1278–1347); bishop and builder', *Archaeologia Cambrensis*, cxxx (1981), pp. 1–18

Chapter Five
ARTISTS, CRAFTSMEN AND ADMINISTRATORS
The History of the King's Works (see above) is the main source of published information on the clerks and craftsmen working on royal buildings. See also:

Binski, P., *Painters*, Medieval Craftsmen (London, 1991)

Blair, J., and Ramsay, N. ed., *English Medieval Industries. Craftsmen, Techniques, Products* (London and Rio Grande, OH, 1991)

Brown, S., and O'Connor, D., *Glass-Painters*, Medieval Craftsmen (London, 1991)

Cherry, J., *Goldsmiths*, Medieval Craftsmen (London, 1991)

Coldstream, N., *Masons and Sculptors*, Medieval Craftsmen (London, 1991)

Dawton, N., 'The Percy Tomb at Beverley Minster: the Style of the Sculpture', in *Studies in Medieval Sculpture*, ed. F. H. Thompson, Society of Antiquaries, Occasional Paper (NS) III (London, 1983), pp. 122–50

De Hamel, C., *Scribes and Illuminators*, Medieval Craftsmen (London, 1991)

Dennison, L., 'An Illuminator of the Queen Mary Psalter Group: The Ancient 6 Master', *Antiquaries Journal*, lxvi/ii (1986), pp. 287–315

Erskine, A., ed., *The Accounts of the Fabric of Exeter Cathedral, 1279–1353*, Devon and Cornwall Record Society, NS, xxiv (1981), xxvi (1983)

Harvey, J., *English Medieval Architects. A Biographical Dictionary Down To 1550* (rev. ed., Gloucester, 1984)

Lancaster, R. Kent, 'Artists, suppliers and clerks: the human factor in the art patronage of Henry III', Journal of the Warburg and Courtauld Institutes, xxxv (1972), pp. 81–107

Lethaby, W. R., *Westminster Abbey and the King's Craftsmen* (London, 1906)

Lethaby, W. R., *Westminster Abbey Re-examined* (London, 1925)

Morris, R., 'The Mason of Madley, Allensmore, and Eaton Bishop', *Transactions of the Woolhope Naturalists' Field Club*, xli/i (1974), pp. 180–97

Sekules, V., 'A Group of Masons in Early Fourteenth-Century Lincolnshire', in *Studies in Medieval Sculpture*, ed. F. H. Thompson, Society of Antiquaries, Occasional Paper (NS) III (London, 1983), pp. 151–64

Staniland, K., *Embroiderers*, Medieval Craftsmen (London, 1991)

Williamson, P., *Northern Gothic Sculpture 1200–1450* (London, 1988)

EPILOGUE
Discussions of the court style will be found in the works on architecture and sculpture given above. There is further discussion in Coales (1987), by N. Rogers (pp. 8–68) and P. Binski (pp. 69–132); and in Parsons (1991), by N. Coldstream (pp. 55–68). The French material was initially assessed in:

Branner, R., *St Louis and the Court Style* (London, 1965).

See also:

Binski, P., 'The Cosmati at Westminster and the English Court Style', *Art Bulletin*, lxxii/i (1990), pp. 6–34

Coldstream, N., 'The Lady Chapel at Ely Cathedral: Its Place in the English Decorated Style', in *East Anglian and Other Studies in Honour of Barbara Dodwell*, ed. P. Noble et al., Reading Medieval Studies, XI (1985), pp. 1–30

Gardner, J., 'The Cosmati at Westminster: Some Anglo-Italian Reflexions', in *Skulptur und Grabmal des Spätmittelalters in Rom und Italien*, ed. J. Garms and A. Romanini (Vienna, 1990), pp. 201–16

Hallam, E., 'Royal Burial and the Cult of Kingship in France and England, 1060–1330', *Journal of Medieval History*, viii (1982), pp. 359–80

Hallam, E., 'Philip the Fair and the Cult of St Louis', *Studies in Church History*, xviii (1982), pp. 201–14

Photographic Acknowledgements

© A.C.L., Institut Royal du Patrimonie Artistique, Brussels: 56; © James Austin: 30; Bibliothéque Royale, Brussels: plate VI; Bilarchiv Foto Marburg: 5; © The Bodleian Library: 80, plate VII; The British Library 53, 88, 100, 116; © Trustees of the British Museum: 58, 82; Nicola Coldstream: 62; The Conway Library, Courtauld Institute of Art: 8, 13, 14, 15, 16, 17, 19, 22, 26, 29, 36, 37, 38, 39, 40, 41, 47, 48, 50, 51, 59, 60, 61, 65, 66, 74, 75 (Conservation Wall Painting Department), 87, 102, 104, 106, 109, 110, 111, 112, 113; Master and Fellows of Corpus Christi College: 70; Malcolm Crowthers: 11, 77, 115; © Dean and Chapter of Durham: 81; © English Heritage: 69; Exeter City Museum: 82; © Glasgow Museums: 96; © Sonia Halliday: plate II; © Clive Hicks: plate IV; Reproduced by courtesy of the Director and University Librarian, the John Rylands University Library of Manchester: 21; © Anthony Kersting: front cover, frontispiece, 2, 18, 35, 55, 57, 63, 78, 79, 83, plates I, III, IX; The Monumental Brass Society: 68, 85, 91, 97, 103; Musée de Cluny: plate X; Museum of London; 117; Pierpont Morgan Library: plate XI; Royal Commission on the Architectural and Historical Monuments of Wales: 94; Royal Commission on the Historical Monuments of England: 1, 3, 4, 6, 7, 9, 12, 20, 23, 24, 25, 27, 28, 31, 32, 33, 34, 43, 44, 45, 46, 52, 54, 64, 67, 72, 73, 76, 86, 89, 92, 93, 95, 98, 101, 107, 108, 114, plate VIII; Veronica Sekules: 79; © Society of Antiquaries of London: 42, 71; © The Board and Trustees of the Victoria and Albert Museum: 99, 105; University of Warwick, History of Art Photographic Collection: 84; © Dean and Chapter of Westminster Abbey: 10; © Christopher Wilson: 90; © Woodmansterne Ltd: 49.

Index

THE DECORATED STYLE

Architecture and Ornament, 1240–1360